Great Sporting Scandals

By the same author and published by Robson Books:

Great Sporting Eccentrics
Great Sporting Mishaps
Motor-racing's Strangest Races

Great Sporting Scandals

Geoff Tibballs

ROBSON BOOKS

First published in Great Britain in 2003 by Robson Books, The Chrysalis Building, Bramley Road, London, W10 6SP

An imprint of Chrysalis Books Group plc

British Library Cataloguing in Publication Data
A catalogue record for this title is available from the British Library.

ISBN 1 86105 686 9

Typeset by FiSH Books, London
Printed by Creative Print & Design (Wales), Ebbw Vale

Contents

Contents

Introduction

Even in these enlightened times Will Carling and Shergar would seem unlikely bedfellows. Yet, apart from both making newspaper headlines for their activities at stud, they do have one other thing in common. Along with the likes of Roy Keane, Hansie Cronje, Mike Tyson, Glenn Hoddle, Tonya Harding, Ben Johnson, Michael Schumacher and Freddie the Fox, they have all been at the centre of some of the most notorious sporting scandals of the past twenty years. Carling's crime was to refer to the executive of the Rugby Football Union as '57 old farts'; Shergar's misfortune was to be kidnapped. And Freddie the Fox? He was the mascot disqualified from first place in the 2001 Mascots' Grand National, after it emerged that the vulpine costume used in the fun run housed Olympic 400 metre hurdler Matthew Douglas. Such professionalism was deemed not to be in keeping with the spirit of the event.

Nowadays sport is a big-money business and where there's brass, there's muck. Hardly a week goes by without the back pages splashing the latest scandal from the world of sport – be it an allegation of drug-taking, match-fixing or general unsportsmanlike behaviour – as part of the prevailing culture of winning at any cost. In truth, while such revelations have become infinitely more commonplace over the past few decades, only drugs are a truly modern blight on sporting society. As far back as 1791 the racing fraternity was shaken by the Escape Affair in which royal jockey Sam Chifney was accused of deliberately 'stopping' a horse. Some 25 years later came the first known case of match-fixing in cricket, when England's William Lambert was warned off for selling a match against Nottingham. Cricket's first major riot erupted in 1879 during England's tour of Australia and then, in 1900, Burnley goalkeeper Jack Hillman set an unwanted footballing precedent when he was banned for a year for trying to bribe opponents Nottingham Forest to throw a match. Despite being offered £2 a head, Forest ran out 4–0 winners and Burnley were relegated. Nor were Victorian sportsmen averse to behaviour that would have made George Best look like a teetotaller. Bobby Peel and Bill Scott were just two of the leading lights of that age to be found drunk and incapable on the field of play – the former in charge of a cricket ball at Bramall Lane, Sheffield; the latter, more alarmingly, on top of a horse at the 1846 Derby!

At one time or another every sport has had its moment of controversy. Even the once genteel pastime of bowls has been witness to the occasional unseemly brawl, while the apparently sedate world of ice skating has been rocked by two major scandals in the past decade – the Tonya Harding/Nancy Kerrigan affair and the so-called Skategate judging row at the 2002 Winter Olympics. And who could forget the outrage when Harvey Smith completed his round at the 1971 British Show Jumping Derby by sticking two fingers up at officials in full view of millions on television?

Some of the scandals have long since faded into obscurity but others have continued to be debated decades after the event in bars, in the media and wherever sports fans gather. Just as every cricket devotee has an opinion on the Bodyline series, so boxing supporters still discuss the Night of the Long Count and football followers argue about the rights and wrongs of Maradona's infamous Hand of God.

When compiling this trawl through sport's most shameful episodes, my biggest problem was deciding what to leave out. For there is enough material to fill several volumes. Ultimately I have tried to present as many different types of scandal as possible (rather than include every failed drugs test or bribery investigation) and to cover a wide variety of sports. As a general rule, I have also tended to omit any scandals confined to people's private lives. Footballers behaving badly off duty are ten-a-penny and, while many such exposes are hugely entertaining (proving that 'three in a bed' is not a term used solely in darts), even Sven and Ulrika would only have found their way into these pages had they been caught *in flagrante* at half-time in the centre-circle at Stamford Bridge. However, I must admit I was tempted to catalogue the fall from grace of Atlanta Falcons' Eugene Robinson who, on the eve of his team's Super Bowl against the Denver Broncos in Miami in 1999, was charged with soliciting a prostitute. Unfortunately for Robinson the prostitute turned out to be an undercover policewoman.

Researching this book would have been an impossible task without the assistance of library staff up and down the country. I am particularly indebted to Nottinghamshire Library Services, The British Newspaper Library at Colindale, and the staff at Sheffield, Derby, Marylebone, Birmingham, Leicester, Lincoln and Charing Cross libraries. I would also like to thank Jeremy Robson for his continued support and enthusiasm.

Geoff Tibballs, 2003

The Escape Affair

1791

The Prince of Wales, the future George IV, kept almost as many racehorses as he kept mistresses. At one point the inveterate womaniser, gambler and general wastrel boasted over forty racehorses in training and relished the opportunity to run them against his aristocratic chums with large sums of money being wagered on the outcome. Among his more colourful associates was Lord Barrymore who once won a bet that he could find a man willing to eat a live cat. In Barrymore, the Prince clearly recognised a kindred spirit.

The Prince's success with his string of racehorses – he had won the Derby in 1788 with Sir Thomas – had brought him admirers and enemies in equal quantities. The latter, led by Jockey Club president Sir Charles Bunbury, the most powerful figure in English racing at the time, were irked that the Prince was using his wealth and connections to dominate the sport. They felt it wrong that one owner should have so many outstanding horses in his stable and privately longed for the opportunity to bring him down a peg or two.

Just as the Prince of Wales was the most celebrated owner in the land, so Sam Chifney was the most famous jockey. Born in Norfolk in 1753, Chifney was a tactical genius and master of the flying finish, known popularly as the 'Chifney Rush', although the 'Chifney Sweep' would surely have earned him more headlines. He was a master horseman with hands so light that he described his method of riding as 'if you had a silken rein as fine as a hair in his mouth and were afraid of breaking it'. He created a veritable racing dynasty, with one son, William, becoming a leading trainer while another, Sam junior, would go on to emulate his father's success in the saddle. However, like the Prince, Sam Chifney senior was not to everyone's taste. There were dark mutterings to the effect that Tattenham Corner was straighter than Sam Chifney.

Since the Prince was able to command the best jockeys, it was inevitable that he and Chifney should form a dangerous liaison. The whispers soon started that the Prince's racing manager, Warwick Lake, had given Chifney orders to 'stop' certain horses so that the Prince and his friends could make a killing on them the next time they ran. Suspicion began to follow Chifney's every ride for royalty.

One of the Prince's main hopes for the 1791 season was Escape, an animal bred by the Prince which had earned its name as a yearling by almost kicking its way out of its horsebox. In the early summer of 1791 Escape was one of four horses entered by the Prince of Wales for the prestigious Oatlands Stakes at Ascot. Both Lake and the horse's trainer, Neale, were adamant that Escape had never been better but Chifney expressed his doubts and begged the Prince to let him ride another of his horses, Baronet, instead. The Prince backed Chifney's judgement and told him: 'Whenever I have two horses in a race, I wish you, Sam, to ride whichever you fancy most on the day, without consulting anyone.' The Prince's faith in his jockey proved totally justified for in a field of twenty Baronet got home narrowly; Escape finished well down the field.

In early October Chifney rode Escape to two victories in a day. Two weeks later, on the 20th, the horse was entered against three decidedly inferior animals in a contest in excess of two miles over the Ditch In course at Newmarket. Escape was a hot favourite at 2–1 and on his way to the course that day Chifney met the Prince and his friends, all of whom were in an optimistic mood. The Prince called out: 'Sam Chifney, Escape is sure of winning today, is he not?' But Chifney was worried that the horse was unfit, having not had a proper gallop since the two races a fortnight earlier, and urged caution, replying: 'Your Highness, I do not think Escape is sure to win today.' In his subsequent account of the Escape Affair in his book *Genius Genuine*, Chifney wrote: 'I then took the liberty of advising his

Royal Highness not to bet upon him, as the odds, from his previous performances, were likely to be high upon him, and much might be lost, though little could be won.'

The Prince instructed Chifney to make the running but the jockey opted to play his usual waiting game. Escape trailed in last of four. When the Prince caught up with his rider, he was not a happy Highness. 'Chifney,' he growled, 'you have lost this race by not making strong play as I desired you.' Chifney's discomfort was eased by the confirmation that the Prince had taken his advice and not bet on the horse and, furthermore, that it would be running again the following day. 'I am very glad your Royal Highness does run Escape tomorrow,' said Chifney. 'This sharp rally today will not fatigue him, has sweated him, opened his pores, and lightened his flesh.' In modern parlance, Escape would be all the better for the run.

So it was that on 21 October Chifney and Escape turned out again at Newmarket, this time over the four miles of the Beacon Course. Eighteenth-century horses were nothing if not versatile. Among Escape's five opponents were Skylark and Pipator, both of whom had beaten him the previous day, and the useful Chanticleer. In view of his poor showing on the 20th, Escape started at a far more generous price of 5–1 and Chifney strongly advised the Prince to back the horse at those odds. The Prince repeated his instructions from the first race. Escape was to make the running, but once again Chifney preferred to bide his time. The waiting game paid off. Escape overhauled Skylark near the finish to win the prize with plenty to spare.

No sooner had the horses passed the post than accusations were being levelled at the Prince of Wales and Sam Chifney. It was said that the Prince had visited the stables shortly before the first race and had given Escape a bucket of water to affect his wind. Lake, upset by Chifney's criticism of the horse's preparation, dropped a heavy hint that the jockey had 'stopped' Escape. The Jockey Club were understandably sceptical about Escape's sudden turnaround in form, their suspicions fuelled by the fact that both Chifney and the Prince had backed the horse to win on the second day after ignoring it on the first. The Prince had placed 400 guineas on Escape to win the second race while it was rumoured that Chifney had bet against the horse on the first day before placing a similar sum on the horse to win the following day. And it had not escaped Bunbury's attention that the beaten favourite, Chanticleer, was owned by Lord Barrymore. The implication was clear: Chifney, with or without the connivance of the Prince, had deliberately pulled Escape on the 20th and then backed him to win on the 21st.

On 22 October Chifney was summoned by the Prince who informed him of the rumours that were circulating – namely that the jockey had pocketed some 600 guineas as a result of Escape's defeat and the same amount following his victory. Chifney denied both charges, insisting that he had made no wager on the first race and had bet a modest twenty guineas with a Mr Vauxhall Clark on Escape to win the second race. It was not illegal for jockeys to bet in those days. Chifney was known to have had financial problems and the Prince felt obliged to add that he had also heard that Chifney had recently been arrested at Ascot Heath for a debt of £300 and that the debt had been paid on his behalf by the same Mr Vauxhall Clark. Again Chifney denied the allegation, whereupon the Prince advised him to put his version of events in his formal statement to the Jockey Club.

Chifney maintained his stance in his sworn affidavit to the Jockey Club and stated that on both occasions he had ridden Escape to win. Bunbury quizzed him repeatedly about the waiting tactics employed in the first race but Chifney stood his ground. Although his fellow stewards apparently accepted the jockey's explanation for Escape's fluctuating form, Bunbury was not satisfied and told the Prince that if Chifney rode his horses, no gentleman would start against him. The Prince interpreted this as a thinly veiled way of telling him that he had been warned off the turf and that either he or his jockey had been guilty of fraud.

Understandably the Prince was highly indignant, viewing the episode as part of Bunbury's vendetta against Chifney and himself. He had no intention of sacrificing his jockey to the wolves and loyally defended him in public, insisting that, as far as he was concerned, Sam Chifney was beyond reproach. More-over, he awarded Chifney an annual retainer of 200 guineas – for being 'an honest and good servant to me' – and withdrew from racing at Newmarket where Bunbury reigned supreme.

Despite receiving the royal seal of approval, Chifney was stigmatised by Bunbury's words and when the Prince decided to sell off his string of horses as a further act of protest, Chifney found himself without an employer. The situation was not helped when Colonel Leigh, manager of the Prince's stud, threw his hat into the ring and bluntly told Chifney that he thought he had cheated on Escape. The conversation was overheard by Chifney's young son William who, years later on reaching adulthood, took his revenge by assaulting the colonel in Newmarket High Street, for which he was sentenced to six months' hard labour. However, the colonel bore no grudges and the two became firm friends. William Chifney went on to train for the Prince but his horses never ran at Newmarket. In 1805 the Jockey Club did try to entice the Prince back to Newmarket, in the hope that 'the affair may be buried in oblivion', but the Prince stayed away. He once told William: 'They treated your poor father and me very badly. I won't run there.'

By then Sam Chifney was a broken man physically, emotionally and financially. Hounded by his enemies, he was forced to commute the Prince's pension for £1200. He headed for London with the intention of patenting and marketing a new bit, The Chifney, but he lost money on the venture and drifted into a sad decline. The most talented jockey of his generation died in 1807 at the age of 52 in Fleet, the debtors' prison.

An Early Case of Match-fixing

1817

William Lambert was the dominant figure in English cricket from the turn of the nineteenth century. Born at Burstow, Surrey, he first appeared at Lord's in 1801, playing for his county against an All England XI, and soon acquired a reputation as a ferocious batsman and cunning slow bowler, being able to extract lift and turn from many a wicket. He was also an outstanding fielder. His friend George 'Squire' Osbaldeston described him as 'the most wonderful man that ever existed at catching a ball', adding that 'as wicketkeeper, fieldsman, bowler and batter, no man ever equalled Lambert'. He was indeed a force to be reckoned with.

Osbaldeston was no slouch himself. Small and stocky with a family motto of 'What man dare, I dare', he was an excellent horseman, first rate shot and one of the leading half-dozen amateur cricketers in England. A professional gambler, Osbaldeston enjoyed a tilt at the single and double-wicket matches that were popular at the time and often recruited the services of Lambert. Together, they were a formidable pair. Lambert made a good living from these matches, playing for the highest bidder.

In 1810 Osbaldeston was involved in a fifty-guinea challenge match with Lord Frederick Beauclerk at Lord's – a single-wicket match contested by two sets of pairs. Beauclerk chose as his partner the fast bowler C T Howard while the 'Squire' opted for the tried and trusted Lambert, who by then was the country's foremost all-rounder. Unfortunately Osbaldeston was taken ill a few days before the match, but his request for a postponement received short shrift from Beauclerk who knew that his rival would almost certainly have to forfeit the game and therefore the money. However, Beauclerk had reckoned without the wily Lambert who persuaded Osbaldeston to rise from his sick bed, score one run, retire and then allow his partner to tackle the two opponents single-handed. This Lambert did to great effect, eventually winning the match for the sick 'Squire' by fourteen runs. He then collected his reward in the form of a parcel from Osbaldeston's carriage, the bundle being said to contain either banknotes or a gold watch. Beauclerk was livid and swore revenge.

He had to wait seven years. The year of 1817 was a momentous one for Lambert. It started auspiciously when, playing for Sussex, he became the first batsman to score a century in each innings of a major match (a feat not repeated for 76 years) but ended in disaster following a controversial fixture between an England XI and 22 men of Nottingham. Having arranged the match for a stake of £150, Osbaldeston was unable to take part owing to a mix-up over the dates. The Nottinghamshire club were most upset and wrote him a vitriolic letter in which they ascribed his absence to an overweening sense of his own importance. Not only was Osbaldeston arguably the most dangerous bowler of his day but also without his financial input the stake money could not be raised. With a crowd of 20,000 expected at the Forest Ground, the county were eager for the match to go ahead and so it was agreed to play the game simply for pleasure, the gentlemen of Nottinghamshire agreeing to contribute £30 towards the visitors' expenses. However, 'simply for pleasure' was an alien term to the cash-conscious Lambert.

Among Lambert's England team-mates that day was Beauclerk, a man who played to win in even the most insignificant contest. It was soon apparent to his lordship that not all of his colleagues were giving their all, a belief brought home in painful fashion when he broke a finger trying to prevent what looked suspiciously like a deliberate overthrow. Undaunted, Beauclerk batted one-handed but his gallantry could not stop England slumping to a shock thirty-run defeat.

When it emerged that large sums of money had changed hands over the result, Beauclerk began to investigate. Soon he had collected enough evidence to prove that Lambert had not played his best and had 'sold' the match. Using his considerable influence, Lord Frederick succeeded in having Lambert 'warned off' from playing at Lord's for the rest of his life. It was a harsh sentence, pursued as much out of malice as any desire to clean up the game, and effectively ended Lambert's illustrious career. He slunk back to Sussex in disgrace while equally guilty parties remained unfettered.

The Derby Ringer

1844

The real drama of the 1844 Derby occurred not on Epsom Downs in front of a huge crowd of enthusiastic Londoners but over a month later at a criminal court in Westminster before a handful of interested spectators. For it was there that the winner of the three-year-olds' classic, Running Rein, was unmasked as a four-year-old named Maccabeus following one of the most shameful episodes in the history of the English turf.

Although the court case was the result of an action brought by Colonel Peel, owner of the runner-up Orlando, against Alexander Wood, owner of Running Rein, the two principal players in this tale of deception and skulduggery were the villain of the piece, the dastardly Levi Goodman, and his nemesis from the Jockey Club, Lord George Bentinck.

Running Rein and Maccabeus were two almost identical-looking bays, originally owned by Goodman. Both had a small white star on their forehead and four black legs. The only outward distinction between the two horses was that the year older Maccabeus had a scar on one of his forelegs. Whether by chance or design, Running Rein soon possessed a similar scar after damaging a foreleg while trying to jump a fence near his paddock. Goodman now considered the colts to be all but indistinguishable to the naked eye and so embarked on a long-term plan to make a financial killing on the 1844 Derby.

To throw any future investigators off the scent, Goodman arranged for Running Rein to switch stables and then in September 1842 he sent Running Rein, Maccabeus and another colt to Epsom trainer William Smith. The following month the horses were broken in by George Hitchcock who subsequently admitted that although he had been told that all three were yearlings, he believed that one was a year older. However, he was reluctant to voice his suspicions to the volatile Smith who had once taken a whip to Hitchcock after the latter had queried the age of a horse that had been sent to him. Running Rein and Maccabeus remained with Smith until February 1843 when Goodman suddenly ordered them to be moved to his own secluded paddocks at Sutton. There they were joined by a useful Irish horse called Goneaway, leased by Goodman for a year to muddy the waters still further. Visiting a Regent Street hairdresser, Goodman purchased a large bottle of hair dye with which he proceeded to paint a pastern – part of the horse's foot – on Goneaway to make it resemble Maccabeus and Running Rein. He then trimmed Goneaway's tail and entered the horse as 'Maccabeus' at the Epsom spring meeting. However, the fact that 'Maccabeus' started at 4–7 in a field of 13 suggested that Goodman had not covered his tracks as well as he had hoped.

The Epsom disappointment seemed to dissuade Goodman from further schemes involving Goneaway and, during the summer, he announced that Maccabeus had died. In truth Maccabeus was alive and kicking and in October of that year was ready to begin his impersonation of Running Rein in a £50 sweepstake at Newmarket. 'Running Rein' trotted up at 3–1 but the ease of his victory alerted the ever-vigilant Lord George Bentinck who, considering the horse to be too big for a two-year-old and too impressive in triumph, promptly encouraged the beaten owners to object to the outcome on the grounds that the winner was really a three-year-old. The stewards duly investigated but a stable lad who had been present at Running Rein's birth two years earlier swore that the Newmarket winner and Running Rein were one and the same horse. For the time being Goodman's plot remained undetected, but Bentinck was too formidable an adversary to let the matter lie.

After backing Running Rein at an early price of 33–1 for the 1844 Derby, Goodman sought to distance himself from the affair by selling the horse to Alexander Wood, a respectable Epsom corn merchant, as payment for a debt. Although

Goodman would keep control of all racing arrangements to ensure that the horse actually took part in the Derby, it would now be running in Wood's name. Naturally, Wood knew nothing of Goodman's duplicity.

Wary of arousing further suspicion in the wake of the Newmarket dispute, Goodman refrained from giving either the real or the fake Running Rein a preparatory race for the Derby. Nevertheless, that spring Bentinck continued to tell anyone who would listen that the horse was a 'ringer'. Five days before the Epsom classic he petitioned the Epsom stewards to have the colt's mouth examined and strongly protested at Running Rein's participation in the Derby. The stewards ignored the request and merely asked Wood to produce a breeding certificate and warned him that there might be an inquiry if Running Rein won.

Twenty-nine horses lined up on the Downs on 22 May, Running Rein (alias Maccabeus) being sent off third favourite at 10–1. Bentinck's money was on the second favourite Ratan. After two false starts, 'Running Rein' stormed to victory, despite striking into Leander at Tattenham Corner – an incident which, as we shall see, would have its own strange twist. But for the time being all eyes – especially those of Bentinck – were on the winner. No doubt at his lordship's instigation, Colonel Peel, brother of the prime minister and owner of the runner-up, Orlando, immediately launched a formal objection. The stewards withheld the prize and agreed to an inquiry, only to be informed that the winning horse had already left the course. It is rumoured that, in order to destroy any evidence, the hapless Maccabeus was swiftly beheaded and buried on a Northamptonshire farm. The real Running Rein also vanished without trace.

Having been foiled at Newmarket, Bentinck was not about to let history repeat itself, so began playing detective. First he uncovered the Goneaway connection and, suspecting that the horse's legs had been dyed to conceal its true identity, set about visiting every chemist between Goodman's home and the London club that Goodman visited on a daily basis. His calls eventually took him to Regent Street where he was told that a man fitting Goodman's description had bought a large bottle of hair dye. The female assistant who made the sale went with Bentinck to Goodman's club and positively identified him. Confronted with the evidence, Goodman admitted the frauds concerning Goneaway, Running Rein and Maccabeus. Goodman was barred from the Turf, Running Rein was disqualified and Orlando declared the winner of the 1844 Derby – just in time for a young officer who had sustained such heavy losses on Orlando that he had been about to blow his brains out when news of the revised placings came through.

The wrangling between Wood and Colonel Peel resulted in a court case that began at Westminster on 1 July. Wood maintained his innocence but when he was unable to produce the horse to back up his statement, he was forced to admit that there had been a fraud even though he himself had played no part in it. Summing up, the judge, Baron Alderson, expressed his regret and disgust at 'noblemen and gentlemen of rank associating and betting with men of low rank... In doing so, they have found themselves cheated and made the dupes of the grossest frauds.'

Curiously 'Running Rein' was not the only overage horse in that year's Derby. Leander, struck into by the illicit winner, broke a fetlock and was destroyed, a vet adding insult to injury by claiming that the horse was anything between four and six years old. Leander's trainer, John Forth, was so angered by the whispering campaign that he later had the horse's corpse exhumed, cut off the lower jaw, boiled it clean and sent it to the vet to prove that the animal was only three. When the vet stood by his diagnosis, Forth dug up the body again and this time sent the upper jaw to another medical man. But the second expert came to the same conclusion as the first and, with nothing left to dig up, Forth quietly retreated from the debate.

As a final footnote to the most crooked Derby ever, Bentinck's satisfaction at uncovering Goodman was tempered by the heavy losses he sustained on Ratan. He had noticed that the horse was drifting sharply in the betting just before the off and it later emerged that Ratan's jockey, Sam Rogers, had laid £10,000 to £1,000 against his own mount and had been backing the favourite, The Ugly Buck, instead. Rogers was banned from riding for three years.

England Walk Off

1862

As the laws of cricket stood in 1862, under Rule 10 it was illegal for a bowler to raise his hand or arm above his shoulder while in the act of delivering the ball, principally because it was thought to be dangerous on rough wickets. 'High bowling', as this illicit practice was known, had been prevalent for years but some umpires had chosen to turn a blind eye to it. However, an unsavoury incident during the Surrey versus England match at the Oval on 26 August 1862 brought about a drastic change in the laws and paved the way for the introduction of overarm bowling.

The match had been eventful from the outset. More than 5,000 spectators could hardly believe their eyes as England, batting first, compiled a record total of 503, surpassing the 473 made by MCC at Lord's in 1820. After nine hours 55 minutes and 1,058 balls, the innings concluded at 5.30 on the second day, leaving the Surrey openers with an awkward period to negotiate before close of play. Surrey came out to bat shortly before six o'clock to face the bowling of Mr V E Walker and the Kent left-armer Edgar Willsher. With Walker claiming an early breakthrough, Surrey were on the ropes when Willsher came in to bowl his third over from the Pavilion End. But just as Willsher unleashed the first delivery, the Pavilion End umpire, John Lillywhite, called 'no-ball'. To add insult to injury, the batsman cut it for four. It was the same story for the remainder of the over, Lillywhite calling Willsher for six no-balls in succession. At the end of the over, Willsher threw the ball angrily to the ground and marched off the field, followed by the rest of the England team.

Confusion reigned supreme. The crowd spilled over on to the pitch and it was announced that play had been abandoned for the day. The *Daily Telegraph* reported: 'On inquiry, we learnt that, on bowling his second over, Willsher was cautioned by John Lillywhite that he was getting high in delivery, and that he should "no-ball" him if he continued to so deliver the balls.' However, *The Times* stated that it was not only the high bowling that the umpire objected to; Lillywhite also deemed Willsher's deliveries to be throws.

Following the curtailment of play, Surrey Cricket Club held a committee meeting at which wholehearted support was expressed for Lillywhite. The umpire offered to step down for the rest of the match and, rather than run the risk of further interruptions and controversies, Surrey accepted the gesture. Willsher duly apologised for his abrupt departure and display of petulance and the match was resumed the next day. Allowed to bowl unchecked and high by Lillywhite's replacement, Willsher took six wickets as Surrey were dismissed for 102. Following on, they reached 154–6 before the game was declared a draw.

The incident provoked much discussion in the press. *The Times* wrote: 'For some time past it has been a moot point regarding "high bowling", and although the "cricket laws" define it, still it has been a growing fashion to get high, and with Willsher it is considered by some particularly so.' The *Daily Telegraph* predicted: 'One thing is certain, that today's proceedings are pregnant with important results to the national game, and after this season Rule 10 will either have to be carried out by umpires in its integrity, or struck out of the laws of cricket.' Two years later cricket's lawmakers voted to remove the restrictions on overarm bowling by 27 votes to twenty, although underarm bowling continued to be practised in the first-class game for many years to come.

Stormy Waters

1871

When the New York Yacht Club's representative *America* defeated the British schooner *Titania* in a challenge match off Cowes in 1851, the victorious owners were presented with a cup, which they subsequently donated to the NYYC as a perpetual challenge trophy in conjunction with a deed of gift outlining the rules and conditions of future races. Six years later the NYYC informed overseas yacht clubs of its new competition and invited 'spirited contest for the championship', promising 'a liberal, hearty welcome and the strictest of fair play'. But then the American Civil War intervened and it was not until 1868 that a challenger came forward in the shape of Englishman James Ashbury to contest what would become the most prestigious prize in yachting, the America's Cup.

The son of a wheelwright who had made his fortune by inventing a railway carriage, Ashbury had ideas above his station. He harboured ambitions of a seat in Parliament and, whether at work or play, insisted on playing by his own rules. Naturally, therefore, he had very definite ideas about the form that the challenge should take, regardless of the rules laid down in the deed of gift. Ashbury proposed a multirace challenge between his yacht *Cambria* (sponsored by the Royal Thames Yacht Club) and the best of the NYYC fleet, but the New Yorkers maintained that their entire fleet be allowed to compete against the sole British boat. Ashbury was further infuriated by the hosts selecting a twisting course off Staten Island, which greatly rewarded local knowledge, and by their allowing centreboard yachts – those with a moveable keel – to race against the challenger. He objected on all three counts but the NYYC refused to back down and on 8 August 1870 the *Cambria* lined up against seventeen US boats for the inaugural America's Cup race.

Predictably Ashbury lost but his mutterings about foul play led to a renewed challenge the following year with a different yacht, *Livonia*. From the outset, he once again endeavoured to impose his will on the NYYC, claiming that the deed of gift called for a 'match' as opposed to a race against an entire fleet, and he went so far as to consult his lawyers on the matter. This time the NYYC capitulated and on 24 March 1871 it resolved 'that we sail one or more representative vessels, against the same number of challenging vessels'. Flushed with this success, Ashbury then repeated his demands that centre-boarders be excluded and that a different course be chosen. Furthermore he loftily suggested that, because he was a member of twelve different yacht clubs, he wished to represent them all and proposed a series of twelve races, with the first to win seven being declared the overall winner.

The NYYC was not in the habit of being dictated to – least of all by an upstart Englishman – but it decided to wait until Ashbury arrived in New York in early October before dismissing his latest requests out of hand. Incensed, Ashbury immediately threatened to withdraw and wrote: 'As you decline twelve races, seven out of twelve to win, I have no alternative but to act strictly up to the deed of trust by which you hold the cup, viz., by sailing the twelve races on behalf of as many clubs against your champion vessel – keel boat or centreboard, as you may select; and the first race *Livonia* won I should in that case formally and officially claim the cup on behalf of the club whose flag I sailed under.'

When this ultimatum was also rejected, Ashbury threatened to sail around the course alone and claim the Cup by default. As the exchange of increasingly acidic letters continued, the fear on both sides was that it would soon be too cold to race anyway. Ashbury may have been tempted to storm off in a huff and take his toys back to England but he realised that failure to compete after such a fanfare would seriously dent his parliamentary ambitions. So he reluctantly agreed to a compromise whereby the Cup would be decided by a best of seven-race series. Three of the races would be held on the tricky inside course favoured by the Americans and three on an outside course preferred by Ashbury. If a seventh race were necessary, it would be staged on the outside course. Centreboarders would be allowed and Ashbury agreed to represent just one club – the Royal Harwich Yacht Club.

Having previously accused Ashbury of 'sharp practice', the NYYC now indulged in a spot of skulduggery of its own. The Englishman's satisfaction at the agreement to a one-on-one match was tempered by the Americans' announcement that they would be selecting four boats to defend the Cup, reserving the right to delay choosing which of the four would compete against *Livonia* until the morning of each race. This allowed the NYYC to pick whichever boat was best suited to the prevailing weather conditions. Ashbury was less than amused by this unexpected development but equally he was aware that it was non-negotiable. For once he yielded without too much of a fuss, but it was to prove the lull before the storm.

The Americans' four boats were *Dauntless, Sappho, Columbia* and *Palmer*, the last two of which were centreboards. The first race for the 1871 America's Cup took place on 16 October and was won by *Columbia*. Two days later – in race two – the same boat triumphed again, only to be on the receiving end of a fierce formal protest from Ashbury. The Cup's sailing rules offered no instructions regarding which way to round the turning mark. In the first race both boats had left all marks to starboard and Ashbury assumed that the same rules applied to race two. However, Franklin Osgood, owner of *Columbia*, sounded out the Cup committee beforehand and was told that the mark could be turned 'as you please'. But nobody passed on this information to Ashbury. In England, according to Ashbury, the rule was that when no instructions were given, all marks had to be left on the starboard hand, which required a complicated, time-consuming gybe at the mark. Thus, although *Livonia* rounded the mark-boat almost two minutes ahead of *Columbia*, her captain lost all of that time – and more – by performing the delicate manoeuvre. Meanwhile *Columbia* simply tacked around, gaining time, distance and the favoured windward side and went on to win by over ten minutes. Never

slow to react to a perceived injustice against himself, Ashbury
was incandescent.

The Cup committee treated his protest with customary
disdain, ruling that it 'could not be entertained' as the
Englishman should have known that the rules make the
method of rounding optional in the absence of any official
instructions. It added that the English rule to which Ashbury
referred applied only to fleet races, not matches.

Ashbury refused to accept the decision and, via another
series of letters in the press, threatened to appeal to higher
tribunals. The NYYC was not for turning.

Amid the mounting acrimony, the races continued. *Livonia*
took race three against *Columbia* before *Sappho* won races four
and five to give the Americans a 4–1 victory overall. That could
have been the end of the matter but Ashbury was not finished
yet. Still claiming that he should have won the second race on
a protest, he insisted that the true score was 3–2 and that
therefore *Livonia* would be at the line for the next two days for
races six and seven. On the 24th Ashbury sailed against
Dauntless in what the Americans had decreed was a non-
competitive race. *Dauntless* won but the indefatigable Ashbury
claimed victory on the grounds that, as far as the Cup
committee was concerned, he had gone over the course alone.
The weather was so bad on the 25th that the mark-boat could
not set out, at which point Ashbury claimed another triumph
and declared that he had won the series 4–3. Not surprisingly,
the NYYC disagreed and the Cup stayed firmly in America.

Back in England, Ashbury was still seething at his treatment
and proceeded to fire off a lengthy epistle to the NYYC
accusing the club of 'unfair and unsportsmanlike
proceedings', adding that if ever again he challenged for the
Cup he would be bringing his lawyers with him. The NYYC
merely acknowledged receipt of his letter. It was the ultimate
put-down.

Unable to admit defeat, Ashbury launched a new offensive in
the form of a pamphlet. This latest attack stung the NYYC into
retaliation and the club felt obliged to write back to the Royal
Harwich: 'We are accustomed to hold that there are certain
acts which a gentleman cannot commit. Whatever the cause,

Mr Ashbury evidently thinks otherwise, and with apparent unconsciousness that it ought to give offence, he seems to look behind every action for an unworthy motive, and seek in every explanation evidences of concealment and want of candour.' By now the New York club was so irritated by Ashbury's behaviour that it wished to sever all ties with him and returned three cups, which he had generously donated.

It will come as no surprise to learn that 1871 was James Ashbury's last challenge for the America's Cup. He did eventually secure a seat in parliament before opting for the quieter life of a sheep farmer in New Zealand.

Open Warfare

1876

The archetypal dour Scot, Davie Strath's outwardly uncompromising demeanour was allied to a shrewd golfing brain. It ran in the family. His elder brother Andrew won the Open in 1865 and when Davie turned professional three years later he was widely expected not only to follow in Andrew's footsteps but to exceed the feats of his sibling. At Hoylake in 1872 he finished runner-up to his good friend, 'Young' Tom Morris, in the first professional tournament to be held in England, but the coveted prize of the Open continued to elude him. That he failed to rectify the situation in 1876 was because his natural talent came second to his sheer bloody-mindedness, as a result of which the championship was thrown into its first great controversy.

If the truth be told the 1876 Open at St Andrews was an organisational nightmare from the start. The Royal and Ancient's autumn meeting had already been delayed by the late arrival of Queen Victoria's son, Prince Leopold, who had eventually turned up to drive himself in as captain just three days before the beginning of the Open. Having been deprived of valuable playing time, the club members felt it only fair that they be allowed to play on that final Saturday in September (the first day of the Open) and so it was agreed that they should tee-off alternately with the Open competitors. The result was less than satisfactory with rank amateurs playing in alarmingly close proximity to the world's foremost professionals. Davie Strath's characteristic air of doom and gloom was not brightened when, following a rare wayward shot, his ball ended up in a bad lie after taking an unfortunate 'kick' off the head of a local upholsterer who happened to be playing on the adjacent fairway. Nevertheless Strath was very much in contention as the 36-hole contest drew to a climax. Bob Martin, who worked in 'Old' Tom Morris's shop at St Andrews, was the leader in the clubhouse with a second round of ninety for a total of 176. This meant that Strath had to complete the last two holes in ten strokes or less to become the new Open champion.

Playing his third shot to the seventeenth – the famous Road Hole – Strath made the cardinal error of not waiting until the green ahead had cleared. According to witnesses, Strath's ball hit one of the players on the green and stopped near the hole when otherwise it might have run through on to the road. From his favourable position Strath got down in two putts for a five. However, he was unable to take full advantage of his fortune and took six on the last to end up tied for the championship with Martin.

It was then that the fur began to fly. The player who had apparently been struck by Strath's ball lodged a protest and demanded a disqualification for a breach of the rules. The rule in force at St Andrews at the time read: 'When two parties meet on the putting green, the party first there may claim the privilege of holing out, and any party coming up must wait until the other party has played out the hole, and on no account play their balls up lest they should annoy the parties who are putting.' Amid further rumours that Strath's card had not been kept accurately by the marker, the matter was referred to the Council of the R&A who proposed a Monday play-off while they sat in judgement on Strath's alleged infringements. But Strath demanded that a decision be reached before any play-off and when the R&A refused to cave in to his bullying, Martin was allowed to walk over the course and claim the Open and its first prize money of £10. Somewhat surprisingly in view of his behaviour, Strath was permitted to keep second place and a prize of £8.

Davie Strath never did win the Open. Two years later he died of consumption in Australia, ironically while on a health trip. Yet his memory lives on at St Andrews to this day. For one of the bunkers guarding the eleventh green on the Old Course is officially known as the Strath bunker in memory of the man whose temperament cost him a place on golf's roll of honour.

The Sydney Cricket Riot

1879

The team that toured Australia under Lord Harris in 1878–9 was the fifth party of English cricketers to visit those distant shores. It was also very nearly the last.

The side was predominantly amateur, bolstered by the inclusion of the Yorkshire professionals, George Ulyett and Tom Emmett. The composition rendered the tourists something of an unknown quantity, much to the consternation of the Australian betting fraternity who wavered as to which team should carry the smart money. The early indications certainly favoured the Australians. The only Test match of the tour – in Melbourne – resulted in a resounding ten-wicket victory for the hosts, a rout which apparently prompted the usually disciplined Lord Harris to hurl his bat around the dressing room in a fit of rage. Following the debacle, England headed for Sydney to play two matches against New South Wales and Lord Harris took with him from Melbourne 22-year-old George Coulthard, who had stood in the Test, to umpire in both fixtures. Although Australian, Coulthard was viewed with deep suspicion by the New South Wales men, not so much because he was Lord Harris's chosen umpire but because he hailed from Victoria. The rivalry between the different Australian colonies (as they were then) was even more intense than that between Australia and England.

The first New South Wales match passed off without incident and ended in further humiliation for the visitors, who went down by five wickets. However, the second match, which began at the Association Ground on 7 February, was a different proposition. Lord Harris won the toss and saw his team post a respectable 267, although this total represented quite a collapse from 217–2. In reply, New South Wales were dismissed for 177, their star player, Billy Murdoch, carrying his bat for an unbeaten 82, and were forced to follow on. The sudden change in fortunes did not go down well with professional bookmakers in the crowd, who had willingly accepted hefty bets on an England victory at generous odds in the belief that the tourists would inevitably suffer another defeat.

Against this backdrop of mounting discontent, New South Wales had reached nineteen in their second innings on the Saturday when Murdoch was dubiously adjudged run out for ten, the fatal decision delivered by Coulthard. Almost immediately murmurings of unrest emanating from the pavilion spilled over on to the pitch as 2,000 spectators invaded the playing area to remonstrate with the umpire. The majority were simply aggrieved at the run out and at the prospect of seeing the local team lose, but those who called for the invasion in the first place were thought to be the very bookmakers who faced heavy financial losses if England won. Coulthard's fellow umpire was Edmund Barton, later Sir Edmund Barton and from 1901–3 the first prime minister of the Australian Commonwealth, but even his diplomatic skills were powerless to quell the rioters. Lord Harris tried to protect Coulthard from the mob but was struck with a whip or a stick. While some of the England players armed themselves with stumps to repel the invaders, the diminutive Lancashire batsman Albert Hornby managed to effect a citizen's arrest of his lordship's assailant but in doing so had most of his shirt ripped from his back. The commotion lasted for half an hour, during which time Lord Harris refused to leave the ground for fear of forfeiting the match. When order was eventually restored, play was suspended for the remainder of the day.

Following an official apology from the New South Wales club and expressions of regret from leading Australian politicians, Lord Harris agreed to continue the match after the Sunday break but he refused to ask Coulthard to stand down. England went on to win by an innings and 41 runs, Emmett finishing with match figures of thirteen for 68.

The Australian press were divided about the unsavoury incident. While the *Sydney Morning Herald* accused 'hundreds of roughs and larrikins' of behaving 'in a most cowardly manner', other publications accused Coulthard of having backed England to win the match. Furthermore it was insinuated that Ulyett and Emmett had deliberately played poorly in the earlier games in order to guarantee bigger odds on an England victory at Sydney. It was all most undignified and when Lord Harris wrote a critical letter that appeared in both the British and Australian press, sporting relations between the two countries became decidedly strained.

The Australians did their best to clamp down on the troublemakers. Two of the rioters, William Rigney and John Richards, were each fined £2 and ordered to pay £1 6s 0d costs. And those in the pavilion who had started the disturbance – including a prominent Victorian bookmaker – had their membership subscriptions of £1 11s 6d returned and were banned from the ground for life. Nevertheless the wounds took a long time to heal and when an Australian touring team arrived in England the following year, such was the ill feeling towards them that they were forced to advertise for fixtures. Indeed, it required a great deal of persuasive talk before Lord Harris finally agreed to lead England in their first-ever home Test match, at the Oval in September 1880.

The man at the centre of the rumpus, George Coulthard, actually went on to play for Australia in the second Test of the 1881–2 series, thus achieving the unusual distinction of umpiring in a Test match before playing in one. By a neat twist of fate his captain in that Test was none other than Billy Murdoch!

The Poisoning of Orme

1892

The doping of horses has been an unwelcome component of racing ever since betting on the sport began. After winning the 1852 Grand National and finishing runner-up the following year, Miss Mowbray was a hot favourite for the 1854 race. Thousands of pounds were placed on her with the result that many bookmakers faced financial ruin if she won. But shortly before the 21 runners were due to assemble in the paddock, Miss Mowbray was found to have been deliberately blistered on her near foreleg, rendering the limb useless and causing her to be withdrawn. The new favourite, Bourton, went on to win by fifteen lengths. And, as recently as 2002, former National Hunt jockey Dermot Browne was banned for twenty years after admitting to doping no fewer than 23 horses. However, that case created nothing more than a minor ripple compared to the furore surrounding the alleged poisoning of Guineas and Derby favourite Orme in 1892.

The son of the unbeaten Triple Crown winner Ormonde, Orme was owned and bred by the Duke of Westminster, a leading light in the Jockey Club as well as being one of the wealthiest men in the land. As a yearling Orme was sent to be trained at Kingsclere, near Newbury, by John Porter, a firm disciplinarian with a reputation for getting the very best out of the horses in his charge. Orme responded to the Porter treatment by winning five out of six races as a two-year-old, his only defeat being a second to Signorina in the Lancashire Plate at the Manchester September meeting when giving weight away. Along with the filly La Flèche (owned by Baron de Hirsch, a friend of the Prince of Wales), Orme was the stable star and expectations were high that between them the pair would make a clean sweep of the 1892 classics.

But behind the scenes there were mutterings of discontent at Kingsclere. The once friendly rivalry between the respective handlers of La Flèche and Orme began to develop into open hostility, while Porter himself was on rapidly deteriorating terms with Lord Marcus Beresford, racing manager for both Baron de Hirsch and the Prince of Wales. It was a simple clash of personalities. Porter did not suffer fools gladly and, in his opinion, the extrovert Beresford fitted snugly into that category. However, Porter was well aware that he could not afford to allow his personal feelings to cloud his business judgement. For all the influential owners at his yard and his previous classic successes, the loss of a client of the calibre of the Prince of Wales could easily produce a snowball effect.

Against this awkward backdrop Orme prepared for the first classic of the season, the Two Thousand Guineas. Although he was not given a preparatory race, he impressed Porter with his work on the gallops and was strongly fancied to pick up the Newmarket prize. On the Friday before the big race Beresford and a small party visited Kingsclere and, accompanied by Porter, looked in on Orme. Porter could not help noticing rivulets of saliva leaking from the horse's mouth and, although he played down its significance in the presence of the visitors, as soon as they had departed he rushed back to the box and examined Orme's mouth. Not only was the stream of saliva increasing but also blisters were beginning to form under the horse's tongue. The mouth appeared to be swollen. Porter judged the problem to be some form of dental infection and, as well as sending for his local vet, a Mr Williams, despatched a telegram to Loeffler, a German expert in such matters who practised at Newmarket, urging him to visit Kingsclere as soon as possible. Meanwhile, as a precaution, Porter moved Orme to a more isolated box and rubbed the horse's throat with mustard lest the symptoms proved to be the onset of coughing.

Loeffler arrived the following morning and immediately attributed the malaise to a septic tooth. After removing an offending molar, he prepared to leave, satisfied that the horse would soon make a full recovery, but Porter had become alarmed by the dreadful stench emanating from Orme's mouth and was now convinced that an attempt had been made to poison the animal. This led to a frank exchange of views between the trainer and the equally forthright Loeffler.

Orme's withdrawal from the Guineas field sent the bush telegraph into overdrive. Rumours of foul play abounded and word spread that the horse might not even be fit to run in the Derby, for which he was the hottest favourite in years. To Porter's growing consternation, the horse was showing no sign of improvement following Loeffler's visit and on the Sunday he sent once more for Mr Williams. With the racing press now full of wild speculation, Porter decided that it was time for the Duke of Westminster to be put fully in the picture. So he despatched Williams to inform the Duke that an attempt had undoubtedly been made to poison the horse.

On hearing from Williams, the Duke promptly offered a £1,000 reward for information leading to the culprit, stating that 'on the 21st of April last, at Kingsclere Stable, in the County of Hants, the racehorse Orme, the property of his Grace the Duke of Westminster, was wilfully poisoned'.

Over the following week it would seem that Orme's condition did steadily improve although Porter, who was no great media communicator, refrained from issuing any public statements regarding the horse's wellbeing. However, he did grant an interview to William Allison of the *Sportsman* in which he appeared to backtrack on the poisoning theory and suggest that accounts of the horse's illness had been greatly exaggerated. Unfortunately for Porter the story was published in the same issue that the *Sportsman* printed a letter from the Duke of Westminster, which read: 'Orme is better but was nearly dead on Sunday and Monday, and was only kept alive by injections of milk and eggs. It is hoped he may recover sufficiently to meet his Derby engagement. I am afraid there can be no doubt that a very virulent poison was administered to him, probably twice – on Thursday and Friday in last week.'

The Duke was furious at being made to look foolish. Fearful that he might lose the Duke's patronage at a time when his relationship with the Prince of Wales' representative was also under a cloud, Porter was coerced into issuing a formal retraction of his interview with the *Sportsman*. In a letter to *The Times* dated 7 May, Porter voiced his objections to Allison's article, criticising it in particular for 'ascribing to me the statement that his Grace the Duke of Westminster had "formed his conclusions too hastily".' He also attacked Allison for saying that, on his visit to Kingsclere in the week following the illness, he had seen Orme 'taking walking exercise'. Porter pointed out that Allison had not been allowed to see Orme. Porter's assertion that Orme had been the victim of poisoning was backed up in the same edition of *The Times* by a letter from Williams the vet who described how he had first visited the sick horse on Friday 22 April and found him to be suffering from a very sore throat and swollen lips. The symptoms had increased on the Saturday and on the Sunday, Williams wrote that:

> ... the horse was much worse. The tongue was protruding from the mouth, and so large that the animal could not close his jaws, and was quite unable to swallow anything. The discharge was of a thick, grey, stringy character, and hung from his mouth in long ropy strings. On each side of the mouth, and extending along the floor of the mouth, there were two large serous abscesses (the one on the left being the larger) some three or four inches long. The presence of these, with the other symptoms, raised my suspicions. I have never seen a case presenting these symptoms except following the administration of some strong irritant.

On Monday Williams lanced the abscesses, 'which discharged freely, and scarified the tongue, which bled to some extent. Towards evening the horse appeared somewhat relieved, and we were able to drench him with a little milk.' Williams concluded: 'In my opinion the horse was suffering from the administration of a powerful irritant poison ... I am positive the teeth in no way have produced this illness.'

While appeasing the Duke, the statements of Porter and Williams put both men on collision course with Loeffler who dismissed the poisoning theory out of hand. Via heated correspondence in the sporting press, Loeffler expressed the opinion that the excess of saliva in the horse's mouth was a natural result of the swollen tongue, which, together with the blisters, had been caused by contact with the sharp edges of a broken tooth – the tooth that Loeffler had then removed. He added haughtily: 'There is nothing more mysterious about the illness than a man with a decayed tooth having a faceache.' As the arguments continued to rage as to whether or not Orme had been poisoned, Loeffler became so distressed by his credibility being questioned that he suffered a nervous breakdown.

When it came to writing his memoirs Porter stuck to the party line, claiming that someone had tried to poison Orme by giving the horse a ball saturated in mercury. As Orme habitually had problems swallowing, Porter suggested that the ball had not passed beyond the mouth and that the irritation had therefore been confined to that part of the body. 'The tongue protruded,' he wrote, 'the teeth had loosened, there was sloughing and the poor creature was unable to swallow naturally either liquid or solid food.' Porter added that Orme's hair had fallen out in clumps and that for ten days the horse could barely stand without assistance. 'Orme hovered between life and death. It was almost a hopeless case.' As to the culprit, Porter pointed the finger at one of his stable lads whom he duly dismissed but never had charged. Indeed, despite the substantial reward and police and private investigations, nobody was ever brought to justice in connection with the Orme affair.

If Orme was poisoned, the motive seems unclear. There was no sudden rush of betting against the horse prior to the Guineas to suggest that the sabotage was part of an organised gambling coup. So was Orme perhaps the victim of inter-stable rivalry, poisoned by a handler of La Flèche desperate for the filly to grab the Kingsclere glory?

Orme's recovery was not sufficiently speedy for him to stake his reputation in the Derby for which La Flèche started 1–2 favourite, only to be beaten three-quarters of a length by the outsider Sir Hugo. The filly's defeat was openly celebrated by the Orme camp at Kingsclere – a further indication of the bitter rivalry between the two sets of supporters. Orme returned to work in mid-June and the following month won the Eclipse Stakes. Two weeks later he took the Sussex Stakes at Goodwood but classic success eluded him when he finished unplaced in the St Leger. The build-up to the Leger was also marred by rumours of nobbling – this time that jockey George Barrett was in the pay of bookmakers. The Duke of Westminster let Barrett know that he would be watching his every move – a warning that so unnerved the jockey that he abandoned his usual tactics and made the running, as a result of which Orme failed to last the distance. As a four-year-old Orme won the Eclipse for the second time (defeating La Flèche in the process) before being retired to stud. While he had proved his superiority over his stable-mate, he was never able to fulfil his true potential due to the mysterious goings-on at Kingsclere in April 1892.

Somebody Stole the Cup

1895

From its introduction in 1872, the FA Cup – eighteen inches high and made of silver by the firm of Martin, Hall and Co. at a cost of £20 – was the most coveted trophy in football. Affectionately known as the 'Little Tin Idol', it may well have seen service to this very day but for the intervention of a gang of Birmingham burglars one September night in 1895.

That year's final had been an all-West Midlands affair between Aston Villa and West Bromwich Albion and following Villa's 1–0 victory at Crystal Palace, the trophy was taken proudly back to Birmingham. Later that summer Villa were approached by William Shillcock, a football and football-boot manufacturer with premises at 73 Newtown Row, Birmingham, regarding the possibility of the Cup being displayed in his shop window. Having taken the precaution of insuring the trophy for £200, the club agreed to the request but little more than a fortnight later – between 9.30 p.m. on Wednesday 11 September and 7.30 the following morning – the FA Cup was stolen. Burglars had broken into Shillcock's shop by removing a portion of the roof and had made off with cash from the shop drawer as well as the 'Little Tin Idol'.

News of the theft spread rapidly. It was tantamount to a national disaster. Anxious crowds gathered outside the shop and the sum of £10 was offered for the trophy's return. One scribe, referring to the fact that the Wanderers and Blackburn Rovers had each won the Cup in three successive years but had opted not to keep it permanently, tried to see the lighter side of the situation. 'The Cup may be returned,' he wrote. 'It probably will. But it must not be forgotten that even when stolen three times it does not become the property of the thief!'

His optimism was misplaced. The 'Little Tin Idol' was never seen again.

The theft cast a shadow over the sporting nation. Poor Shillcock, who had also insured the Cup against burglary, was alarmed to see customers deserting his shop in their droves, clearly holding him responsible for the loss of such a treasure. He later wrote despairingly: 'It was an incident which seemed to me at the time a great and unprecedented calamity. I pictured myself a ruined man. I seemed to see myself a hated individual – to see my business boycotted.'

When three months of extensive police inquiries drew a blank, the Football Association was forced to consider the question of a replacement trophy. It was initially suggested that the £200 insurance money should be used to provide a new trophy in gold but that proposal was overruled in favour of making a precise copy of the missing Cup, based on models presented to the Wolves players when they won the competition in 1893. The new Cup, made by Vaughton's Ltd, cost £25 – conveniently the exact fine imposed upon Villa for losing the trophy while it was in their charge.

The postscript to the theft of the FA Cup occurred 63 years later when, in February 1958, the *Sunday Pictorial* carried the confession of a local petty criminal named Harry Burge. Then 83 years old (46 of them having beem spent at Her Majesty's Pleasure), Burge admitted that he and two accomplices had carried out the burglary at Shillcock's. But any hopes that the famous old trophy was safely stored in his attic were shattered when Burge revealed that they had melted it down to make counterfeit half crowns.

Thus ended the sad tale of the original FA Cup and the most notorious theft in football – that is until a dog named Pickles turned Norwood into a place of interest, when he famously discovered the World Cup in 1966.

Monkey Business in Wales

1896

Arthur Gould was the first superstar of Welsh rugby, so much so that he acquired two nicknames – 'Monkey' for his ability as a child to climb trees and the 'Great Crack of Newport' possibly for reasons that are better left unexplained.

Hailing from a family of rugby players, he made his first XV debut for Newport at the age of sixteen and quickly established himself as an outstanding centre three-quarter. In fact he was a superb all-round athlete and could run 100 yards in 10.2 seconds, a talent that enabled him to win numerous sprinting competitions, picking up over £1,000 in prize money. By contrast rugby was a strictly amateur sport and Gould was obliged to earn a living as a public works contractor. When in 1890 he announced that he was joining his brother Bob in the West Indies on contract work building bridges, the Mayor of Newport presented him with a cheque for fifty guineas and a gold ring. Gould vowed to return if he made his fortune and, sure enough, within eighteen months he was back in Newport playing rugby and captaining the local team.

His dark curly hair and black moustache earned him a host of admirers and his charismatic personality inspired all around him, never more so than in 1893 when he starred in Wales' first Triple Crown. His finest hour that year was against England in Cardiff, his two tries helping Wales to a famous victory, prompting scenes which saw him paraded shoulder-high through the streets.

By 1896 he had just turned thirty and was ready to announce his retirement. He had played in more first-class matches, scored more tries and dropped more goals than any other Welshman and it seemed that the whole of South Wales wanted to honour his achievements as captain of both club and country. Newspaper columns suggested a testimonial and after the proposal had been fully endorsed by the Welsh Rugby Football Union, over £400 was collected to buy Gould a house in Newport. But what appeared to be nothing more than a generous gesture by a grateful nation smacked of professionalism to the other three home unions. The Rugby Football Union in London and the International Rugby Board were furious at the gift and calls were made for the Welsh RFU to confiscate Gould's house. The Welsh RFU stood firm, arguing that it was merely a token of esteem rather than payment for playing, and threatened to withdraw from the International Board.

England alone backed down. Still scarred from the previous year when 22 clubs from Yorkshire and Lancashire had broken away to form the Northern Union (the forerunner of Rugby League) and mindful of the fact that English clubs still wanted to play Welsh clubs, the English RFU opted to steer clear of further controversy and dismissed the Gould affair as an internal Welsh problem. Scotland and Ireland, however, were less forgiving of any hint of professionalism and flatly refused to play Wales again until 1899.

Meanwhile the Welsh outcasts went ahead with honouring their favourite son. On Easter Monday 1897 they gathered in large numbers in Newport to sing Gould's praises and see him presented with the keys to a splendid detached villa. By way of repayment he proceeded to serve Welsh rugby admirably as a referee and national selector right up until his death in 1919.

Drunk at the Wicket

1897

Bobby Peel made an instant impact on Yorkshire cricket. On his debut for the county against Surrey in 1882, the slow left-armer – seen as the natural successor to Edmund Peate – destroyed the visitors to finish with figures of 9–29. With his high action and deceptive loop – in contrast to Peate who was more of a round-arm bowler – Peel went on to take 1,273 wickets between 1888 and 1897 and to play for England on twenty occasions. Among his admirers was Lancashire's Archie MacLaren who wrote: 'He was never worried by a perfect wicket and always appeared to have some conjuring trick up his sleeve with which to outwit his opponents... I place Peel first on my list of great left-handed bowlers that I have seen on account of his wonderful judgement, his diabolical cleverness and his great natural ability.'

High praise indeed, but it wasn't only his bowling that made Peel such an invaluable member of the Yorkshire side. He regularly made over 1,000 runs in a season, and made two unbeaten double centuries – 226 in a second-class game against Leicestershire in 1892, and 210 against Warwickshire four years later. A quiet man, Peel was said to be unflinching under fire, a man to rely on when the team was struggling. Sadly his prodigious talent was matched only by his prodigious thirst.

Upon the retirement of George Ulyett in 1893, Peel became the senior professional in the Yorkshire dressing room. His captain was Lord Hawke, a firm disciplinarian who was not afraid to make unpopular decisions, having rebuilt the side following the departure of many of the old guard. By 1897 Peel was forty years old, but proved that he still had much to offer by taking 8–53 against Kent in July of that year. However, instances where mind and body operated in perfect harmony were becoming increasingly infrequent as Peel began to hit the bottle as frequently as he hit the stumps. His team-mates strove to protect him from the wrath of his captain but Lord Hawke lived up to his name. Very little escaped his steely gaze.

The middle of August saw Yorkshire entertain Middlesex at Bramall Lane, Sheffield. Peel had been doing plenty of entertaining of his own. The match marked his return to the side after a month's absence, the result of being 'indisposed' on the final day of the previous fixture. The euphemism was equalled by *Cricket* magazine who diplomatically described the Middlesex game as 'his first appearance after a long illness'. Hopes that Peel had mended his ways during his enforced lay-off were dashed when, one morning in the course of the Middlesex match, he came down to breakfast at the team hotel looking, as team-mate George Hirst put it, in 'a proper condition'. Manhandling the drunken Peel back to his room, Hirst managed to get him undressed and into bed, praying that he would somehow sleep it off. The loyal Hirst then set off for the ground where he explained to Lord Hawke: 'Peel was taken very queer in the night, m'lord. He apologises but won't be able to turn out this morning.' If he suspected the real reason for Peel's absence, Lord Hawke did not betray it.

With Yorkshire in the field, Lord Hawke duly informed the twelfth man that he would be playing. Then, to the fury of Hawke and the dismay of Hirst, it became apparent that there were twelve men out in the middle because there, red-faced, ball in hand, was the grinning figure of Peel in what Hirst described as 'a properer condition than before'. All too aware that Peel was roaring drunk, Hawke stormed over and ordered him to leave the field whereupon Peel replied cheerfully: 'Not at all, my lord. I'm in fine form this morning.' According to some accounts, Peel proceeded to demonstrate his 'fine form' by bowling at the sightscreen in the mistaken belief that it was a Middlesex batsman. Others claim that he urinated on the wicket. Whatever the transgression, Lord Hawke had no choice but to lead him bodily from the field.

That evening Hirst, desperately trying to save his friend's career, went looking for Peel but found him sleeping off his excesses. The following morning he urged Peel to write an immediate apology to the captain.

'That I never will,' replied Peel.

Hirst warned him that he would be finished unless he apologised.

'Never,' insisted Peel. 'They'll have to send for me; they can't do without me.'

Lord Hawke did indeed send for him...but only to sack him.

Peel's sudden departure from Yorkshire cricket caused outrage among the county's supporters, not only because he had been such a stalwart servant of the club but also because he was an extremely popular figure, the archetypal working-class hero. But Lord Hawke was unrepentant. In his *Recollections and Reminiscences*, published in the 1920s, he wrote that Peel's sacking 'had to be done for the sake of discipline and the good of cricket'. As for Peel, he drowned his sorrows by becoming a publican in Leeds. It must have been the ultimate in job satisfaction.

Taking a Dive

1900

Joe Gans was the first native-born black American to win a world boxing title. His meticulous approach allied to his undisputed artistry in the ring earned him the nickname of the 'Old Master' yet much of his career was shrouded in controversy amid allegations that he deliberately threw fights. One highly suspicious bout caused such a furore that it led to boxing being banned throughout the state of Illinois for twenty years.

Born in Baltimore, Maryland, in 1874, Gans first made his mark at the city's Monumental Theater where he took part in a 'battle royal' – a brutal contest in which a number of black fighters entered the ring simultaneously and fought until only one was left. That last man standing was Joe Gans and his performance attracted the attention of boxing manager Al Herford who, in 1891, encouraged the sixteen-year-old to turn professional. Over the course of the decade he lost just three fights and on 23 March 1900 earned his first shot at the world lightweight title.

But while Gans may have been honest, Herford was not. Black boxers were subjected to considerable hostility in those days and Herford managed to persuade Gans that it would be wiser – and more profitable – if he were to lose certain fights. His challenge for the world title was against Frank Erne in New York City and although Gans was leading comfortably in the twelfth round, as soon as he sustained a cut eye he asked the referee to stop the fight. Some onlookers smelled a rat, and the doubts were scarcely dispelled two years later when Gans destroyed Erne inside two minutes.

In the interim Gans fought 'Terrible' Terry McGovern in Chicago on 13 December 1900. On paper it was a no-contest. The skilful Gans should easily have been able to deal with a slugger like McGovern but alarm bells began to ring several days before the fight when large sums of money were bet on a McGovern victory. Rumours started to sweep Chicago that Gans would fall in an early round so that his backers, including Herford, could make a financial killing. To be charitable to Herford, since press reports in the build-up to the contest had predicted race riots if McGovern, a white man, were to lose to a black fighter, his motives may have been guided almost as much by self-preservation as by monetary gain. Whatever the reason, Gans put up a lamentable display, offering precious little resistance to his opponent's wild blows. He had already been knocked down four times when, to the sound of catcalls and jeers, he failed to beat the count in round two.

The reaction ringside was mirrored in the newspaper columns. Referee George Siler said in the *Chicago Tribune*: 'I do not wish to accuse any fighter of faking, but if Gans was trying last night I don't know much about the game.' The *Philadelphia Evening Item* described the contest as 'a fake of the first water', adding that it 'outdid the most barefaced ring fraud that ever played in New York'. Naturally Herford and promoter Lou Houseman denied all allegations of a fix, but the stench of corruption would not blow away. A number of prominent Chicago politicians had lost big money on the fight and, together with the clergy, they campaigned to have boxing banned within the city limits. By 1906 the sport was outlawed throughout Illinois and remained illegal for the next twenty years.

Gans and Herford survived the scandal (although both steered clear of Chicago until the fuss had died down) and after he had captured the world crown from Erne at the second attempt, the 'Old Master' was at last able to demonstrate his real ability without any pressure from his corner. However, Herford again revealed his true colours early in 1906 when he vanished with the purse after Gans had defeated Mike Sullivan. Gans eventually surrendered his crown to Battling Nelson in 1908 and two years later he died from tuberculosis. To the end, he never admitted having taken a dive, but nobody who was ringside at Chicago ever had the slightest doubt.

Boxing on Trial

1901

The formulation of the Queensbury Rules in 1867 made boxing respectable. The primitive days of bare-knuckle bouts were all but consigned to history although the last championship fight without gloves, between John L Sullivan and Jake Kilrain, took place as late as 1899. In their place came structured, properly supervised contests. No more untimed rounds, no more spectator riots, no more fatalities in the ring. At least that was the idea.

To cater for boxing's new look and the well-heeled Victorian gentlemen who came to watch the noble art of self-defence, the National Sporting Club was formed in 1891, replacing the aristocratic Pelican Club. The NSC's base in London's Covent Garden quickly established itself as a stronghold of the sport, offering first-class facilities to watch the leading pugilists of the day, but in 1901 its future – and indeed the future of British boxing – was thrown into doubt when ten people were charged with manslaughter following the death in the ring of American fighter Billy Smith.

Death was an occupational hazard of boxing in the brutal, bloody, bare-knuckle days, but in some 5,000 fights staged by the National Sporting Club in the ten years since its formation, Smith's was only the fourth fatality. However, the club was only just recovering from the adverse publicity occasioned by the demise on its premises of British bantamweight Walter Croot in a world title fight with America's Jimmy Barry on 6 December 1897. Croot was comfortably ahead on points when, with less than a minute remaining of the twenty-round bout, Barry caught him with a stunning right to the jaw. Croot fell with such force that he suffered a broken skull as his head struck the hard floor of the ring. He died from his injuries a few days later. Barry and the NSC were eventually exonerated of any blame but the regrettable incident led to the club installing safety-conscious, padded floors in its rings. Four years on, even the precaution of padding could not save Billy Smith.

Twenty-five-year-old Smith (real name Murray Livingstone) had travelled from Philadelphia to the NSC for an international featherweight contest against Londoner Jack Roberts to take place on 22 April 1901. There were to be fifteen three-minute rounds with a purse of £100 going to the winner. Smith looked the more accomplished boxer over the opening rounds and had built up a lead of 4½ points by the seventh. Until then the fight had been relatively uneventful but shortly before the end of that seventh round both men accidentally slipped. In trying to avoid a blow, Smith lost his balance and the back of his head hit first the lower rope and then the padded floor. As the round ended Smith was helped to his corner and was seen to be dragging one leg behind him. A witness remarked that the previously strong Smith suddenly looked to be 'giving way', apparently through fatigue. Both men emerged for round eight but after a minute or so Smith sank to his knees and was counted out. While Roberts celebrated an unexpected victory, Smith had to be removed from the ring by his seconds. He was taken unconscious to Charing Cross Hospital where he died two days later.

The inquest heard that his death had been caused by compression of the brain, the result of either a blow or a fall. The dragging of the leg was symptomatic of a brain injury. The coroner heard that while Smith had minor bruises on his right arm and lips, there were no other outward signs of injury and witnesses testified that although he had been hit by Roberts during round eight, the punches were by no means excessive. Dismissing a suggestion by Smith's brother that the deceased had been drugged, the coroner praised the NSC for having a padded floor instead of bare boards and the jury returned a verdict of accidental death.

Nevertheless the police pursued charges of manslaughter against Roberts, Arthur Bettinson of the NSC, referee John

Douglas, timekeeper Eugene Corri, and the six seconds involved in the contest – William Chester, Arthur Gutteridge, Arthur Lock, William Baxter, Ben Jordan and Harry Greenfield. The case was heard at Bow Street Court in May and generated considerable interest, not least because boxing itself was on trial. As a private institution, the NSC had been permitted to stage boxing matches provided they were considered to be scientific exhibitions. However, the prosecution argued that far from being a scientific exhibition of the art of self-defence, the Roberts–Smith contest amounted to nothing more than a prize fight – 'fought for money, exhibited for money, and between trained boxers who had every inducement to punish each other as severely as possible'. In particular, grave concern was expressed about the rule that stated that a boxer who did not rise within ten seconds of a knockdown would be deemed counted out, the prosecution suggesting that this encouraged the combatants to inflict maximum damage on each other. The implication was clear: boxing was a barbaric sport with no place in twentieth century society.

The defence pointed out that there were more deaths on the football field than in the boxing ring, adding that both boxers were examined by a doctor before the fight. Furthermore, as seen from the medical report at the inquest, there were no marks of violence on Smith. Douglas, an experienced referee, testified that before the fight he had warned both men about boxing fairly and that he would disqualify them if they did 'anything that was underhand', and expert witnesses maintained that the ten-second knockout rule had been inserted for the purpose of making boxing more scientific and less dangerous. After lengthy deliberation the jury were unable to reach a verdict, so the judge ordered a retrial.

It was now that the celebrated barrister Edward Marshall Hall, who was defending Roberts, came into his own. In an impassioned speech he professed himself to be an admirer of boxing 'as a sport which fosters and encourages the true spirit of Englishmen'. Hall added that Roberts was in the dock because of 'a cruel accident', a view supported in his summing-up by Mr Justice Grantham who affirmed that Smith did not meet his death as a result of a punch. Mindful of the increasing number of stabbings brought before him, the judge went on to say that he preferred man to 'use the weapon that God has given him, namely his fists' rather than knives. The jury took the hint and this time required just two minutes to find all defendants not guilty. Boxing was acquitted.

Tour de Farce

1904

A sensational story in cycling is when one of the riders *passes* a drugs test. For much of the past forty years the sport has been perceived as being about as clean as Monica Lewinsky's favourite blue dress, and, even before illegal stimulants came to be in widespread use, showpiece events such as the Tour de France were frequently shrouded in accusations of tampering, intimidation and downright cheating. Never was this better illustrated than in the second ever Tour, in 1904, when no fewer than thirteen riders – including the first four to finish – were disqualified for a variety of transgressions at the end of a race marred by sabotage and riots.

The Tour de France was born in 1903 to boost the circulation of *L'Auto* newspaper and the inaugural event (won by French rider Maurice Garin) proved such a success that the organisers retained the same formula for the following year. Defending champion Garin, nicknamed the 'Little Chimney Sweep' in honour of his former trade, was the favourite once more in his capacity as leader of team La Française where he was joined by his brother César and the 1903 runner-up, Lucien Pothier. Their principal rivals were the Peugeot team, led by Hippolyte Aucouturier.

On 2 July the riders set out from Paris on the first stage to Lyon. Aucouturier was beset by repeated crashes and punctures and only kept in contention by taking an illegal tow from a car thanks to a wire fitted to a piece of cork which he held between his teeth. Another rider, Pierre Chevallier, eschewed such subtlety. Finding himself dropped from the main bunch, he simply hitched a ride in a car as darkness descended. And Pothier stayed in touch with the leaders by allowing his team's sporting director to pace him in a following car. This, too, was strictly against the rules. The tactic worked to such an extent that towards the end of the stage Pothier and Maurice Garin, both of whom had also taken illicit feeds en route from race organiser Georges Lefèvre, were able to break away from the pack. In their splendid isolation they suddenly found themselves flanked by a car full of menacing-looking men wearing goggles who strongly advised them to let the local rider, Antoine Fauré, win the stage. For six kilometres the car tried to run the pair into roadside ditches but somehow they survived and Garin was first to cross the line at Lyon.

However, Fauré's supporters were not to be denied and, as the second stage reached the Col du Grand Bois near St Etienne, a hundred-strong mob brandishing cudgels confronted the riders at three o'clock in the morning. Fauré was allowed through but Garin and his team-mates were pelted with rocks and prevented from proceeding. The Italian rider Giovanni Gerbi sustained broken fingers at the hands of the thugs, as a result of which he was forced to retire. The rioters were eventually dispersed when Lefèvre arrived on the scene and fired his pistol over their heads. Although apparently innocent of inciting any unrest, Fauré was disqualified when the stage finished at Marseille, as was Ferdinand Payan who had been found guilty of taking pace from a spectator's car. Aucouturier was declared the stage winner in a large group sprint, the riders being fearful of making a solo attack after the night's disgraceful violence.

Stage three – Marseille to Toulouse – was mapped to go through Nîmes, Payan's home region, and his angry fans had warned the race organisers that, in light of his disqualification, they could expect more trouble. The warning went unheeded and when the leaders reached the gates of Nîmes they were forced to slow to a crawl to avoid sharp nails and shards of broken glass that had been scattered in the road. At a snail's pace they became sitting targets for a hail of stones hurled by Payan's followers in the city centre. While Garin was punched in the face and Pothier received a blow to the arm, Aucouturier defended himself admirably, felling an assailant with a neat uppercut. As the riot intensified, Lefèvre's car found itself in the middle of the melee with its tyres slashed. This time it was his fellow official, Jean Miral, who rode to the rescue and fired shots into the air to put the saboteurs to flight. When the dust had settled Aucouturier was named stage winner, although Garin led overall.

Stage four to Bordeaux passed off peacefully, principally because it took place entirely in daylight, and was won by Pothier, but Aucouturier took stage five to Nantes. The final stage to Paris saw Garin extend his overall lead to some six minutes from Pothier, despite having to negotiate logs and farm wagons that were deliberately placed across the road leading into the capital. Thus Maurice Garin was declared the winner for the second successive year, ahead of Pothier, César Garin, Aucouturier and Henri Cornet, a twenty-year-old Frenchman.

But the race had a sting in the tail. Four months after the event the Union Vélocepedique de France announced at the end of a lengthy inquiry into the chaos that the first four finishers and nine other riders had been excluded from the result for various 'irregularities' and that therefore the fifth-placed man, Cornet, was now the official winner. Three riders, including Pothier (who had already been fined 500 francs for his crime of taking pace) and Chevallier, were banned for life, and Maurice Garin was banned for two years. The other transgressors received less severe sentences. The inquiry revealed a trail of premeditated destruction from first to last – powdered emery and itching dust placed in riders' shorts; spiked drinks; fouled drinks; and a bicycle frame filed through so that it collapsed as soon as the rider climbed aboard. Such antics belonged more to a circus than the world's most prestigious cycle race.

The fortuitous nature of his victory ensured that Cornet was without honour in his own land and he became christened 'Rigolo' or 'The Phoney'. Maurice Garin never rode in the Tour de France again, and his career was effectively over at the age of 33. Instead he bought a filling station in Northern France and worked the pumps right up until his death in 1956.

The race organisers sought to learn from the 1904 debacle. They divided the Tour into eleven shorter stages and eliminated night riding. They were confident of a good clean race. For two years their optimism appeared justified, but then in 1907 three riders were disqualified for taking a short cut by train...

The Stripping of Jim Thorpe

1913

Presenting a bronze bust of himself to Jim Thorpe to mark the American's victory in the 1912 Olympic pentathlon, King Gustav V of Sweden said: 'Sir, you are the greatest athlete in the world.' To which Thorpe, who also won the decathlon, replied humbly: 'Thanks, King.'

Thorpe returned home from those Stockholm Olympics as America's favourite son. Accorded the ultimate honour of a ticker-tape parade through New York City, a bemused Thorpe remarked: 'I heard people yelling my name, and I couldn't realise how one fellow could have so many friends.' It seemed he could do no wrong. Yet within a few months his world came crashing down when he was unceremoniously stripped of his Olympic titles for being a professional.

The Jim Thorpe story began in 1888 near Prague, Oklahoma, on Sac and Fox Indian land. Both of his parents (who died when Thorpe was a teenager) were part Native American and he was given the name Wa-Tho-Huck, meaning 'Bright Path'. As a child he sometimes used to run twenty miles home from school. 'I never was content,' he said, 'unless I was trying my skill in some game against my fellow playmates.' An opportunity to test his prowess arose in the spring of 1907. Attending Carlisle Indian School in Pennsylvania, Thorpe wandered past the track area where the high jumpers were attempting unsuccessfully to clear 5ft 9in. Dressed in his ordinary work clothes, he cleared the bar at the first attempt to set a new school record. His fame spread and by 1911 he was being hailed as 'the greatest all-round athlete in the world', excelling at track and field, American football and baseball. Nothing was beyond him.

Chosen to represent the United States at the 1912 Olympics, Thorpe took part in no fewer than four events. On 7 July he won the pentathlon and the following day he tied for fourth place in the high jump. Six days later he came seventh in the long jump and finally he tackled the decathlon for the first time ever. Despite never having thrown a javelin until two months earlier, he swept to victory, setting a new world record and a standard that would have still earned him a silver medal at the 1948 Olympics.

Returning home with two gold medals, Thorpe picked up where he had left off, starring in football games. But that winter Roy Johnson, a journalist on the *Worcester (Massachusetts) Telegram*, started digging into Thorpe's past and discovered that in the summers of 1909 and 1910 he had received $25 a week playing minor league baseball for Rocky Mountain in North Carolina. Naively Thorpe had used his real name, unlike other collegians who adopted pseudonyms to preserve their amateur status. Although his transgression was relatively trivial, Thorpe was, strictly speaking, a professional athlete and therefore ineligible to compete in the Olympics.

Asked by the Amateur Athletic Union for his response to the accusation, Thorpe readily confessed to his sins but asked for leniency. He wrote: 'I did not play for the money there was in it . . . but because I liked to play ball. I was not very wise to the ways of the world and did not realise that this was wrong and it would make me a professional in track sports . . . I hope I will be partly excused by the fact that I was simply an Indian schoolboy and did not know all about such things. In fact, I did not know that I was doing wrong because I was doing what I knew several other college men had done except that they did not use their own names.'

The Amateur Athletic Union did not heed Thorpe's plea for clemency and immediately cancelled all of his records post 1909. On 27 January 1913 the all-American hero was formally stripped of his gold medals by the International Olympic Committee. Fortunately he still had public opinion on his side, witnessed by the fact that the runners-up in both the pentathlon and decathlon refused to accept the gold medals that Thorpe had won.

No sooner had he been ruled a professional than he was approached to play major league baseball, which he did first for New York Giants, then Cincinnati Reds and Boston Braves. He also played football, notably for the Canton Bulldogs, making his last appearance – for the Chicago Cardinals against the Chicago Bears – on 30 November 1928. It was not an auspicious farewell. One reporter wrote of his performance: 'In his forties and muscle-bound, Thorpe was a mere shadow of his former self.'

Without sport, Thorpe's life seemed empty. He began to drink heavily, drifting through a succession of menial jobs – painter, ditch digger, deck hand, bar bouncer. He also worked occasionally as a Hollywood extra, mainly playing Indian chiefs. His fame resurfaced in the 1950s when a poll of sportswriters voted him the greatest athlete of the first half of the century and then Burt Lancaster starred in a biopic of Thorpe's life. Sadly Thorpe's carelessness over contractual details cost him dear and he was reduced to living in a California trailer where he suffered a fatal heart attack on 28 March 1953. The following year his body was moved to Mauch Chunk, Pennsylvania, a small town that agreed to change its name to Jim Thorpe in return for the honour of being his final resting place.

Thorpe's tragic decline reinforced the view that he had been harshly treated back in 1913. A campaign to reinstate his Olympic records and medals had begun in 1943 based on a rule, in effect at the time of the Stockholm Games, which stated that officials had thirty days to contest an athlete's amateur status. Thorpe's standing had not been raised until six months after the Olympics but the IOC refused to be swayed during his lifetime and it was not until 1982, after intense lobbying, that it finally agreed to restore Jim Thorpe's gold medals. The following January the medals were presented to his children.

The Suffragette Derby

1913

By 1913 the suffragette movement was in full flow. The struggle to obtain equal rights for women – in particular the vote – had been gathering momentum for over 25 years, only to be repeatedly rebuffed in Parliament. The increasing frustration manifested itself with the foundation of the Women's Social and Political Union and an escalation to militant activities, orchestrated by a Manchester suffragette, Emmeline Pankhurst, and her daughters Christabel and Sylvia. Together with their growing band of supporters, they chained themselves to railings, heckled political meetings, and refused to pay taxes. Among their number was 38-year-old Emily Davison of Morpeth, Northumberland, an extremist who served six jail sentences for such crimes as breaking a window in the House of Commons, setting fire to pillar boxes in Westminster, and lashing a Baptist minister with a dog-whip on Aberdeen station in the mistaken belief that he was the Chancellor of the Exchequer, Lloyd George. In prison she regularly went on hunger strike to bring attention to the plight of women but the authorities kept her alive by force-feeding her. She remained convinced that the cause needed a martyr and, to this end, threw herself thirty feet down an iron staircase, only to escape with spinal injuries. Davison was released from her latest sojourn in prison shortly before the 1913 Derby and immediately set about planning her most spectacular protest to date. On the night before the big race, her roommate saw her sewing the colours of the suffragette movement inside her coat. When asked what she was intending to do, Davison replied: 'Look in the paper and you will see. I'm going to the Derby tomorrow.'

The favourite for the Derby was the 6–4 shot Craganour who had won five of his six starts as a two-year-old including the Champagne Stakes at Doncaster and the Middle Park Plate at Newmarket. As a three-year-old he had officially been beaten a head by Louvois in the Two Thousand Guineas although most observers felt that he was a desperately unlucky loser and that the result was solely attributable to the elderly judge's poor eyesight. Now he was strongly fancied to make amends for that controversial defeat by taking his revenge on Louvois at Epsom. Among his other principal rivals were Agadir, ridden by Walter Earl, and King George V's colt Anmer, ridden by Herbert Jones, but it was the 100–1 outsider Aboyeur who set the early pace and who was still leading as the fifteen runners rounded Tattenham Corner. What happened next was described to readers of the *Daily Sketch* by an eye-witness:

> The leaders, in a bunch of nine, had just swept round the bend at Tattenham Corner, fighting all the way for the inside place, and the King's horse was some yards behind with no hope of catching them up, when suddenly a woman darted out from the opposite rails.
>
> Like a rabbit she ran across the course to intercept Anmer and as the horse was hugging the rails she stood up in front of him holding both her hands above her head, and then sprang at him. She caught the reins or bridle in her hands, and there hung suspended for a second as Anmer rushed on at a speed of over thirty miles an hour.
>
> Then the horse plunged as Jones shook the reins to get rid of the swaying woman, who still hung on like a limpet, and Anmer rolled over towards the inside rails with Jones underneath. The woman was hurled clear and fell onto her side near the horse's flanks. There she lay like a dead thing with the people gazing at her open-eyed until the ambulance carried her away.

The fact that it was the King's horse that Davison brought down merely added to her notoriety. When she ran on to the course, she severely hampered Agadir, whose jockey somehow managed to swerve and avoid her, before seizing Anmer's reins. This prompted some writers to speculate that she had deliberately targeted the royal horse but, given the speed at which they were travelling, this seems unlikely. Instead it would appear to have been a lucky chance – lucky, that is, in terms of the publicity generated for the suffragette movement by the incident.

Anmer's jockey, Herbert Jones, was dragged along the course for several yards with one of his feet caught in the stirrups. He was taken unconscious to the Jockeys' Room but, because the door was too narrow to admit a stretcher, he had to remain outside until he could be taken to Epsom Cottage Hospital. Although bruised and concussed, he was discharged the following day. Emily Davison sustained a fractured skull and died in the same hospital on 8 June – four days after the race – without ever regaining consciousness.

Sympathy for Davison was in short supply. The majority of the public were more concerned about the health of horse and jockey and dismissed Davison's reckless deed as that of a madwoman. Even those who agreed with the goals of the suffragette campaign could not tolerate the methods being used to obtain them. King George, in his private diary, described Davison's action as 'a most regrettable, scandalous proceeding'. And in a telegram of good wishes to the recuperating Herbert Jones, Queen Mary wrote that she was 'very sorry indeed to hear of your sad accident caused through the abominable behaviour of a brutal, lunatic woman'.

Not surprisingly, the suffragettes themselves made great capital out of their colleague's death. Davison achieved her aim of martyrdom and was given a ceremonial funeral through the streets of London, an occasion attended by tens of thousands of women of all ages and classes. Sympathisers across the world sent hundreds of wreaths. She was finally laid to rest in the family vault in Morpeth, beneath a purple cloth inscribed by her mother, 'Welcome the Northumbrian hunger striker'.

By then the result of the 1913 Derby had almost been forgotten, yet the drama of the race had not ended with Davison's untimely intervention. The closing stages had developed into a fierce tussle between Craganour and Aboyeur. In a blanket finish Craganour, ridden by Johnny Reiff, passed the post a head in front of the outsider to gain what was thought to be a thoroughly deserved victory. Although minor skirmishing had taken place up the straight, Edwin Piper, Aboyeur's jockey, did not object to Craganour and the red flag was raised to indicate that the result stood. However, moments later it was lowered as the stewards themselves took the almost unprecedented step of holding an inquiry without any of the parties concerned staging an objection. To the astonishment of the huge crowd, Craganour was disqualified for not keeping a straight course and placed last, the race being awarded to Aboyeur.

While the racing world expressed sympathy for Craganour being cheated of another classic, conspiracy theorists started to question the stewards' motives. Craganour's owner was the popular C Bower Ismay, younger brother of J Bruce Ismay, the man vilified in some quarters for his role in the previous year's *Titanic* disaster. J Bruce Ismay was chairman of the White Star Line, under whose flag the *Titanic* sailed, and had been roundly condemned for saving his own life while over 1,500 others perished. Could it be that with the tragedy still so fresh in everyone's minds, the Epsom stewards could not allow themselves to hand British horse racing's most prestigious prize to an Ismay?

The Good Friday Agreement

1915

Good Friday 1915. While war was raging in Europe, the Football League was limping towards the end of its last season before play was suspended for hostilities. The holiday clash between bitter local rivals Manchester United and Liverpool should have offered a welcome relief from the grim reality of trench warfare, but instead it has passed into history as one of soccer's blackest days following the exposure of a match-fixing scam that eventually saw eight players banned for life.

One of the central figures in the drama – although ultimately not one of those banned – was Billy Meredith, the Welsh wing wizard who, in his prime, was thought to be the finest player in Britain. Meredith's trademark was to chew a toothpick during matches to aid concentration. He had previously chewed tobacco until the cleaners refused to wash the spit off his shirts! A staunch advocate of player power, at a time when Jimmy Hill was just a twinkle in his father's eye, Meredith was no stranger to controversy. In 1905 he became embroiled in the climate of backhanders, bungs and bribes that prevailed at Manchester City and was banned for eight months for offering Aston Villa's Alec Leake £10 – the equivalent of three weeks' wages – to throw a game with City. The ensuing scandal resulted in City off-loading no fewer than seventeen players, four of whom, including Meredith and Scottish striker Sandy Turnbull, crossed Manchester to join United the following season. Their new colleagues included centre forward Enoch 'Knocker' West who had been signed from Nottingham Forest in 1905. West and Turnbull were fiery characters. Predating the actions of another United star by the best part of a century, Turnbull was suspended by the club in 1914 for swearing at the manager in front of his team-mates while West, a former Nottingham collier, was banned for a month in 1911 after brawling in a match with Aston Villa.

By the 1914–15 season West and Turnbull were nearing the ends of their careers. Between arguments with the management, Turnbull made only a dozen appearances that campaign while Meredith, now over forty, missed more than a third of the matches through injury. United felt both losses deeply and, as they came to face Liverpool at Old Trafford on 2 April, they were fighting a desperate battle against relegation. Liverpool, by contrast, were sitting comfortably in mid-table.

Although United had everything to play for in the Easter fixture, their performance was strangely lacklustre. Given the boost of an early George Anderson goal, they showed little interest in pressing home their advantage and only remained in front by dint of their opponents' complete indifference. Neither side seemed to want to break into anything resembling a trot and what tackles there were owed more to Aled Jones than Vinnie Jones. When Anderson overcame minimal resistance from the Liverpool rearguard to score a second goal for United, there was little by way of jubilation from the players. The visitors even contrived to miss a penalty to leave United the 2–0 winners. Rarely has the term 'strolled to victory' been more apt.

At the final whistle even the United fans jeered the teams. The *Sporting Chronicle* said Liverpool were 'too poor to describe'. Vague rumour first became firm suspicion when it emerged that a large number of bets had been placed nationwide on United to win 2–0. Betting on the actual scoreline was a rarity in those days and the deluge of wagers – sufficient for the odds on a 2–0 win for United to plunge from 12–1 to 5–1 – prompted some bookmakers to withhold payment and alert the police as to their misgivings. Within two weeks handbills were circulating in Manchester offering a £50 reward to anyone with information relating to the allegation that the match had been fixed. Following their involvement in the Manchester City bribery case ten years earlier, Meredith and Turnbull were the obvious suspects, but it was West who would emerge as the prime mover. For the time being, however, everyone involved hid behind a wall of silence, reasoning that without evidence there was little the authorities could do. But it only needed one player to speak out for the wall to crumble.

The Football Association and the Football League joined forces to begin a painstaking inquiry, the outcome of which was announced some eighteen months later. The commission of inquiry report stated:

> The allegation of squaring the match carried with it a charge of conspiracy by some of the players, and as a result of long and searching investigations we are satisfied that a number of them were party to an arrangement to do so, and joined together to obtain money by betting on the actual result of the match. It is proved that a considerable sum of money changed hands by betting on the match, and that some of the players profited thereby.

Eight players were banned for life – West, Turnbull, Laurence Cook and Arthur Whalley of United (although only West played in the Liverpool match); and Jackie Sheldon, Tommy Miller, Tom Fairfoul and Bob Purcell of Liverpool.

The whistle-blower had been George Anderson. It transpired that Sheldon, a former United player, had acted as the go-between, introducing some of the participants to each other a week before the game in the Dog and Partridge public house near Old Trafford. Following that match-fixing meeting, bets had been placed all around the country – as far afield as Nottingham and London – with a view to making a quick financial killing before soccer was suspended for the war. Nottingham bookmakers revealed abnormally heavy betting on the 2–0 win in West's home village of Hucknall Torknard.

The press condemned the guilty eight for their selfish, contemptible behaviour at a time when the whole country was supposed to be pulling together. The *Athletic News* referred to the players' 'diabolical machinations' and added: 'The money they have handled will pollute their lives, for they have enriched themselves in a manner which not only disgusts the public and defrauds bookmakers, but threatens the very existence of the game.'

Seven of the players took their medicine quietly but Enoch West vehemently protested his innocence and sunk much of his savings into bringing a libel case against the Football Association and Hulton Newspapers. Among the witnesses at the trial was Billy Meredith, who had also been accused by Anderson of being party to fixing the match. Under cross-examination Meredith denied any prior knowledge of the fix but said that he first became suspicious soon after kickoff when none of his team-mates would pass to him. At half-time he asked the captain why they were starving him of the ball and was told they were doing their best. According to Meredith, it got even worse after the second goal. 'No one could have played in that game without suspecting there was something wrong.'

At first the evidence against West appeared largely circumstantial but then Sheldon took the stand and revealed that West had been a key instigator of the meeting at the Dog and Partridge. While insisting that he himself had played no part in the scam, Anderson then revealed that West had made £70 from bets on the result. The judge found against West who promptly launched an appeal, only to lose again. His case was not helped when the appeal court judges recalled his original statement that he had no relatives in his home village who might, if tipped off, have been responsible for placing the bets. On the contrary it had emerged that no fewer than sixty of West's family lived in Hucknall Torknard!

The fix enabled Manchester United to avoid relegation by two points. At the end of the war all of the players' bans were lifted except for West's but by then Sandy Turnbull had been killed by a German shell. Billy Meredith survived the scandal and played on into his fifties but George Anderson was sentenced to eight months in prison in 1918 for his part in an even larger betting scam. As for Enoch West, his ban was not lifted until 1945 when, at 59, he was far too old to resume playing. He continued to maintain his innocence right up until his death in 1965.

Cook Boils Over

1915

Just three days after the Manchester United–Liverpool nonevent, soccer was plunged into further scenes of disgrace when Oldham Athletic left-back Billy Cook refused to leave the field after being sent off at Middlesbrough on Easter Monday.

Short, stocky, bald, and uncompromising to the point of being intimidating, Cook had joined Oldham from Rossendale United for £200 in 1908. A hero of the 1913 FA Cup win at Everton, he was one of the Latics' true stalwarts although by 1915 he was in his 33rd year. Having finished third the previous season, Oldham were mounting another determined challenge and were lying in fourth place – just two points behind leaders Manchester City – when they made the Easter pilgrimage to Middlesbrough, a team they had trounced 5–1 earlier in the campaign.

Before a crowd of 7,000 on a typically grey, wet Teesside day, the match began disastrously for the visitors who found themselves three goals down after just twenty minutes. Trying to claw themselves back into the game, they received little assistance from the referee, Mr H Smith of Nottingham, whose dubious decisions included rejecting a seemingly valid appeal for an Oldham penalty. They did eventually manage to reduce the arrears, but ten minutes into the second half Mr Smith awarded 'Boro a penalty for a foul by Cook on Carr. Tinsley scored from the spot to complete his hat trick and virtually put the game out of Oldham's reach. Three minutes later Cook's frustration boiled over when he marred what had previously been a clean contest with another rash tackle on Carr.

Without hesitation, the referee ordered Cook off but he refused to go. As the Oldham players crowded around him in protest at the decision, claiming that the slippery pitch was as much to blame as their fullback, Mr Smith took out his watch and announced that he was giving Cook one minute to leave the field. The sixty seconds expired but Cook showed no intention of departing. So Mr Smith calmly walked off, followed by 22 bemused players.

Learning that the match had been abandoned with over half an hour still to play, the crowd became understandably restless, venting their anger on the hapless official. Some spectators said the referee should have continued the game with Cook playing; others suggested that the police should have been called to remove the Oldham fullback by force.

The sporting press hit out at Cook's behaviour, the *Athletic News* saying that the incident was 'without precedent in the history of the premier combination'. Oldham proceeded to exacerbate the situation by selecting Cook to play in their next game, at Manchester City, even though some Oldham directors had decided that he should not play again until the Football League announced his punishment. Reacting to calls to come down hard on Cook, the League suspended him for a year, although since football itself was soon to be suspended, the immediate effect was minimal. For their part, Oldham were severely reprimanded and fined £350.

The Cook affair heralded a miserable end to Oldham's season. The 4–1 score at Middlesbrough was allowed to stand and successive home defeats to Burnley on 20 April and Liverpool four days later saw them miss out on the title to Everton by a single point. It was the closest Oldham have ever come to winning the League Championship.

Somewhat surprisingly in view of his serious transgression, Cook was chosen to represent the Football League against the Irish League in 1919, but ironically an injury sustained in that game effectively ended his career.

The Black Sox Scandal

1919

Since its inception in 1903 the World Series contest between America's top two baseball teams had developed into one of the nation's most eagerly anticipated sporting events. The game as a whole was enjoying a boom period and in the immediate aftermath of the war attendance records were set in many ballparks. Consequently the 1919 World Series – fought out between the Chicago White Sox and the Cincinnati Reds – proved a real money-spinner, generating fifty per cent more revenue than any previous decider. Such was the demand for tickets that it was decided to cash in by making it a best of nine series instead of the traditional best of seven. The level of betting rose accordingly and with so much money in circulation it followed that anyone who was somehow able to acquire prior knowledge of the result could strike it rich.

Professional gamblers had been unwelcome visitors to ballparks for years. As early as the mid-nineteenth century, when the sport was still in its infancy, there were rumours of games being fixed but in 1919 the number of gamblers visibly present at ballparks increased dramatically, prompting Charles Comiskey, owner of the Chicago White Sox, to post notices proclaiming, 'No Betting Allowed In This Park'. The signs had little effect and speculation was rife that several players enjoyed unhealthily close relationships with gamblers. One small-time gambler, Joseph 'Sport' Sullivan, was said to be profiting from inside information supplied by Chicago's first baseman Arnold 'Chick' Gandil who allegedly told Sullivan in advance if a pitcher or hitter was sick, injured or out of form.

Having carried all before them in 1919, Chicago were hot favourites for the World Series but their status was undermined by unrest within the camp, mostly caused by the miserly Comiskey. Although no team played better that year, few were paid so poorly. Comiskey was able to get away with paying low salaries because of a reserve clause in players' contracts but prevented them from changing teams without the permission of the owner. The dictatorial Comiskey was untouchable. He had little concept of ethics. When they won the pennant in 1917, Comiskey promised his players a sizeable bonus but instead all they received was a case of champagne...cheap champagne at that. Before the 1919 season he promised his ace pitcher Eddie Cicotte an extra $10,000 if he won thirty games. When Cicotte reached 29, Comiskey put him on the bench, using the excuse that he should rest in readiness for the forthcoming pennant games. He even charged, the players for having their kit cleaned, whereupon they registered their displeasure by wearing the same dirty strip for weeks on end. Eventually Comiskey seized the uniforms from the lockers and handed the players hefty fines as punishment for their insubordination.

There were also internal divisions within the playing ranks. The team was divided into two distinct cliques – one led by second baseman Eddie Collins, the other by Gandil. The Collins faction was well educated, sophisticated and able to prise a salary as high as $15,000 out of the reluctant Comiskey. Gandil's group, who came from the poor side of the tracks and earned on average just $6,000, bitterly resented the difference. The situation at Chicago was wide open to exploitation by unscrupulous gamblers.

At 33, Gandil was in the twilight of his career. Sensing that this could be his last chance to make big bucks from baseball, he summoned Sullivan to his room in Boston's Hotel Buckminster on 18 September – two weeks before the 1919 World Series was due to begin – and told him that for $80,000 he and several of his Chicago team-mates would ensure that the White Sox lost the series. 'I think we can put it in the bag,' Gandil told the gambler.

While Sullivan set about raising the cash, Gandil approached some of his colleagues. For a fix to succeed, he needed the co-operation of the pitchers, notably Cicotte and Lefty Williams who between them had won 52 games that season. Cicotte needed little persuasion to join the scam, simply demanding up front the $10,000 he reckoned he was owed by Comiskey. Williams, outfielder Oscar 'Happy' Felsch and shortstop Swede Risberg all expressed an interest and when utility player Fred McMullin overheard Gandil discussing the plot with Risberg, he, too, demanded a piece of the action.

So far so good, but one key component of the team was missing – star outfielder 'Shoeless' Joe Jackson, a local hero who had earned his nickname after playing a minor league game in his socks because a new pair of baseball shoes were hurting his feet. Sullivan and his cohorts were particularly keen for Jackson to be involved. Jackson's alleged participation in the fix has been the subject of many a barroom debate – and brawl – down the decades. According to his subsequent testimony, he rejected Gandil's initial offer of $10,000 and, even when the figure was doubled, he refused to go along with the plan. Gandil then supposedly told Jackson he could take it or leave it because the fix was going to happen anyway, with or without him. Did Jackson back down or did Gandil lie to the gamblers and say that Jackson was in just to keep them happy?

The other Chicago player whose involvement is suspect was third baseman Buck Weaver. While attending several meetings of the conspirators, he claimed that he declined to be part of the plot.

By now Gandil had raised the asking price to $100,000. Since Sullivan did not have access to that kind of money, he enlisted the help of other well-known gamblers: William 'Sleepy Bill' Burns, a former White Sox pitcher; New York Giants' first baseman Hal Chase; and Abe Attell, a one-time featherweight boxing champion. But these were small fry compared to the principal financier, Arnold Rothstein, a man known in New York City circles as a gambler who would bet on anything he could fix.

Fielding almost the same team that had won the championship two years earlier, a White Sox victory in the series was seen as a formality. Early betting quoted the Reds at 5–1 and it was at that price that Rothstein, Sullivan and co. wagered nearly half a million dollars on Cincinnati causing a major upset. The Reds' price tumbled dramatically in the lead-up to the contest. The players' hopes of keeping the conspiracy a secret began to evaporate as rumours of a fix spread like wildfire.

Although Gandil had received assurances that everyone involved would be paid up front, only Cicotte was rewarded in advance. On the night before game one, Cicotte found $10,000 under a pillow in his hotel room. The next day his second pitch hit Reds' leadoff Morrie Rath – the signal that the fix was on. Cicotte was hammered 9–1 by the Reds in that opening game but there were murmurings of discontent among the other players who hadn't seen a dime for their treachery. After lengthy discussion, they agreed to throw game two as long as the money came by the end of the day. Williams lost the second game 4–2 and Gandil demanded the $40,000 the players were owed for losing the first two games. He was given just $10,000. The players felt betrayed and contemplated backing out of the deal. Meanwhile those team-mates who were not in on the fix were growing suspicious. Catcher Ray Schalk was sure that something was wrong with the pitching and following game two he and the team's manager, Kid Gleason, became involved in a heated argument with Gandil and Williams over their poor performances.

To the fury of those gamblers who were betting on individual games, Chicago won the third game 3–0. Now it was Attell's turn to feel betrayed and he refused to hand over any more money. Faced with the collapse of the entire operation, Sullivan managed to come up with $20,000 before game four with the promise of a further $20,000 if Chicago lost. Gandil split the $20,000 evenly among Risberg, Felsch, Williams and Jackson. For some reason McMullin and Weaver missed out. A succession of Cicotte blunders saw the White Sox slump 2–0 and then Williams contrived to lose the fifth game 5–0 and leave Chicago trailing 4–1 overall. One more win and the Reds would be home and dry.

But once again the second instalment of $20,000 never materialised. Angry that they had been duped after keeping their side of the bargain, the players decided they had nothing to lose by trying to win. At least if they fought back to capture the series they would pocket $5,000 each. Therefore Chicago suddenly found their form, winning games six and seven 5–4 and 4–1 respectively. The rogue players had every intention of maintaining the momentum but moneyman Rothstein had other ideas. Instead of betting on individual games, he had bet on Cincinnati to win the series and now he could see that his investment was at serious risk. So he despatched one of his henchmen to visit Williams, who was pitching in the eighth game, and explain that the series was to end the next day. Fearing for the safety of both himself and his wife, Williams made sure that Chicago lost 10-5. The World Series went to Cincinnati.

Among journalists who had queried the legality of the series was Hugh Fullerton, a sports writer for the *Chicago Herald and Examiner*. Like others, he had heard the rumours of a fix and urged club owners to banish the gamblers but the owners, fearful that the public would desert baseball if any wrongdoing was proved, preferred to sweep the matter under the carpet. When Joe Jackson's conscience finally got the better of him and he tried to see Charles Comiskey to ask what to do with his $5,000, Comiskey refused to entertain him. Jackson then sent him a letter hinting that the games might have been fixed, but Comiskey never replied.

Comiskey and his fellow owners might have continued to bury their heads in the sand had the problem of gambling not escalated during the 1920 season. Rumours surfaced about a number of fixed games and in September of that year a Cook County, Illinois, grand jury looked into reports that the Chicago Cubs had thrown games against the Philadelphia Phillies. The investigation soon spread to the 1919 World Series. With the owners under fire and Comiskey anxious to conceal his own knowledge of the fix, Jackson, Cicotte and later Williams were encouraged to come forward and admit everything they knew.

Jackson denied deliberately playing badly during the series, insisting that he was playing to win. Gandil, the ringleader, admitted nothing. All eight players plus Sullivan, Burns, Attell, Chase and several of Rothstein's henchmen were indicted for conspiracy to defraud the public. Curiously Rothstein, who allegedly pocketed $270,000 from fixing the 1919 World Series, did not face any charges. With a sense of poetic justice he was subsequently murdered by a rival gambler whom he had accused of fixing a poker game.

The indictment of the eight players (who came to be known as the Black Sox) shattered the illusions of their thousands of fans. The story goes that as Jackson left the courthouse a small boy, his eyes filled with tears, looked up at his hero and pleaded: 'Say it ain't so, Joe.' The phrase passed into folklore although Jackson later claimed it was the invention of an imaginative reporter on the *Chicago Daily News*.

The trial, which began in June 1921, was deeply unsatisfactory, not least because the signed confessions that Jackson, Cicotte and Williams had given before the grand jury had mysteriously gone missing from the Cook County district attorney's office. They would turn up four years later in the hands of Comiskey's lawyer, George Hudnall, who never explained their reappearance. In the meantime the trial dragged on for a month amid claim and counterclaim. Jackson accused Gandil of keeping the majority of the money, adding: 'I didn't think Gandil was crossed as much as he crossed us.' However, with no firm evidence, no confessions and only a vague picture of what had happened, the jury was left with little alternative than to deliver 'not guilty' verdicts all round.

The players' relief was short-lived. The following day Kenesaw Mountain Landis, the newly appointed first commissioner of baseball and the man hired to clean up the sport, barred all eight from organised baseball for life. 'Regardless of the verdict of juries,' he decreed, 'no player who throws a ball game, no player that undertakes or promises to throw a ball game, no player who sits in conference with a bunch of crooked players and gamblers where the ways and means of throwing a game are discussed and does not promptly tell his club about it, will ever play professional baseball.'

While Weaver continued to protest his innocence, Jackson, Cicotte and Risberg were reduced to playing in outlaw leagues. Jackson's supporters campaigned long and hard for his reinstatement, claiming that he was too uneducated to understand what he was involved in. When age caught up with him, he moved to Greenville, South Carolina, where he ran a liquor store until his death from a heart attack in 1951 – the first of the eight to die. As he lay dying he murmured: 'I am going to meet the greatest umpire of all – and He knows I'm innocent.'

By the Sword Divided

1924

The history of the Olympic Games is littered with allegations of home bias. Whether it was London in 1908, Seoul in 1988 or Atlanta in 1996, competitors from the host nation often appear to have been looked upon favourably by the judges. Paris in 1924 was no exception. Accusations of officials leaning towards the French were as frequent as complaints about the hostile Parisian crowds, never more so than in the men's team foil and individual sabre competitions, where the behaviour of a Hungarian fencing judge by the name of Kovács prompted such anger that the ensuing arguments ended in two bloody duels.

The team foil saw France meet Italy in the final pool at the Vélodrome d'Hiver with the winners expected to go on and take the gold medal. Trailing 3–1, Italy's hopes in the fifth assault rested on the shoulders of Aldo Boni who took on Lucien Gaudin. The contest was perfectly balanced at four touches each when the jury controversially awarded a decisive fifth touch to the Frenchman. An incensed Boni immediately let forth a stream of invective in the direction of the offending judge, Kovács, who went to the Jury of Appeal to demand an apology. Boni not only refused to apologise but also denied abusing Kovács whereupon the latter summoned a witness, the Italian-born Hungarian fencing master Italo Santelli. Somewhat reluctantly, Santelli confirmed Boni's outburst, following which the Italian team withdrew from the competition in protest, singing the Fascist hymn as they left the arena.

However, that was not the end of the matter. Back in Italy the furious fencers issued a statement accusing Santelli of testifying against them because he feared that Italy would beat Hungary, the team that he had coached. Santelli saw the accusation as an affront to his reputation and standing in the sport and, even though he was over sixty years old, he challenged the Italian captain, Adolfo Contronei, to a duel. Government licence was obtained but before the two men could meet, Santelli's 27-year-old son Giorgio invoked the duelling code and demanded to be allowed to take his father's place.

The duel was fought with heavy sabres at Abazzia, near the Hungarian border. It was all over in just two minutes when Giorgio slashed Contronei on the side of the head, drawing blood. Doctors rushed in and, after inspecting the deep cut, called a halt to the duel. Santelli family honour was satisfied.

Meanwhile Kovács had managed to upset another Italian fencer, Oreste Puliti. The Italian team, led by Puliti, had already beaten the Hungarians to win the team sabre title and were strongly fancied to add the individual event. Indeed, four of their number – Puliti, Marcello Bertinetti, Giulio Sarrocchi and Bino Bini – were in the final pool of twelve. Then Kovács and his colleagues ordered an extra qualifying round where the Italians had to fight off against each other. Puliti won through but Kovács claimed that the other three had deliberately thrown their matches against Puliti to increase his chances of taking gold. Puliti responded by threatening to cane Kovács – a gesture that resulted in the Italian's disqualification. His three team-mates stormed out in sympathy. The fencing competition was proving a highly charged affair.

Two days later Puliti and Kovács happened to bump into each other at a music hall. The tension quickly bubbled over into a full-blown row and when Kovács haughtily informed Puliti that he couldn't understand him because he didn't speak Italian, Puliti struck the Hungarian a blow to the face, suggesting that perhaps that was something Kovács could understand. Although the two men were quickly pulled apart before further physical blows could be landed, the verbal war resumed, resulting in the arrangement of a formal duel. This took place four months later at Nagykanizsa on the

Yugoslav–Hungarian border, but when an hour's fighting failed to separate the combatants, the duel was declared a draw. Both men seemed happy with the outcome, shook hands and went their separate ways.

A Right Royal Mix-up

1926

In the 1920s women tennis players dressed as if going on an Antarctic expedition. Shirts were buttoned up to the neck, skirts flowed right down to the ankles and beneath these outer garments were layer upon layer of stays and petticoats. It was a wonder they could move about the court. Then along came Suzanne Lenglen, the toast of France. She dared to bare her forearms and wear a dress cut just above the calf. British crowds in particular were stunned that a player should choose to reveal an ankle.

Furthermore, she wore lipstick, wept openly during matches, pouted, and sipped brandy between sets. Some called her shocking and indecent but most overcame their reservations and warmed to her displays of raw emotion. Mlle Lenglen was to become Wimbledon's biggest attraction.

She had more than enough talent to back it up. Trained from youth by her father Charles who, for hours on end, made her aim the ball at a handkerchief which he moved from spot to spot to build up her accuracy, Lenglen developed an astonishing range of rhythmic ground strokes. Unencumbered by the rigid clothing that blighted her contemporaries, she was able to move freely and effortlessly about the court whether it was launching her own shots or anticipating those of her opponents. Lenglen was in a class of her own and between 1919 and 1925 she won Wimbledon every year except 1924 when illness forced her to withdraw after the fourth round.

Her health was probably her most dangerous opponent. At the 1921 US Championships, having lost the first set heavily to the American Molla Mallory, Lenglen walked weeping and coughing to the umpire and said she was unable to continue. After defaulting the match, she was dubbed 'cough and quit Lenglen' by the bullish American press. She gained her revenge the following year by crushing Mallory 6–2, 6–0 in just 26 minutes. Referring to the traditional post-match handshake at the net, Lenglen smiled: 'I could have said something to her. Instead I decided just to have a little cough...'

Naturally the six-times champion was the major draw at the 1926 Wimbledon. The fascination with the 27-year-old French girl showed no sign of diminishing as tennis fans ranging from the humble man in the street to King George and Queen Mary clamoured to see her matches. The difference was that the man in the street had to queue and pay. As the undoubted star of the ladies' game, Lenglen was used to being treated as such by officials of the All-England Club. The old secretary, Commander George Hillyard, had always made a point of informing her of the times of her next day's matches when she left Wimbledon each day. However, in 1926 the club had a new secretary, Major Dudley Larcombe.

Lenglen was already smarting from a ruling by the French Federation concerning her choice of partner in the women's doubles. Over the years she had formed a formidable – indeed invincible – union with the American girl, Elizabeth Ryan. Together they had never lost a tournament match and had collected no fewer than six Wimbledon doubles titles, but now Lenglen had been virtually ordered to play with a French compatriot, Didi Vlasto. To make matters worse, the draw pitted Lenglen and Vlasto against Ryan and her new partner, Mary K Browne, whom Lenglen had struggled to beat in the first round of the singles. Faced with such a potentially awkward tie, Lenglen asked the referee, Frank Burrow, to schedule only that doubles match on the first Wednesday of the tournament. It was fixed for 4.30 p.m. but, unbeknown to Lenglen and against her express wishes, Burrow then added a second round singles match against Evelyn Dewhurst at 2 p.m. Since Lenglen did not read the newspapers during Wimbledon fortnight and because Major Larcombe had failed to inform her of the change, Lenglen was left in the dark until Vlasto told her about it late on the Wednesday morning.

Unable to contact the referee, Lenglen decided to stick to the timetable that she had been officially given. So she arrived at the All-England Club at 3.30 p.m. in readiness for her doubles match, only to be told tersely that she was late and that furthermore her nonappearance had offended Queen Mary who had turned up earlier with the specific intention of watching Lenglen play Mrs Dewhurst. Pointing out that she had been officially notified of only the doubles, she steadfastly refused to play the singles match first, adding that if the referee were to insist upon it, she would scratch from the championships there and then. Ignoring the pleas of the French team captain, Jean Borotra, she then stormed off, exiting SW19 in a state of extreme agitation.

Under ordinary circumstances such a tantrum would have resulted in expulsion from the tournament, but Lenglen was no ordinary player. She was too valuable a commodity for Wimbledon to lose and the organisers feared, understandably, that the spectators might be unhappy were she to be scratched. As both her singles and doubles opponents also had no desire to see her scratched, referee Burrow was given the face-saver of postponing her two matches until the Thursday, even allowing her to play her doubles tie first.

When Lenglen returned on Thursday, the grey weather matched the atmosphere on court. Lenglen and Vlasto lost to the American pair after having twice been at match point, but rain prevented her from playing her singles match. This eventually took place on the Friday. Lenglen won despite, to quote Burrow, 'complaining of pain in her arm and feeling ill'.

Her only match on the Saturday was a mixed doubles with Borotra, but when Lenglen took to the court she was amazed to hear sections of the crowd booing her for her behaviour earlier in the week. The golden girl had fallen from grace. Although Borotra managed to ease the tension first by doing without a warm-up and then by clowning around, Lenglen could still sense an air of animosity towards her. The final straw appeared in Monday's programme with the referee's wording for the singles of 'Mlle Lenglen (if well enough to play) versus Miss C Beckingham'. Burrow subsequently maintained that his choice of words was intended purely as a precaution but there is little doubt that Lenglen saw them as inflammatory.

Shortly afterwards it was announced that she had retired from both the singles and the mixed doubles and was heading back to Paris. In doing so, she again snubbed Buckingham Palace where she was due to be presented to Queen Mary. Lenglen had gone to the trouble of having a dress specially made for the occasion but the wife of the French Ambassador in London had put her off attending by telling her that she would not be welcome at the Palace following her petulance at Wimbledon. In fact the ambassador's wife was wide of the mark. The British public may have turned against Lenglen but there is no evidence that Queen Mary bore any resentment. She was almost certainly disappointed not to see Lenglen's singles match but, contrary to the Wimbledon pronouncement, she was not offended.

Suzanne Lenglen never hit another ball at Wimbledon. Later that year she put her unhappy summer behind her and turned professional. Yet within twelve years she was dead, the victim of pernicious anaemia, her health apparently having been undermined by the long hours of practice she endured as a young girl. The other tragedy was that a player who had brought pleasure to so many for so long should have departed Wimbledon for the last time in such acrimonious circumstances.

A Winter of Discontent

1926

The New Zealand Rugby League team's 1926–7 tour of England and Wales was in trouble from the moment the All Blacks appointed an Australian, Ernest Mair, as manager. His man management skills inspired nothing but contempt with the result that seven of the players expressed a desire to go home before the ship had even reached Southampton. Throughout the tour Mair refused to listen to the players' grievances, adopting a high-handed approach that led to bitter showdowns and one of the most shameful episodes in New Zealand sporting history.

The players that sailed from Auckland aboard *RMS Aorangi* on 3 August 1926 were strictly amateur and as such they expected the New Zealand Rugby League to foot essential expenses. Yet less than a week into the voyage Mair announced that he was refusing to pay their laundry bills on the grounds that laundry came under the heading of 'personal expenses' and was therefore not subject to the players' agreement. He also declined to pay travelling expenses to transport each man from his home to the Auckland waterfront in order to catch the ship. Dissent broke out in the ranks and the NZRL backed down over the laundry bills. However, the travelling expenses eventually had to be settled by the English Rugby Football League simply to ensure that the tour went ahead.

These disputes were just the tip of the iceberg. The players began to miss their wives – a situation exacerbated by the fact that Mrs Mair had somehow secured an invitation to join the tour in a semi-official capacity. Then in the heat of the mid-Pacific Mair brusquely informed the players that the ship's chief steward insisted on their wearing collars and ties at meal times. When the team's vice-captain, Neil Mouat, tried to reason with the steward, the latter denied all knowledge of any such edict. The next stage of the journey was a long rail crossing of Canada and once again Mair scarcely endeared himself to the party by ordering the players to perform the Maori haka several times a day. On the crossing to Southampton the players at least had the distraction of the ship's fancy dress ball but when Mouat and team-mate Arthur Singe missed a team meeting because they were sleeping off the effects of the ball, Mair promptly fined the pair £1 each.

The players had had enough and seven of their number – Mouat, Singe, Frank Henry, Lou Peterson, Alphonsus Carroll, W W Devine and J Wright – said they wanted to return to New Zealand. Far from attempting to reconcile any differences with his men, Mair immediately contacted the English RFL and requested that return berths to New Zealand be booked for the seven rebels on the first available ship. Possibly to Mair's disappointment, the tour captain, Bert Avery, managed to placate the disenchanted players so that the first match – against Dewsbury – could take place.

However, trouble flared again when the players returned to their Harrogate hotel after the match. Singe became involved in an ugly street brawl with fellow Aucklander Craddock Dufty, as a result of which Mair informed Singe that he was granting his wish and sending him back to New Zealand. For good measure he told Peterson that he was no longer welcome either. Then Mair changed his mind and decided that Singe and Mouat (who he saw as the principal troublemakers) should go on the boat to New Zealand but the rest could stay. The manager had clearly lost all control over, and respect from, his troops and the seven responded by saying that they would play no further part in the tour so long as Mair was in charge. This put the NZRL in something of a quandary because all seven were forwards and, with no replacements on hand, the tour would effectively end almost as soon as it had begun.

So the RFL were brought in to act as intermediaries and listen to the rebels' complaints, which not only concerned Mair's authoritarian attitude but also his playing tactics. In what was something of an understatement, an RFL council meeting concluded that 'a number of the players did not see eye to eye with the team manager and coach Mr Mair on matters of discipline and tactics on the field'. The matter was resolved temporarily by Mair being pressured into agreeing 'to forego any question of tactics or coaching on the field for the next few matches, and if this proved successful, to allow it to continue'. In other words, Mair had been relieved of his duties for the time being.

This uneasy truce allowed the rebels to participate in the first Test against England at Wigan on 2 October, which New Zealand lost 28–20, but following another outbreak of indiscipline at the Harrogate hotel, the landlady said she wanted the whole team out by the weekend. Mair saw this as an opportunity to stamp his authority again and to send home the seven but the All Blacks' financial manager, G H Ponder, intervened, pointing out the consequences for the tour if the rebels were to leave. Instead Ponder diplomatically suggested that Mair take a prolonged break. His pride hurt, Mair refused to go on leave but did agree to relinquish all selection duties for the next month, leaving the task to a triumvirate of Ponder, Avery and Mouat.

Mair returned to the fold in mid-December whereupon five of the rebels who had been chosen to play against Yorkshire promptly withdrew their services, leaving the team to lose by a single point, 17–16. When the same quintet also refused to play in the next game – against Hunslet – the English RFL finally lost patience. It ordered Mair to stay out of team affairs and told the New Zealanders to sort themselves out or the remainder of the tour would be cancelled.

The tour staggered on with little enthusiasm from either side. By the final game – the third Test on 15 January – all of the rebels had gone. Henry had returned to his home town of York and, with the series already lost, the other six left for New Zealand on the eve of the Test. Even that was not plain sailing as, before leaving England, they demanded £10 a head from the RFL on the grounds that they were destitute. The RFL gave in just to see the back of them. In their absence, New Zealand lost the Test 32–17 before a paltry Leeds crowd of

6,000. The English public had delivered its verdict on the temperamental tourists.

Back home the New Zealand Rugby League described the tour as a 'fiasco' and banned the seven rebels for life. Mair was sacked and he returned to his native Queensland. Meanwhile each of the non-rebels in the party was rewarded with a special medal by the NZRL 'in recognition of his loyal services English tour 1926–1927'. It would be fair to say that it had been earned.

The Battle of the Long Count

1927

It was the most infamous round in the history of boxing – round seven of the world heavyweight title rematch between the holder Gene Tunney and former champion Jack Dempsey at Soldier's Field football stadium in Chicago. Tunney survived a knockdown and the loss of his crown only by virtue of an extended count, which most witnesses put at fifteen seconds but which may even have been as long as seventeen seconds. Such was the chaos and confusion surrounding the long count that five radio listeners across the United States reportedly died of heart attacks brought on by sheer excitement. All in all, it was one hell of a night.

Until the autumn of 1926 Jack Dempsey – the Manassa Mauler – was the undisputed heavyweight champion of the world. He had worn the crown with distinction for seven years and although time was starting to take its toll, there was no sign of any rival being able to take his title. On 23 September 1926 Dempsey was booked to meet ex-US marine Gene Tunney in Philadelphia. At 31, Tunney was only two years younger than Dempsey but while the age difference may not have been a contributory factor in the champ's eventual downfall, fitness undoubtedly was. For whereas Tunney had worked his way up for a title shot with a succession of tough fights – including four the previous year – Dempsey had fought just three times in the past six years and not at all in the last three. Quite simply, Dempsey was ring rusty.

Not that Dempsey's supporters saw it that way. Unable to conceive anything but a victory for their man, they made Dempsey a firm favourite to retain his title. So it was that

120,757 fight fans packed Philadelphia's Sesqui-Centennial Stadium on a night of torrential rain expecting to cheer another triumph for the Mauler, only to receive a nasty surprise when a sluggish Dempsey was comfortably outboxed by the slick, skilful Tunney. The world heavyweight division had a new champion. When asked by his wife Estelle what had gone wrong, Dempsey famously replied: 'Honey, I just forgot to duck.'

The eagerly awaited return fight took place a year later – on 22 September 1927 – before a crowd of 104,943 who between them had paid over two and a half million dollars for the privilege. Like the first fight, it took place in heavy rain and once again it was Tunney who controlled the early exchanges from the moment he landed a telling blow to Dempsey's head in the opening round. Tunney said later: 'I knew after the first round that I had Dempsey. I knew, further, that it would be only a question of time when I would knock him out.'

For his part, Dempsey realised that there was little prospect of outpointing the fleet-footed Tunney. His only hope was for a knockdown. But for the first five rounds he was chasing shadows as Tunney, with his sharp jabs and quick footwork, built up a healthy points advantage. Dempsey looked positively pedestrian in comparison. There was none of the old fire, none of the old ferocity. Then in round six Dempsey finally roused himself and began stalking Tunney like the Mauler of old. Tunney started the seventh with a left and right to the head before Dempsey replied with several blows to the champion's body. As Tunney tried to back off towards the ropes, Dempsey threw a right, which narrowly missed its target, followed by a long left hook that caught Tunney square on the jaw. Tunney staggered back against the ropes and Dempsey, moving in for the kill, pummelled him with a combination of punches that sent Tunney crumbling to the floor – the first time in his career that he had been down.

Tunney later reflected: 'Everybody saw Dempsey land that left hook to my jaw, but never knew how much it surprised me. I never saw the punch. Not seeing it surprised me – I was always cocksure about my eyesight in the ring.'

Instinctively Dempsey hovered over his stricken opponent, but in doing so forgot that under local Illinois rules the aggressor had to retire to a neutral corner before the count could commence. The rule stated:

> When a knockdown occurs the timekeeper shall immediately arise and announce the seconds audibly as they elapse. The referee shall see first that the opponent retires to the farthest neutral corner and then, turning to the timekeeper, shall pick up the count in unison with him, announcing the seconds to the boxer on the floor. Should the boxer on his feet fail to go, or to stay in the corner, the referee and timekeeper shall cease counting until he has so retired.

Ironically the neutral corner rule was instituted in the wake of Dempsey's fight with the Argentinian Luis Angel Firpo four years previously. On that occasion, too, Dempsey had stood menacingly over his opponent after knocking him to the floor, waiting to hammer him with punches as soon as he got to his feet – a tactic that prompted concern from the antiboxing brigade. However, since then Dempsey had fought only once – his first meeting with Tunney – and, although the local amendment had been explained to both fighters beforehand, he was clearly unfamiliar with the rule which he had unwittingly helped bring into existence. Moreover many athletic commissions, including New York City, operated under different rules. There the count started from the moment the boxer hit the floor. It was still the referee's job to force the standing boxer to a neutral corner, but while that was being done the count continued.

With Tunney down, referee Dave Barry began the count, Dempsey hovering at his shoulder. One, two...then Barry suddenly stopped when he realised that Dempsey had not retreated to a neutral corner. Above the roar of the crowd, Barry could be heard yelling: 'Get to a neutral corner, Dempsey.' At first Dempsey failed to react. He was too pumped up, his eyes staring wildly at Tunney. So Barry took him by the arm and shepherded him towards the correct corner. Still Dempsey appeared confused. The rules stated that he had to go to the farthest neutral corner. Tunney had gone down perilously close to Dempsey's corner so the farthest corner was Tunney's, but that was not considered neutral. Eventually one of Dempsey's seconds pointed a finger in the right direction. Referee Barry resumed the count, beginning again at one, but by then three or four valuable seconds had been lost. Afterwards Barry explained his version of the confusion:

> Dempsey, possibly through force of habit or perhaps through forgetfulness, endeavoured to circle around me into his own corner, which would have brought him right behind Tunney. The timekeeper's count had started, but seeing Dempsey's action I thrust my left arm in front of him and ordered Jack to a neutral corner. Dempsey persisted, however, and tried to circle around me in the other direction. Then, apparently realising that he was really penalising himself, he turned and walked to the furthest neutral corner. I immediately faced the timekeeper and by holding up the index finger of my right hand signalled him 'One'.

Timekeeper Paul Beeler had three stopwatches, one in his hand and two on the table. He said:

> When Tunney was floored I began to count. With my eyes on the watch, I tolled off the seconds. I looked up and saw Dave Barry pushing and waving Dempsey to a neutral corner. Barry then picked up the count. I called 'five' and he called 'one', showing that the count started from that second. I had a split second in which to decide whether to go with Barry's count or continue my own original count. I went along with Barry; he was in charge.

All the while Tunney was sitting there with a bewildered expression. He pulled himself into a sitting position but made no attempt to rise to his feet until the count reached nine. By then he had spent anything between fifteen and seventeen seconds on the floor, time in which he had been able to regain his composure and take the heat out of the situation.

Back on his feet, Tunney spent the remainder of the round avoiding Dempsey's frenzied attacks. When the bell went, Dempsey knew that his chance had gone. Sure enough in the next round it was Dempsey's turn to be dumped on the canvas. Tunney was in control once more and soon Dempsey had sustained cuts on both eyes. At the end of the tenth and final round, Tunney was the clear winner. The drama of the seventh was but a distant memory.

However, nobody was in a hurry to forget. Announcing his intention to file a formal protest, Dempsey's manager, Leo Flynn, called the fight:

...The biggest injustice I have ever seen in a ring. Tunney is the pugilistic champion of the world by grace of what was either a queer decision or a colossal case of inefficiency in the simple matter of counting seconds. A dozen stopwatches showed Tunney down for fifteen seconds in the seventh. Even if Tunney could have got to his feet at the end of the count, Jack would have floored him again. He needed those extra five seconds mighty bad.

Dempsey could barely conceal his anger when talking to the man from the *New York Times* straight after the fight:

Intentionally or otherwise, I was robbed of the championship. Every stopwatch around the ring caught the time as about fifteen seconds, and the inefficiency of the referee or the timekeeper or both deprived me of the fight. Everybody knows I am not a whiner. When Tunney beat me last year I admitted that he was the better man that night. I am not an alibi artist, but I know down in my soul that I knocked Tunney out tonight.

Predictably Tunney took a different view, claiming that he could have got up earlier than he did but had deliberately waited until the count reached 'nine'. 'I was not hurt,' he insisted, 'but considered it just as well to take my time.'

The Illinois State Athletic Commission backed referee Barry unequivocally and maintained that Dempsey was the architect of his own misfortune. 'He beat himself by being slow in getting back to his corner,' said one of the judges, George Lytton. 'Dempsey knew the rules. He wanted to be on top of Tunney just as soon as the latter rose. He thought he could get away with that infraction. He guessed wrong.'

Lytton also revealed that Dempsey could have been disqualified before the fateful seventh round for repeatedly hitting below the belt and using the barred rabbit punch. The referee's failure to punish Dempsey for these offences blows a sizeable hole in the argument of Dempsey apologists who claim that Barry was in the pay of the Tunney camp. They also say that Barry deliberately slowed the count from 'five' to 'nine' to allow the fallen champion more time to recover. Timekeeper Beeler confirmed that Barry did slow the count – which was how Beeler's watch came to show seventeen, and not fifteen, seconds when Tunney finally rose – but believed that it was accidental. 'It's difficult to count seconds accurately without using a stopwatch,' said Beeler, 'the general tendency being to count them slower than they actually are. That's what referee Barry did.'

That sounds plausible enough until the Dempsey camp follow it with a devastating counter. How come when Tunney floored Dempsey in round eight, he was allowed to stand at the referee's shoulder as he counted? Why was Tunney not forced to retreat to a neutral corner? Why did the referee not stop the count to steer him to a neutral corner? Was it just inconsistency in the heat of the moment or were more sinister forces at work? It depends on which side you listen to.

And so the debate rages on. The Battle of the Long Count turned out to be Jack Dempsey's last serious venture into the ring. He retired following the fight, boxing only in exhibitions from then on. Gene Tunney picked up a cool $990,445 from his night's work. To fulfil his dream of receiving a million-dollar cheque he wrote promoter Tex Rickard one for the balance and then pocketed his seven-figure fee. Tunney had one more fight, successfully defending his title against New Zealander Tom Heeney in July 1928 before he, too, retired.

Curiously, while that dramatic night in Chicago ended Dempsey's career, it did wonders for his public image. Until then he had been perceived as a villain of the ring – a brutal, ruthless assassin – but the possible injustice of his defeat to Tunney cast him in the role of wronged hero and he kept the sympathy vote for the remaining 56 years of his life. In American sport winning is everything. Jack Dempsey proved the exception to the rule. But then rules never were his strong point.

The Expulsion of France

1931

The game of rugby union was in a dire state in France. Whereas at club level in Britain the match was still sometimes seen as little more than a pleasant afternoon's diversion between bouts of socialising, in France it was literally a matter of life and death.

Nowhere did the desire to win at any cost burn more fiercely than in the southwest of the country around Bordeaux and Toulouse, where teams from Paris were regarded as the natural enemy and where local rivalry was equally intense. Among the most passionate rugby supporters was local industrialist Jean Bourrel whose goal was to convert Quillan, a small town nestling at the foot of the Pyrenees, into the region's leading club side. To this end he lured the best players from the likes of Perpignan and Toulouse with offers of money and jobs at his factory. The policy worked to the extent that Quillan went on to lift the French national championship three years in a row from 1927, but they won few friends outside the town, being perceived as nothing more than a team of mercenaries. Bourrel's mercenaries merely served to fuel the hatred between Quillan and their local rivals – a hatred that manifested itself in an episode of extreme savagery when the Quillan hooker, Gaston Riviere, died from his injuries after being viciously kicked by Perpignan players during the 1927 fixture between the two clubs.

Sadly this was not an isolated incident. As the violence escalated, a Pau player also met his death on the pitch and then in 1930 an eighteen-year-old wing, Michel Pradie, was killed playing in a cup match for Agen. Matches became so competitive that referees officiating at home defeats found themselves in grave danger of being attacked by spectators and some players were even found to have hidden lethal stiletto knives in their socks. This was not sport; it was civil war.

Violence was not the only blight on French rugby at the time. The professionalism championed by Jean Bourrel had spread right across the country. In truth it was nothing new. The strictly amateur British Unions had long harboured suspicions about the French. As far back as 1912 Stade Bordelais had placed adverts in Scotland offering to find a well-paid job for an accomplished fly half, as a result of which the Scottish Rugby Union was so incensed that the French authorities were forced to ban members of the offending club's committee for life. With the game in France becoming ever more combative, financial inducements and player poaching were commonplace. French rugby was professional in everything but the name.

In 1930 the top dozen French clubs – *Le Douze* – broke away from the nation's official body in a row over player payments. Within a year those twelve clubs were openly paying their players.

This blatant affront to amateurism, coupled with the prevailing violence in the French game, was too much for British rugby to take. In 1931 France were kicked out of the Five Nations Championship (ironically it was they who had coined the term 'Five Nations' back in 1910). Announcing the expulsion, the Home Unions Committee declared solemnly:

> We are compelled to state that owing to the unsatisfactory state of the game of Rugby Football in France, neither our Union, nor the clubs or Unions under its jurisdiction, will be able to arrange or fulfil fixtures with France or French clubs until we are satisfied that conduct of the game has been placed on a satisfactory basis in all essentials.

And so France went into rugby exile. They were allowed back in 1939, only for the Second World War to delay their re-entry for a further eight years.

The Bodyline Controversy

1933

Following the loss of the Ashes to the visiting Australians in 1930, the leading thinkers in English cricket were united in the view that something had to be done about Don Bradman. The 21-year-old had, almost single-handedly, destroyed the England bowling in that series, finishing with an average of 139.14. The outlook for the next decade was bleak unless England could come up with some means of curbing Bradman's phenomenal strokeplay.

The task of doing so was handed to Surrey's Douglas Jardine. Studying film of the 1930 Oval Test – in which Bradman made 232 – Jardine felt he had spotted a chink in the prodigy's armour. On a damp pitch Bradman had looked momentarily uncomfortable when facing deliveries from England's fastest bowler, Harold Larwood, which lifted sharply. Clutching at that straw, the Oxford-educated Jardine and the former Nottinghamshire miner Larwood formed an unlikely alliance to combat Bradman. But in the process they also created arguably the biggest controversy in sporting history, one which seriously jeopardised Anglo-Australian relations.

Jardine's plan was to encourage his fast bowlers to aim short-pitched deliveries on the leg stump and to crowd the batsman with a cordon of on-side fielders close to the wicket. 'Leg-theory', as it was known, was nothing new. Ironically the Australians had pioneered it through fast bowlers such as Warwick Armstrong, but Jardine – via his battery of pacemen – was to take it to new levels of aggression and intimidation and to earn it a more graphic description: 'Bodyline'.

Jardine first outlined his ideas during the Surrey–Nottinghamshire game at The Oval in August 1932. He invited Larwood and his Nottinghamshire fast-bowling partner, the left-armer Bill Voce, to dinner at the Piccadilly Hotel. Larwood later recalled:

> Jardine asked me if I thought I could bowl on the leg stump, making the ball come up into the body all the time so that Bradman had to play his shots to leg... We thought Don was frightened of sharp-rising balls and we reasoned that if he got a lot of them over the leg stump he would be put off his game and intimidated, and eventually, having to direct his shots to leg all the time, would give a catch to one of the on-side fieldsmen.

Larwood was slight for a fast bowler at 5ft 8in tall and weighing just eleven stone yet he delivered the ball at speeds upwards of 90mph. His secret lay in the strength of his forearms, developed from years of working in the pit. His Nottinghamshire team-mate, Joe Hardstaff senior, nicknamed Larwood 'Silent Killer'. Hardstaff explained:

> I used to field at cover point and as Harold came up on that smooth, carpet-slipper run of his, and I moved in to the batsmen, I used to listen hard to find out what kind of delivery he was going to bowl. If I could hear his feet tip-tapping over the turf, I knew he would be well within himself. But when I couldn't hear him running up, I used to look at the batsman and think 'you're a split second away from trouble, son', because I knew that Harold was coming in on his toes and he was going to let slip the fastest he'd got.

The naming of Jardine's party to tour Australia in 1932–3 betrayed his intentions, containing as it did four fast bowlers – Larwood, Voce, the tall bespectacled Yorkshireman Bill Bowes, and the Middlesex amateur Gubby Allen. The accent was clearly going to be on speed, not spin.

Jardine was a single-minded individual who did not set out to win friends, especially among the Australian press. Aloof and reserved, he was a PR nightmare. When Bill Woodfull was hit over the heart by a short-pitched delivery while batting for an Australian XI against the tourists at Melbourne in mid-November, newspaper pictures of him reeling back in agony immediately turned the Australian public against England.

Bradman was twice out cheaply to Larwood in that match, prompting the *Evening Standard* correspondent to predict: 'In Larwood, assuming that he maintains his "demon" speed of the present match, lies the answer to the Bradman problem. Bradman does not appear to like supercharged fast bowling.'

Both Bradman and Woodfull struggled for runs in the lead-up to the Test series. Jardine was convinced that the Australians were on the run and when Bradman pulled out of the first Test at Sydney with a virus, a Larwood-inspired England eased to a ten-wicket victory. The shell-shocked Australians were confident that it would be a different story when Bradman returned for the second Test at Melbourne. Between matches Jardine succeeded in further antagonising the locals by refusing to play on a wet ground at Hobart for fear of incurring injuries to his fast bowlers. It was by no means an unreasonable stance but the Tasmanian crowd, who had come to watch England's finest, thought differently and made their feelings known. Jardine eventually backed down and agreed to play, but he still flatly refused to bowl his top men.

Before the second Test Jardine told Allen that he wanted him to bowl more bouncers and to a stronger leg-side field. Allen declined, replying: 'If you don't like the way I bowl, you'd better leave me out – but I would add that if you do, every word you've said here today will be made public when I get home.' Jardine decided not to push the matter. Allen played, and in all of the remaining Tests. As it turned out the slow Melbourne wicket did not suit the England pace attack and a century from Bradman (following a first-innings duck) steered Australia to victory by 111 runs. So there was everything to play for as the circus moved to Adelaide in January 1933 for the third Test.

Two days before the Test Jardine was jeered by 3,000 spectators when he led England in the nets, his subsequent complaint resulting in onlookers being excluded from watching England practise the next day. With Jardine's popularity with the Australian cricketing public plummeting by the day – and about to plunge to hitherto uncharted depths – there was widespread rejoicing when the England captain was dismissed cheaply on the first morning. On the fastest wicket they had encountered to date on the tour, England rallied to post a total of 341 and waited to see how the Australians would cope with Larwood and co. Although the 'bodyline' tactic had been used on occasions in the first two Tests it had not proved decisive but now, in favourable conditions, it was unleashed in all its venom. The stumps became immaterial as deliveries were speared at the batsman's body. Off the last ball of Larwood's second over, the Australian captain Woodfull was hit over the heart, just as he had been at Melbourne in November. Dropping his bat, he staggered from the wicket, clutching his chest in pain whereupon Jardine called across to Larwood: 'Well bowled, Harold.' After an over of respite from Allen, Larwood was about to start his third over when Jardine stepped forward and signalled for his fielders to form the infamous leg-trap. Everybody knew what was coming, not least the ailing Woodfull. To a crescendo of boos, Larwood surged in and unleashed a fearsome delivery that knocked Woodfull's bat clean out of his hands. Such was the hostility from the crowd that a pitch invasion was feared, never more so than when Larwood captured the prize wicket of Bradman, caught in the leg-trap by Allen, precisely according to the plan drawn up at the Piccadilly Hotel. With Australia reeling at the end of the day's play, the MCC manager, Pelham Warner, visited the Australian dressing room to inquire after Woodfull's health. Woodfull's response left no room for misinterpretation. He said:

> I don't want to speak to you, Mr Warner. Of two teams out there, one is playing cricket, the other is making no effort to play the game of cricket. It is too great a game for spoiling by the tactics your team are adopting. I don't approve of them and never will. If they are persevered with it may be better if I do not play the game. The matter is in your hands. I have nothing further to say. Good afternoon.

Woodfull's comments were leaked to the press and there was further uproar when Bert Oldfield was forced to leave the field after being hit on the head trying to hook a short ball from Larwood. Although the injuries to Woodfull and Oldfield had both occurred when the leg-trap field was not in operation, the Australian Board of Control had become infuriated by England's shock tactics and on 18 January fired off an unprecedented telegram to the MCC:

Body-line bowling has assumed such proportions as to menace the best interests of the game, making protection of the body by the batsmen the main consideration. This is causing intensely bitter feeling between the players as well as injury. In our opinion it is unsportsmanlike. Unless stopped at once it is likely to upset the friendly relations existing between Australia and England.

There was even talk of Australia leaving the Commonwealth, a fear expressed by Jardine's old cricket master at Winchester who, on hearing of his former pupil's actions, famously remarked: 'He could well win the Ashes – and lose the Empire!'

Unwilling or unable to accept the extent of Jardine's tactics and the gravity of the situation, the MCC condemned the Australian Board's telegram and expressed complete confidence in the England captain. After England had gone on to win that bellicose third Test by 338 runs, rumours circulated that the remainder of the tour might be cancelled, but, in the wake of two financially disastrous visits by the West Indies and South Africa, the Australian Board needed the money from the Ashes series. And whatever its faults, bodyline generated tremendous interest at the box office.

It also sold newspapers. Naturally the English press tended to side with the tourists, *The Times* from its distant London base taking the view that 'It is inconceivable that a cricketer of Jardine's standing, chosen by the MCC to captain an English side, would ever dream of allowing or ordering the bowlers under his command to practise any system of attack that, in the time-honoured English phrase, is not cricket.' To cover itself in the absence of any first-hand knowledge, the paper added that if 'Jardine has made more use of the "leg-theory" than other captains before him the development is largely due to the fashion of the two-eyed stance and the modern batsman's habit of covering the stumps with his legs, thereby preventing the bowler from getting a clear view of the wicket, and incidentally making it more likely that he himself will be hit.'

In the *Daily Telegraph* former Test player Percy Fender also leaped to England's defence. He wrote:

There can be no question about the legality of attacking the leg stump, and if there were the slightest question of a bowler going out more for the body than the wicket, the umpires are there on the spot, and would act without hesitation... The Press and the public, being 120 yards from the wicket, cannot see enough to warrant the belief that the success of our bowlers is due to anything more than that they have discovered a hole in the Australian betting, and are making full use of it.

Apparently Fender, thousands of miles from the wicket, could see enough.

Jardine was rarely short of self-belief but he decided that it was an appropriate time to ascertain whether his tactics had the backing of his players. The majority gave the captain their support, at which Jardine asserted that the Australians' bitterness was little more than a case of sour grapes. 'The general impression to be formed after the second Test match,' he later wrote, 'was that there was nothing wrong with leg-theory provided it was mastered.' However, he said that he would refuse to lead England into the fourth Test at Brisbane unless the Australian Board withdrew its accusation of 'unsportsmanlike' behaviour. A half-hearted apology was duly made on the morning of the match, allowing Jardine to help England reclaim the Ashes with a six-wicket victory.

That match passed without incident and, with the Ashes safely won, Warner thought it might be prudent for Jardine to drop bodyline for the fifth Test. Jardine would not hear of it. 'We've got the bastards down there,' he snapped, 'and we'll keep them there.' England triumphed again – this time by eight wickets – the highlight for the Sydney crowd being when Jardine received a taste of his own medicine in the form of a few painful blows to the ribs. Bradman finished the series with an average of 56.57, having scored just 396 runs, less than half his 1930 total. For the only time in his career he had been reduced to the level of a mere mortal.

The end of the series did not mark the end of the controversy. While Jardine and Larwood remained resolutely unapologetic for their actions, Warner felt obliged to denounce bodyline. 'One of the strongest arguments against this bowling,' he wrote, 'is that it breeds anger, hatred and malice, with consequent reprisals.' Having publicly supported Jardine during the tour, the MCC was put in a quandary, particularly with the Australians due to visit England in 1934. That tour was already in doubt unless Jardine could be persuaded to abandon bodyline, but he was not one for sacrificing his principles. Instead he announced that he would not be available to lead England in the 1934 series. The MCC breathed an audible sigh of relief.

Without a leader to back him, Larwood suddenly felt an outcast and he, too, declared himself unavailable to face Australia. He angrily rounded on what he saw as a 'conspiracy to bury leg-theory and brand me as a dangerous and unfair bowler. The MCC have given way to political or other influences determined at all costs to placate Australia.' Voce also found himself out of favour and took out his frustrations when the Australians played Nottinghamshire at Trent Bridge. After his batsmen had been on the receiving end of a hostile spell of bodyline, Woodfull told Nottinghamshire that if Voce took the field the following day, the Australians would not. Voce was conveniently taken ill overnight.

The MCC finally decided to act and labelled the 'persistent and systematic bowling of fast, short-pitched balls at batsmen standing clear of the wicket' as 'unfair', adding that 'it must be eliminated'. Umpires were given the power to have repeat offenders removed from the attack. To all intents and purposes, bodyline was dead. Normal service could be resumed.

The Italian Job

1933

The new Melaha circuit at Tripoli was heralded as the fastest motor racing venue in the world with cars attaining speeds of up to 140mph. On 7 May 1933 it attracted the world's leading drivers for the Tripoli Grand Prix and, with Libya being an Italian colony, the Italian dictator Benito Mussolini, himself a motor racing fan, ordered a major publicity coup to mark the occasion. The celebrated Italian aviator, Marshal Balbo, had recently been appointed governor of Libya and it was he who answered Mussolini's demands by organising a national lottery, to be run in conjunction with the race.

Tickets went on sale in Italy months in advance and thousands of people invested their small change in the hope of winning seven and a half million lire, the equivalent of around £80,000. Three days before the race thirty tickets were drawn, each bearing the car number of one of the competing vehicles. As the lucky ticket-holders contemplated riches beyond their dreams, little did they know that Mussolini's grand vision was about to turn sour.

It all started on the eve of the Grand Prix. The Italian driver Achille Varzi was sitting in his elegant hotel room when he received a visit from a stout, bald-headed gentleman who introduced himself as Enrico Rivio, a timber merchant from Pisa. Rivio explained that he had drawn the lottery ticket bearing the number of Varzi's car and that, in the event of Varzi winning, he was prepared to split the prize money with him. To illustrate his sincerity, Rivio produced an official document, drawn up by his solicitor, granting the driver a share of the spoils. Varzi was puzzled by such an unexpected act of generosity from a complete stranger until he began reading between the lines. Then it dawned on him that he was being asked to make sure he won the race.

Once his guest had departed, Varzi telephoned his compatriot and old rival, Tazio Nuvolari, the most exciting driver of his day. No record of their actual conversation exists but the bizarre events of the following day's race strongly suggest that they decided upon some form of collusion to ensure that Varzi was first to take the chequered flag.

The temperature soared to over 100 degrees in the shade on race day. The splendid grandstand – the British driver Dick Seaman described the circuit as 'the Ascot of motor racing' – housed Arab sheikhs in their flowing robes while nearby, in a special box, sat the thirty hopeful ticket-holders, nervously gripping the slips of paper that could prove their passport to riches. There was a butcher from Milan, an old lady from Florence, a student, a baron who had fallen on hard times, and there was Signor Rivio, the sweat of anticipation glistening on his bald pate.

In a display of pomp and ceremony, Marshal Balbo flagged away the starters. The early stages of the thirty-lap race did not follow the script with the intrepid Englishman Tim Birkin setting the pace in his privately entered green Maserati. However, the Italians began to assert their authority and by lap 12 Giuseppe Campari's Maserati led from Nuvolari and Baconin Borzacchini. Birkin was hanging on gamely in fourth but, to the dismay of Signor Rivio, Varzi's Bugatti appeared to be struggling. Mechanical problems soon accounted for Campari, who was seen drowning his sorrows with a bottle of Chianti, allowing Nuvolari to take over from Borzacchini and the Frenchman, Louis Chiron, as Birkin dropped back.

With just five laps of the $8^{1}/_{2}$-mile circuit remaining, Varzi finally gave his backer some cause for hope by moving up to third, but no sooner had he done so than the Bugatti started making ominous noises. Two cylinders were dead and the car was slowing. To call in to the pits for a change of plugs would have eliminated any chance of victory so Varzi was left with little option but to soldier on and pray for divine intervention...or at least the intervention of his fellow drivers.

At that point the hapless Varzi was on the brink of being lapped by Nuvolari but then events started to take a strange twist, the remaining few laps being conducted in a manner more befitting the Keystone Cops than Grand Prix racers. On lap 27 Borzacchini inexplicably slowed and kept looking over his shoulder. Moments later he cut a corner so fine that he hit an empty oil drum marker and his car skidded to a halt with a burst tyre. Although forced to retire, Borzacchini did not seem unduly perturbed by his misfortune.

Borzacchini's exit allowed Varzi up into second place but he still trailed Nuvolari by some thirty seconds at the start of the final lap. Nuvolari had seen his lead eroded by a series of unnecessary pit stops, which had baffled his mechanics to the point that they had run out of things to repair. Indeed, on his latest stop one of the crew suggested that he must have been coming in to go to the toilet, although the language was more colourful. Nevertheless Nuvolari still looked a certain winner until, with just half a mile to go, he, too, began peering anxiously over his shoulder. His Alfa slowed alarmingly until, 100 yards from the finish, it ground to a halt. Nuvolari leaped out and screamed in typically animated fashion: 'No petrol! No petrol!' Mechanics rushed to his assistance but in the meantime the ailing Varzi trundled into view. Nuvolari suddenly managed to get going again but not in time to prevent Varzi crossing the line, almost in slow motion, the winner by one-tenth of a second. The exhausted Varzi was carried shoulder-high by the crowds cheering his heroic victory. None cheered louder than Signor Rivio.

That evening, as Varzi, Nuvolari and Borzacchini were seen sipping the most expensive champagne, rumours began to circulate that the race had been fixed and that the reason Borzacchini and Nuvolari had been looking over their shoulders during the race was that they had been waiting for Varzi. These three were named as the prime suspects with Campari and Chiron also suspected of being involved. The following morning Libya's supreme sporting authority held an emergency meeting at which there were calls for all five to be disqualified and for their competition licences to be withdrawn. Despite there being no satisfactory explanation for the curious finish to the Grand Prix, the demands were rejected, not least because to have banned five of Europe's best-known drivers would have seriously dented the sport's image. Instead they escaped with a mild warning. However, to avoid a repeat of the scandal, the lottery system was changed so that in future ticket numbers were drawn just five minutes before the race when the drivers were already in their cars and were therefore immune to temptation.

Slow Boat to Hamburg

1936

Eleanor Holm Jarrett was the golden girl of the US Olympic team. Despite once confessing that she 'trained on champagne and caviar', the pretty 22-year-old wife of singer and band leader Art Jarrett was unbeaten in competitive swimming for seven years and was hotly fancied to retain the 100 metre backstroke title that she had won at the 1932 Olympics. But she had an Achilles heel in that she loved to party, and it was her love of the high life that resulted in her being kicked off the team in disgrace before she even reached the controversial 1936 Berlin Olympics.

Germany was in the grip of the Nazi movement and a number of countries expressed misgivings about sending teams to Berlin for what they feared would be a Hitler propaganda exercise. To allay fears of an American boycott, Hitler promised that there would be no anti-Semitic demonstrations and instructed his propaganda minister, Joseph Goebbels, to have any such signs removed from the streets of Berlin. Avery Brundage, president of the American Olympic Committee, was clearly won over by Hitler's charm offensive for he defiantly told objectors that Germany was pursuing 'the spirit of the Olympics' and arranged for a team of around 350 Americans to sail for Hamburg aboard the luxury liner, the *SS Manhattan*.

Among them was Eleanor Holm. In the three years since her Beverly Hills wedding to Art Jarrett, she had established herself as a partygoer of international standard. She sang in her husband's band at Hollywood's Coconut Grove and socialised with stars of stage and screen. Swimming was important to her, but not important enough to get in the way of a good party.

Indeed, she had admitted attending a late-night party only hours before winning the final Olympic qualifier earlier in 1936. But no matter how much she drank or how little she slept, her performances in the pool remained unaffected. Even on a steady diet of alcohol she was streets ahead of rivals who had trained assiduously during months of self-denial.

To one with such a vibrant lifestyle, the prospect of spending nine days at sea with no alcohol and plenty of early nights was scarcely appealing. Nor was the third-class accommodation in which the athletes had been quartered by the AOC. Holm was used to travelling first class...and without her every move being monitored by the eagle-eyed team chaperones.

The *Manhattan* sailed from the United States on 15 July. Holm was soon bored but her reputation had gone before her and on the 17th a Mr Maybaum of the United States Lines, the ship's owners, invited her to a party in the first-class lounge. The only team member to be invited, she spent the night mingling merrily with such illustrious guests as actress Helen Hayes and her playwright husband Charles MacArthur. It was six o'clock in the morning when the party finally ended and by then Holm had drunk so much that she had to be helped back to her cabin. Her wayward behaviour did not escape the notice of the team officials who immediately warned her as to her future conduct. Holm resented being treated like a naughty schoolgirl caught behind the bicycle sheds and carried on drinking over the next few days, reminding concerned friends who advised her to slow down that she was 'free, white, and 22'.

On 23 July the ship stopped at Cherbourg and Holm, ignoring her previous warning, spent several hours at a champagne party. At around 10.30 p.m. the appropriately named Ada Sackett, chaperone of the swimming team, discovered her star athlete staggering along the ship's deck in the company of a young man. Sackett immediately escorted Holm to the cabin that she shared with two other swimmers, Olive McKean and Mary Lou Petty, but as soon as the chaperone had left, Holm compounded her sins by poking her head out of the porthole and shouting obscenities – a tirade that was only ended when her roommates dragged her inside and persuaded her to sleep. Sackett returned at midnight, accompanied by the team doctor, J Hubert Lawson, who found Holm 'in a deep slumber which approached a state of coma'. His diagnosis was 'acute alcoholism'.

At 6 a.m. a bleary-eyed Holm was informed that the AOC had voted for her to be thrown off the team for 'violation of training rules'. In addition to the drinking, she was also accused of gambling and admitted winning a couple of hundred dollars shooting craps shortly before the party. Stunned by the decision, she impetuously went to Brundage's stateroom, but he refused to see her and she was reduced to pleading her case through a crack in the door. He remained unmoved. As news of her sacking spread throughout the ship, 220 of her team-mates signed a petition pleading for her reinstatement. She begged for another chance, but her appeal was dismissed.

Opinion was largely in favour of Holm. Lawson Robertson, head of the US men's track-and-field team, thought Holm was getting a 'rough deal' while predictably Art Jarrett could not understand what the fuss was about. 'She always seems able to win,' he said, 'even if she doesn't go in for the heavy training of some of those athletes. They ought to give some more of those swimmers champagne. Maybe they could win a couple of races.' And one American journalist wrote of Brundage, a former pentathlete who excelled at the discus: 'Avery Brundage has a discus where his heart belongs.' But Dean Cromwell, University of Southern California track coach, disagreed. 'She asked for it,' he told the *New York Times*. 'In fact, she begged for it. If it had just been one time it would have been different, but it had been going on for a week. We cannot get the reputation for being boozers.'

When it became apparent that there was no hope of reinstatement, Holm went on the offensive, claiming that at least a hundred other athletes had broken the training rules during the voyage. 'I like a good time,' she protested, 'particularly champagne. All I did was drink a couple of glasses. I was not exactly a child.' She added that there was no general bar on athletes drinking and pointed out that the heaviest drinkers on the ship were the US team officials.

Specifically she targeted Gustavus T Kirby, treasurer of the AOC, whom she accused of presiding over a mock marriage and trial 'ostensibly given as an entertainment feature'. She said that Kirby had 'so handled the dialogue having to do with marital situations that it was open to questionable interpretations and altogether unsuitable for youthful ears. The reaction to the whole show was such that it was the talk of the boat for days afterward.' An indignant Kirby hit back, insisting: 'We were all merry and the whole thing was done in the spirit of fun without anything offensive whatsoever. Only an evil mind could see anything improper in the performance.'

Having travelled all that way, Holm had no intention of missing out on the Olympics altogether and covered the Games as a celebrity reporter for the Hearst International News Service. She cried when watching the opening parade from the stands instead of being part of it. However, she quickly recovered her appetite for partying and was entertained by the Nazi hierarchy as a special visitor to the Olympics. She later recalled: 'I had such fun! I enjoyed the parties, the *Heil Hitlers*, the uniforms, the flags... Goering was fun. He had a good personality, lots of chuckling. So did the little one with the club foot (Goebbels). Goering gave me a sterling silver swastika. I had a mould made of it and I put a diamond Star of David in the middle.'

On returning to the US after the Games she found that being kicked off the team had made her a bigger star than ever. In 1938 she tried her hand at acting, starring as Jane opposite another Olympic swimmer, Johnny Weissmuller, in the movie *Tarzan's Revenge*. She divorced Jarrett and married impresario Billy Rose, but controversy was always a near neighbour and when she and Rose split acrimoniously in 1954, the case kept tabloid readers entertained for weeks and became known as 'The War of the Roses'. Whether it was swimming, partying or divorcing, Eleanor Holm lived most of her life in the headlines.

Stella the Fella

1936

The Germans would stop at nothing in their quest for Olympic glory in 1936, which was how Hermann Ratjen came to bind up his genitals and call himself 'Dora' to finish fourth in the women's high jump. The deception did not come to light for another 21 years when Ratjen finally confessed, saying that he had been pressured into it by the Nazi Youth Movement. Yet Ratjen's case has since been overshadowed by that of another sex change competitor at those Berlin Olympics, the Polish sprinter Stanislawa Walasiewicz.

Born in the Polish village of Rypin in 1911, Walasiewicz moved with her family to the United States when she was two years old. They settled in Cleveland, Ohio, where she grew up under the name of Stella Walsh. An outstanding athlete, she made her first bid for the US Olympic team in 1928, but was ruled ineligible on account of her Polish citizenship. Two years later she became the first woman to break the eleven-second barrier for the 100 yards and, as the world's fastest sprinter, was confidently expected to bring back gold from the 1932 Los Angeles Olympics. Prior to the Games she was set to become a US citizen but when she lost her job with the New York Central Railroad she accepted a post with the Polish consulate and decided to compete for Poland instead.

American bitterness over her decision was magnified when she duly took gold in the 100 metres, narrowly defeating Canada's Hilde Strike. A Canadian official noted that Strike's conqueror ran with 'long man-like strides'.

Walsh's place at the head of women's sprinting was threatened four years later by the arrival of a new kid on the block, Helen Stephens, a six-foot-tall farm girl from Missouri. When Stephens beat her in a fifty-yard dash, Walsh arrogantly dismissed her rival as a 'greenie from the sticks'. Walsh's reaction merely served to spur Stephens to greater achievements and the Pole was soundly beaten into second place in the 1936 Olympic final.

Walsh did not take kindly to defeat and muttered that Stephens was so fast that she had to be a man! When a Polish journalist repeated the accusation, German officials were obliged to issue a statement saying that Stephens had passed a sex test. Meanwhile some were starting to question Walsh's own credentials. One athletics fan wrote to the head of the IOC:

> As ... one who upholds the participation of feminine athletes in athletics I feel Stella Walsh has been allowed to take part in a field where she doesn't belong. Her deep bass voice, her height and $10^{1}/_{2}$ inch shoes surely proclaim her a borderline case if there ever was one ... Rules should be made to keep the competitive games for normal feminine girls and not monstrosities.

Stephens retired after the Games, thus bringing an end to hostilities between the two athletes. Walsh eventually became an American citizen in 1947 but because she had competed for Poland she was ineligible to try for the US Olympic team. That rule changed in 1956 following her marriage to a US citizen but by then she was 45 and her sprinting days were well behind her.

That might have been the last the world heard of Stella Walsh but for a freak incident on 4 December 1980. After buying bunting from a Cleveland discount store to welcome the visiting Polish national basketball team, she was caught up in an armed robbery and shot dead in the store's parking lot. To the astonishment of medical men and athletics officials alike, the autopsy revealed that Stella Walsh had male sexual organs. The athlete who had set eleven women's world records and won two Olympic medals was really a man.

The Bronx Bull

1947

Jake LaMotta was born to box. As a kid in the Bronx, he was persuaded by his father to fight other boys in the neighbourhood for the entertainment of adults. The money that was thrown into the ring helped pay the family's rent. Like most kids raised on those mean streets, a life of crime was just a solitary mistake away but after an early stint in reform school, LaMotta decided to channel his energies legally and became a professional boxer at the age of nineteen.

Two years later, in 1943, LaMotta inflicted Sugar Ray Robinson's first defeat in 41 pro fights. Robinson gained his revenge within three weeks but 'The Bronx Bull', as LaMotta was known, steadily worked his way up the middleweight rankings, defeating the likes of Tommy Bell, Bert Lytell, Jose Basora and Holman Williams on the way. Despite his impressive record, LaMotta was repeatedly denied a shot at the world middleweight title. The frustration began to build.

In June 1947 he was offered $100,000 to take a dive against Tony Janiro. LaMotta wanted no part of it but started to wonder whether his refusal to co-operate with the shady underworld figures who controlled American boxing at the time was hampering his chances of a title fight.

In November of the same year he was lined up to fight Billy Fox, an undefeated black light heavyweight from Philadelphia, at Madison Square Garden, New York. Fox had won 43 consecutive fights, all on knockouts, and had underworld backing in the shape of his diminutive manager, 'Blinky' Palermo, and the mobster Frankie 'Mr Grey' Carbo. Keen to see their boy win and protect their long and short-term investments, Palermo and Carbo told Joey LaMotta to offer his brother $100,000 to lose the fight. At first Jake declined but when he ruptured his spleen in training he figured he had nothing to lose and instructed Joey to reopen discussions. Four days before the fight Palermo and Carbo visited LaMotta at his New York nightclub. He still had no interest in their money but he agreed to take a dive on condition that he would be promised a shot at the world middleweight title. The deal was done.

LaMotta and Fox climbed into the ring together on 14 November, but even beforehand the rumours of a fix had sent the bookies running for cover. However, LaMotta quickly discovered that losing to Fox would be no easy matter. LaMotta later revealed:

> The guy you're throwing to has to be at least moderately good. I mean, this fight is in Madison Square Garden, and all the fight writers are there and a big crowd, so this little scuffle has got to look like a fight. But the mob guys, like lots of others, are plain stupid. Fox can't even look good. The first round, a couple of belts to his head, and I see a glassy look coming over his eyes. Jesus Christ, a couple of jabs and he is going to fall down? I began to panic a little. I was supposed to be throwing a fight to this guy, and it looked like I was going to end up holding him on his feet.
>
> I don't know how we even got through the first round without me murdering him. Sometimes I thought the air from my punches was affecting him, but we made it to the fourth round. By then if there was anybody in the Garden who didn't know what was happening he must have been dead drunk... Dan Parker, the Mirror guy, said the next day that my performance was so bad he was surprised that Actors Equity didn't picket the joint... Finally the referee had to stop it – what else could he do? I was against the ropes with my hands down pretending I was taking a beating, and Fox had hit me about fifteen times with everything he had, which wasn't enough to dent a bowl of yoghurt.

Fox's victory was not only hollow, it was transparent. At the end of the shambles, the crowd booed and demanded their money back, prompting the Boxing Commission to conduct an investigation at which LaMotta attributed his lacklustre display to his training injury. Unable to prove that he was lying – although there was more than a hint of suspicion – the

Commission could do little more than slap him with a $1,000 fine and a seven-month suspension for failing to report an injury. Nevertheless the controversy surrounding the contest was such that LaMotta had to wait nineteen months for his promised title fight. However, the delay had not blunted his appetite and he defeated the champion, Marcel Cerdan, on a technical knockout. LaMotta was the world champion at last but to win the most coveted prize of all he had seriously compromised his reputation.

LaMotta retired in 1954, having lost his title to old adversary Sugar Ray Robinson, and then in 1960 testified before a committee headed by US Senator Estes Kefauver that was probing organised crime in general, including the involvement of gangsters in boxing. LaMotta admitted that he had twice been approached to throw fights and finally owned up to having taken a dive against Billy Fox, claiming that he had done so only because his injury was so bad that he thought he would be unable to win. In the light of LaMotta's own appraisal of Fox's inadequacies, this assertion seems highly dubious. LaMotta could have broken both arms and probably still beaten Fox that night.

Fox said he knew nothing about the fix and professed to be stunned by LaMotta's confession. 'I was disgusted,' he sighed, 'not with myself, but with what my manager was trying to do.'

The story of Jake LaMotta was resurrected in 1981 when Robert De Niro portrayed him in the Academy Award winning film *Raging Bull*. Time was less kind to 'Blinky' Palermo and Frankie Carbo; their criminal activities earning them sentences of fifteen and 25 years respectively.

Gorgeous Gussie's Naughty Knickers

1949

Teddy Tinling had been associated with Wimbledon in various roles for many years, initially as a player and then as an official assisting at the championships. He had also turned his hand to dress design and it was in that capacity that he created the outfit which scandalised the All-England Club in 1949, leading to denunciation in parliament and pulpit.

In the immediate post-war period women tennis players dressed in a masculine style – wearing shorts or culottes – but Christian Dior's sensational 'New Look' designs of 1947 created a desire for a return to femininity. Tinling wanted to adopt the Parisian style by putting women tennis players in dresses. He wrote: 'I was the first to rebel against the uniform appearance of the post-war tennis players. I felt that by looking like modern-day Amazons, the sportsgirls were renouncing their birthright.'

He found his ideal model in Gertrude Agusta Moran (or 'Gussie' as she was known to her friends), an avant-garde Californian who used to walk around barefoot at home and sleep in a T-shirt. She had a walk, said Tinling, 'that had so much bounce she appeared to be treading on a succession of rubber balls'. Like Tinling, Moran was bored with the dull outfits traditionally worn at Wimbledon. She wanted something with colour and asked Tinling to design her sportswear for the 1949 championships. Although there was nothing to that effect in the Wimbledon entry form, Tinling was left in no doubt by the authorities that only an all-white ensemble would be acceptable, which meant that he had to find the necessary 'colour' from style rather than pigment. He came up with a soft knitted rayon dress trimmed with white satin. The number four seed was delighted but was worried about what to wear underneath. Since she had no time to shop for anything, Tinling got his French fitter to produce some panties made from the leftovers of the dress fabric and, to liven them up and show off Moran's suntanned legs, he added half an inch of lace trim. Tinling said: 'I felt what we wanted was some lace with a bold design that would at least be visible from time to time in the stands when Gussie served.'

The daring creation was unveiled the day before the tournament at the annual pre-Wimbledon garden party at Hurlingham. It caused a sensation, being the first time that ladies' knickers had been deliberately put on public display in a sporting environment, and press photographers jostled furiously to capture the posterior for posterity. The following morning Moran was besieged by reporters at her hotel, all wanting to know whether she was going to wear the frilly panties in her first-round singles match. Taken aback that so small a garment had attracted so much publicity, Moran suddenly developed cold feet and, to the dismay of the Wimbledon crowd, elected instead to wear a staid shirt and a pair of old shorts. But the public were not about to give up on her and nurtured high hopes that she would wear her new outfit for her second-round match with Betty Wilford on 20 June.

Between designing tennis wear, Tinling was working as a callboy for the two main courts. When he went to collect Moran, whose game was scheduled for Number One Court, he was delighted to see that she was wearing the dress and panties. She gave him a knowing smile and walked out on to court where she was greeted by a roar of applause. Hordes of photographers immediately began scrambling for position at the back of the court, searching for a spot where they could lie flat on the ground to obtain the most risqué shot of Moran as she served. Around a hundred reporters covered the match but Moran's victory was treated as incidental. All eyes were on her naughty knickers.

She became an instant celebrity. She was asked to judge beauty contests and the Marx Brothers, who were in London at the time, invited her to join their act. A racehorse, an aircraft and even a restaurant's special sauce were all named in her honour as the whole of Britain raved about 'Gorgeous Gussie'. Wimbledon had never seen anything like it – nor did some committee members wish to see its like again. For while Princess Marina thought the provocative panties to be great fun, one of the Wimbledon committee told Tinling acidly: 'You have put sin and vulgarity into tennis.' The All-England Club went on to reprimand Tinling for 'drawing attention to the sexual area' and the club president, Louis Greig, boomed: 'I will never allow Wimbledon to become a stage for designers' stunts. Wimbledon needs no panties for its popularity.' Tinling was able to see through the unintentional double entendre. Questions were asked in parliament (although Prime Minister Clement Attlee, a man not usually associated with setting fashion trends, complimented Tinling on the outfit) and the English vicar of St Andrew's Church in Buenos Aires preached a sermon on the sins of Gertrude Moran's lace panties. Her infamy knew no bounds.

Moran's new-found celebrity status quickly proved a double-edged sword as she began to grow increasingly uncomfortable in the media spotlight. 'After the lace panties,' she complained, 'everyone was always staring to see what I was wearing and I couldn't concentrate on my tennis.'

Afraid that the hullabaloo was affecting her game, she dressed more soberly for her third-round singles match, but surprisingly lost. However, when she and Pat Todd reached the final of the ladies' doubles, to be played on Centre Court in the possible presence of 82-year-old Queen Mary, the All-England Club got their knickers in a twist once again. Officials warned Moran that HRH might not approve of the outfit and advised restraint. Wanting to give Tinling's design one more airing that summer, she stayed in her hotel until the last minute, regularly telephoning Wimbledon to find out whether or not the royal guest was expected. In the event the weather was too hot for the ageing monarch to attend, thereby allowing Moran to wear the panties in the final. It proved an error of judgement. She was so self-conscious that she hardly dared to bend down during the knock-up. Her play suffered, she and Todd losing in straight sets to Margaret du Pont and Louise Brough. The following day's papers published photographs of the winners walking behind Moran with what Tinling described as 'unabashed and unconcealed curiosity'.

After Moran had been voted Best Dressed Sports Woman by the US Fashion Academy, there was renewed interest in what she would be wearing for the 1950 Wimbledon tournament. The United Press International wire service put out a story that read: 'The lips of every woman and the eyes of every man are asking the same question, "What will she wear this time?"' So it was something of an anticlimax when she paraded a relatively tame, Tinling-designed ensemble of shirt and shorts, christened the 'Peek-a-Boo suit'. In that same year she joined the professional circuit where she proved one of the biggest draws for having worn the smallest.

Tinling was reportedly paid just £10 for his most contentious creation. It brought him credibility as a designer but also a barrowload of trouble from certain factions within the All-England Club who never forgave him for encouraging indecency on the hallowed courts. As a result he found himself alienated from Wimbledon and it was another twenty years before he was able to renew his formal association with the tournament he loved.

The Baseball Midget

1951

Bill Veeck, owner of the St Louis Browns, was known as the Barnum of baseball. A supreme showman who never allowed considerations of taste to get in the way of a good publicity stunt, his finest – and most controversial – hour was the occasion when he introduced a 3ft 7in midget to bat in a game against the Detroit Tigers.

The Browns were enduring a torrid time in the 1951 season, languishing at the bottom of the league. With the Tigers faring only marginally better, the prospect of a double-header between the two on 19 August scarcely set the pulses racing. However, Veeck's bizarre selection of the diminutive Eddie Gaedel as part of a celebration to mark the fiftieth anniversary of both the American League and the Falstaff Brewing Company, the Browns' radio sponsor, ensured that none of the 18,369 fans present at Sportsman's Park in St Louis that Sunday would ever forget the experience.

The promise of a party attracted the Browns' biggest home crowd for four years. On arrival, fans were handed a free can of the sponsor's beer, a slice of birthday cake and a box of ice cream plus salt-and-pepper shakers in the shape of miniature Falstaff beer bottles. But Veeck had one more surprise up his sleeve.

After the Tigers won the first game, a bulky actor dressed in Elizabethan costume wheeled on to the grass a three-tier, 7ft-high papier-mâché cake. 'Ladies and gentlemen,' bellowed the announcer, 'as a special birthday present to manager Zack Taylor, the management is presenting him with a brand-new Brownie.' On cue Gaedel jumped out of the cake wearing elflike slippers and a miniature Browns uniform bearing the number one-eighth. The spectators roared their approval, little knowing that the mini Brown was actually going to play in the second game against the Tigers.

Weighing just 65lb and only slightly taller than a baseball bat, Gaedel had been recruited by Veeck from vaudeville. 'How would you like to be a big-league ballplayer?' Veeck had asked when pitching the idea. 'Eddie, you'll be the only midget in the history of the game. You'll be appearing before thousands of people. Your name will go into the record books for all time. You'll be famous, Eddie. You'll be immortal.' Veeck was never prone to understatement.

So it was that Gaedel sat in the Browns' dugout and changed into his baseball shoes before the start of the second game. Rookie Frank Saucier was expected to lead off for the home team but then Gaedel popped out of the dugout waving three toy bats and it was announced that he was pinch-hitting for Saucier. As Gaedel approached the plate to tumultuous cheers, the Tigers' manager, Red Rolfe, leaped from his seat and protested that the Browns were turning the game into a farce but his opposite number, Taylor, showed umpire Ed Hurley a valid player's contract for Gaedel, which Veeck had fortuitously mailed to the league office the previous day…when the office was closed. After examining the document, Hurley signalled for Gaedel to step to the plate. The objection was overruled.

The rules of baseball state that a batter is out after three strikes. If a pitch crosses home plate in the strike zone (between the armpits and knees of the batter) and the batter does not swing, that is a strike. Swinging and missing the ball also constitutes a strike. Confident that the Detroit pitcher would never manage to hit Gaedel's strike zone, that, because of his stature and taking into account his crouched stance, measured one and a half inches, Veeck strictly forbade the little man from swinging for glory. To reinforce the point, he told Gaedel that he had placed a sniper on the roof to shoot him if he swung. The Tigers' pitcher, Bob 'Sugar' Cain, consulted with catcher Bob Swift, unsure whether to throw underarm or overarm. In the end he delivered a perfect fastball, some four feet above the plate, a strike to every major-leaguer – except this one. The next ball followed a similar pattern but as Cain began to see the funny side, he lobbed the next two high over the batter's head. Gaedel's bat never left his shoulder and after four pitches out of the strike zone he duly trotted to first base, tipping his cap to his adoring fans on the way. There he made way for a pinch runner and received a standing ovation as he crossed the field, his job done. He was paid $100 for his unscheduled appearance but would probably have done it for nothing. 'For a minute,' he said afterwards, 'I felt like Babe Ruth.'

In spite of Gaedel's heroics, the Browns lost the game 6–2, but that was just the start of Veeck's problems. For while most of the press accepted it as a harmless prank, others thought it was an insult to both baseball and midgets. The *New York World* said it 'made a mockery of the sport' and 'exploited a freak of biology in a shameful, disgraceful way'. Priests joined in the condemnation, swiftly followed by American League president Will Harridge who was infuriated by a stunt that, he believed, held the game up to ridicule. Incensed, Harridge banned Gaedel from baseball and introduced a new rule making it mandatory that all player contracts be filed with and approved by the league president. Under pressure from the press, Harridge also tried to expunge Gaedel's name from the record books, but Veeck had promised his man immortality and was not prepared to give up without a fight, arguing that if Gaedel's batting were decreed nonexistent, Cain's pitching in that game should be treated similarly. The league backed down and the name of Eddie Gaedel remains in the record books to this day. Sadly he had only ten years to enjoy his fame, dying from a heart attack at the age of 36 after being mugged in his home town of Chicago in 1961. Among those who attended his funeral was Bob Cain.

The Francasal Mystery

1953

When a 10–1 outsider Francasal trotted up by two lengths in the Spa Selling Plate at Bath on 16 July 1953, the leading London bookmaking firms immediately smelled the whiff of foul play. For the horse had been heavily backed in the minutes leading up to the race but the bookies had been unable to lay any of the money off owing to a mysterious breakdown in telephone communications to the racecourse.

Shortly before the two o'clock race at Bath bets on Francasal totalling £6,000 were struck all over the country in units as small as £10 or in more substantial amounts placed by professional punters. Particularly heavy betting was reported in Bournemouth and Bristol. Under normal circumstances some of this money would have been communicated to the course, thereby lowering the horse's price and easing the load on off-course bookmakers, but the telephone breakdown between Bath telephone exchange and Bath racecourse prevented this happening. Consequently Francasal went off at 10–1 and the bookies stood to lose £60,000.

Looking into the fault on the line, the Post Office found that an overhead cable had been cut about a mile from the racecourse. The police were called in and, although confident that lightning had caused the break, sent the severed ends of the inch-thick cable to a forensic science laboratory for closer examination. Meanwhile the big bookmaking firms announced that they were not paying out on the race until the police investigation was complete.

The forensic report stated that the break was not caused by lightning but by a blowtorch – an act of deliberate sabotage.

Unravelling the web of deceit led to five men standing trial in January 1954 on charges of conspiracy to defraud in what became a tale of two horses.

The five were Henry Kateley, 42, a commission agent from Maidenhead, Berkshire; 47-year-old Maurice Williams, a decorator from Kentish Town, London; William Rook, 57, an engineer from Burnham, Buckinghamshire; Gomer Charles, 46, a Cardiff bookmaker; and Victor Robert Colquhoun Dill, a 56-year-old bloodstock dealer from Hampstead. The court heard that Kateley was the head of the conspiracy and that he and avid punter Williams, whom he had known since childhood, recruited Dill to lend an air of respectability. Dill had been awarded the Military Cross in 1918. At the other end of the spectrum Charles was known to be a shady character, having been warned off all racecourses in May 1951 following a Jockey Club inquiry. His ban was lifted in July 1953.

The plot first took shape in March 1953 when Dill went to France and asked an associate to find him a good two-year-old horse capable of winning an English selling plate. A promising animal named Santa Amaro was suggested and, acting on Dill's report, Kateley flew to France the following month, buying the horse for £2,000 in the name of Williams. Then in early July a similar-looking horse, Francasal, was secured from a French trainer for £820. The paperwork listed Williams as the owner of this horse, too. Francasal had run twice without success and, as the respective purchase prices reflected, was rated inferior to Santa Amaro.

Everything was now in place for the two horses to be switched, a move that took place at a horse-transport contractor's stables at Sonning Common in Oxfordshire. While the real Francasal remained at Sonning, Santa Amaro was taken to the Epsom yard of trainer Percy Bailey by Kateley and Rook, the latter already having four horses in training there. Kateley informed the trainer that the horse was running in a £188 English selling plate – a race where the victor is auctioned immediately after the race – at Bath on 16 July, and that as soon as the race was over it was to be bought in (i.e. ownership retained), whatever the price.

In the meantime Dill, acting under the name of Colquhoun, had taken over the bookmaking business of J Davidson & Co. Between March and July a large number of accounts had been opened with other bookmakers for the purpose of laying bets. These accounts lay idle until 16 July.

At 1.30 p.m. – half an hour before the race – two men burned through the telephone cable near Bath racecourse. With bookmakers effectively kept in the dark, Williams put £3,500 on Francasal and Charles bet £2,500, the money being distributed by J Davidson & Co. among half a dozen different bookmakers. After the race the winning horse was bought in by Rook for 740 guineas and quickly smuggled away. But when the severed phone lines were discovered and the bookmakers refused to pay out, the conspirators were forced to flee without collecting their winnings. Once the two horses were traced, the game was up.

The defendants claimed that the horse contractor must have accidentally loaded the wrong horse into the box bound for Epsom. They denied making any deliberate switch and insisted they were merely taking part in a betting coup. After the jury failed to reach a verdict, a retrial found four of the five men guilty. Rook was acquitted, but Kateley was sentenced to three years' imprisonment, Williams and Charles both got two years, and Dill was jailed for nine months. Francasal was duly disqualified from first place in the Spa Selling Plate, a race in which he had never even run.

Piggott's Six-Month Suspension

1954

On 2 June 1954 Lester Piggott gained the first of his nine Derby wins on the 33–1 shot Never Say Die, in the process becoming, at just eighteen years of age, the youngest jockey ever to ride the winner of the Epsom classic. Hot on the hooves of this historic success, however, came a crushing setback when, on the same horse, he was deemed responsible for a rough finish to the King Edward VII Stakes at Royal Ascot and handed a punishment unprecedented in its severity.

Piggott has never exactly gone out of his way to win friends with the result that his career has seen numerous brushes with authority, culminating in his three-year prison sentence in 1987 for tax evasion. The seeds for his uncompromising riding style were sown early when he worked for his trainer father Keith, a hard taskmaster who instilled a ruthless streak in his son. By the summer of 1954 the young Piggott had already served nine suspensions, mostly for careless riding. He remarked recently: 'When I was young, I didn't want to get beaten and go back with excuses. It was every man for himself. You went out to win. Yes, I did cut up one or two, and them me.'

Piggott's win-at-all-costs attitude had irked senior riders as well as the Jockey Club. Sir Gordon Richards, that noted gentleman of the turf, not only had little time for Piggott's lack of respect but also was somewhat envious of his precocious talent. After all, Richards had famously taken 28 attempts to win the Derby; Piggott had needed only three. The contrasting approaches to racing and life in general of the old maestro and the brash young pretender were already on a seemingly irreversible collision course when the pair clashed at Ascot on 18 June, little more than two weeks after Piggott's Derby triumph.

In the closing stages of a keenly fought race, Piggott cheekily went for a gap on the rails on Never Say Die at the same time as Richards launched his challenge aboard Rashleigh on the outside. Sandwiched between the two as both horses wandered off line under intense driving was Piggott's cousin, Bill Rickaby, on Garter. The horses flashed past the post with Rashleigh in first place and Never Say Die back in fourth, but the Ascot stewards immediately held an inquiry into the scrimmaging that took place inside the final furlong. Initially the stewards lodged an objection to Rashleigh but, without the benefit of camera patrol film, they were forced to rely on their own eyes and the evidence of the jockeys concerned. When summoned by the stewards, Richards laid the blame squarely on Piggott's young shoulders. 'Lester's horse charged into Garter,' he said, 'and hit my quarters and almost turned me round. Then Never Say Die charged Garter again, and Garter turned me broadside on.' Not surprisingly, Piggott saw things rather differently, claiming that Richards had deliberately pushed Garter across to block his path.

The stewards were left with a dilemma, but not much of one. Who should they believe, the respected Richards or the prickly Piggott? In the end they obeyed the laws of human nature and decided that Piggott was the cause of the interference. He was suspended for the remainder of the meeting and reported to the Jockey Club.

If Piggott thought the Ascot stewards had wronged him, it was nothing compared to the sense of injustice he felt when the Jockey Club delivered its verdict two weeks later. The Jockey Club stewards, headed by the Duke of Norfolk, decided that it was time to come down hard on the boy wonder. In a savage statement they announced that they had 'taken notice of his dangerous and erratic riding both this season and in previous seasons, and that in spite of continuous warnings, he continued to show complete disregard for the rules of racing and for the safety of other jockeys.' As a punishment they withdrew his jockey's licence and said that he would not be allowed to reapply for it until he had spent a minimum of six months at a training establishment other than his father's. Keith Piggott was clearly considered a bad influence.

Many senior figures in the racing world welcomed the ban, believing that Lester Piggott had finally received his comeuppance. However, the public who had warmed to the callow youth, and those members of the press who had championed his undisputed talent leaped to his defence, saying that he had been victimised by the authorities. Nor was he without support in the weighing room. Fellow jockey Geoff Lewis told John Karter, author of *Lester: Return of a Legend*, that Piggott had been treated unfairly. 'Lester was going for a legitimate gap, but Gordon and the older jockeys were getting tired of his recklessness and if the opportunity arose to shut the door in his face they would do so. That was what happened at Ascot.'

The ban hit Piggott in a place that was always emotionally if not anatomically close to his heart – his pocket. From earning over £10,000 a year as a top-flight jockey, he was reduced to living on a mere £5 a week as a humble stable lad. In one of his rare public utterances on the subject, he described it as 'bloody hard labour and less than a fiver a week while serving it'. To rub salt into the wounds he missed the winning ride on Never Say Die in the St Leger for which his replacement, Charlie Smirke, picked up over £1,300.

Piggott's sentence was served with Newmarket trainer Jack Jarvis who reputedly acknowledged in later years that his greatest failure as a trainer was that 'I never made a gentleman out of Lester Piggott'. His suspension was lifted early – on 4 October – a fortnight after the St Leger and shortly after the retirement of Sir Gordon Richards.

During his enforced lay-off, Piggott's weight had ballooned to 9st 7lb and he had to sweat and starve before resuming his riding career. Typically his first ride back in public – on Cardington King at Newmarket – was a winner, prompting wild scenes of jubilation among racegoers at Headquarters. Lester Piggott was back with a vengeance. For all their efforts, the Jockey Club would never quite manage to tame him.

The Rocket Richard Riot

1955

'When he's worked up his eyes gleam like headlights – not a glow, but a piercing intensity. Goalies have said he's like a motorcar coming on you at night. He is terrifying. He is like lightning.'

That was how Frank Selke, erstwhile manager of the Montreal Canadiens ice hockey team, once described his star player, Maurice 'Rocket' Richard, the *enfant terrible* of the National Hockey League. With eyes that seemed as black as coal, allied to blinding speed, a devastating shot and a distinctly nasty streak, the burly Richard became a cult figure among fans of the Canadiens. He was the first National Hockey League player to score 500 goals in a career and the first to score fifty goals in a season. More than that, he was a role model for French Canadians – a fearless hero who would let nothing and nobody stand in his way, or, as one scribe put it, 'a resistance leader whose flag was the Montreal Canadiens jersey'. His nemesis was National Hockey League president Clarence Campbell, viewed by French Canadians as an arrogant, power-crazed individual who treated them as an inferior species. So when Richard and Campbell went head-to-head in the spring of 1955, there was no question as to where the fans' loyalty lay. The ensuing scenes of violent public disorder represented ice hockey's darkest hour.

Joseph Henri Maurice Richard was born in Montreal on 4 August 1921. Although he studied to be a machinist at Montreal Technical School, his ultimate goal was to play in the NHL. Overcoming ankle and wrist fractures, he made his senior debut for the Canadiens in 1942–3 and, despite breaking his ankle again sixteen games into his rookie season, received a glowing testimony from team coach Dick Irvin who predicted: 'Not only will he be a star, but he'll be the biggest star in hockey.' Earning his nickname from his phenomenal acceleration, the following season the 'Rocket' starred in the Canadiens' first Stanley Cup success for thirteen years, and in 1944–5 he notched an astonishing fifty goals in fifty games. His all-consuming passion to win struck fear into the hearts of goalminders. Veteran players used to tell rookies to watch for the fire coming out of those eyes. All too often his intensity on the ice boiled over into acts of physical retribution on those who had sought to stifle his skills, a trait that scarcely endeared him to opposing players or fans. He was hated in New York where a ball peen hammer was once thrown at him while he sat on the bench.

Richard continued to blaze a trail through the early 1950s although as a team the Canadiens were forced to play second fiddle to the dominant Detroit Red Wings. The rivalry between the teams was frightening and nobody exemplified it better than Richard, whose frustration and resentment built steadily as he saw trophy after trophy slipping away.

By the mid 1950s French Canadians in Quebec were becoming increasingly disenchanted. The drive and determination of the French-speaking Richard inspired them in their quest for independence. Every time he stood up to opposing players or league officials, the people of Quebec felt as though he was standing up for French Canadians against their English oppressors. Former referee Red Storey says: 'Hockey was a religion in Quebec and Richard was the Pope.'

One man epitomised the enemy – Clarence Campbell. Richard made no secret of his contempt for the NHL president, and accused him in a newspaper column of running a dictatorship. A confrontation was brewing.

Visiting Boston on 13 March 1955, Richard was high-sticked by the Bruins' Hal Lycoe, suffering a head wound which would need eight stitches. Richard exploded with rage, swinging his stick like a baseball bat, raining blows on Laycoe's head and shoulders with such ferocity that the stick splintered. When linesman Cliff Thompson tried to intervene, the two fell to the ice and Richard twice punched the official in the face. It was the second time Richard had hit an official that season. He tried to explain his actions: 'I don't remember what happened. When I'm hit I get mad and I don't know what I do.'

The explanation cut no ice with Campbell. Seizing his moment, he convened a disciplinary meeting on 16 March and, acting as judge and jury and dismissing Richard's claim that he had mistaken Thompson for a Bruin, banned the 'Rocket' from the last three games of the regular season plus the entire Stanley Cup play-offs. Canadiens fans were furious and Campbell's office was bombarded with abuse and even death threats. One fan warned: 'I'm an undertaker and you'll be needing me in a few days.' But Campbell refused to be intimidated and stuck to his guns.

The following evening the Canadiens entertained their archrivals, the Detroit Red Wings, at the Forum in Montreal. In the circumstances Campbell was advised to stay away, but he had no intention of bowing to the bullies. Extra police were drafted in as the Forum was surrounded by 800 angry demonstrators, many carrying placards that read 'Vive Richard' and others holding up images of their hero. Campbell arrived late with three lady friends and tried to slip quietly into his seat but nearby fans spotted him. Eggs, peanuts and programmes were hurled in his direction, but Campbell remained calm until, with the Richard-less Montreal trailing 4–1 at the end of the first period, the spectators renewed the barrage. Overshoes, bottles and tomatoes joined the missiles. Ushers and police attempted to keep the fans at bay but one broke through the guards and, after offering to shake Campbell by the hand, slapped him across the face instead. As Campbell reeled from the blow, the irate fan followed up with a punch. Further debris showered down on the ice, the booing turned to a roar of hatred, and someone in the crowd threw a smoke bomb in Campbell's direction, sending spectators coughing and choking towards the exits as the Forum organist struck up the tune 'My Heart Cries For You'. With the Forum evacuated, Campbell awarded the game to Detroit.

Outside, the angry fans teamed up with ticketless Montrealers who had been unable to get in to see the sellout game and embarked on an orgy of violence and destruction.

Exclusive stores on the city's St Catherine Street were damaged and looted, cars were overturned and set on fire. By 11 p.m. the number of rioters had swelled to over 10,000, confronted by 200 police officers trying to quell the chaos. Trouble raged for more than four hours, resulting in some 60 arrests and $100,000 worth of damage. It became known as the 'Richard Riot'.

With more trouble expected the following night, Richard went on the radio to appeal for calm. The plea worked. He took his punishment and played down his role in the wider scheme of things. 'I'm not a politician,' he protested, 'I'm just a hockey player.' Nevertheless he remained a hero to French Canadians long after his retirement and when he died in May 2000, over 115,000 people turned out and silently paid their respects.

Trouble in Trinidad

1960

Notwithstanding the Montreal riot, crowd problems at sporting events were relatively uncommon in the 1950s. It was an era when good behaviour abounded both on and off the field, when sport was largely seen as competitive fun, the last decade before big money turned it into a matter of life and death. For English cricket it was a period synonymous with the village green, cucumber sandwiches, and vicars on bicycles where, even on the greater stage of the Test match, defeat was met with polite applause. That is not to say that spectators were anything less than partisan, and nowhere was this more apparent than in the West Indies. When the England touring party set off for the Caribbean in the winter of 1959 they were perhaps mindful that on the previous MCC tour to those parts bottles had been thrown on to the pitch during the third Test at Georgetown, Guyana. Little did they know that those scenes would pale in comparison to events during the second Test at Port of Spain, Trinidad, in January 1960.

A cloud was hanging over West Indies cricket on account of the omission from the series of exciting fast bowler Roy Gilchrist, who had been sent home from the tour of India for disobedience. So unpopular was the ban with the West Indies cricketing public that, after the first Test with England in Bridgetown, Barbados, had ended in a dull draw, an organised mob of dissidents urged a wholesale boycott of the second Test. However, Trinidadians love their cricket and turned out in such numbers to support their team at the Queen's Park Oval that the third day attendance of 32,000 set a new record for a sporting event in the West Indies. It also meant that the spectators had to be crammed together like sardines, and this congestion proved a contributory factor in the subsequent unrest.

Prospects of a West Indies victory looked slim from the outset with England posting a healthy first innings total of 382. The hosts began their reply at the end of the second day but it was on the following morning that the rot began to set in. The third over of the day saw Conrad Hunte adjudged by West Indian umpire Sandy Lloyd to have been caught by Fred Trueman in Brian Statham's leg trap, a controversial decision which precipitated an alarming collapse to leave the West Indies on 45–5 at lunch. The terrible twins, Trueman and Statham, did the damage, the former dismissing Garfield Sobers for a duck. Fortunes barely improved during the afternoon session and by 4.15 the score had lurched to 98–7 when Sonny Ramadhin called fellow tail-ender Charran Singh, who was making his Test debut, for a quick single. As Singh scampered down the wicket, Ted Dexter swooped from cover to run him out, the verdict confirmed by the raised finger of Chinese umpire Lee Kow.

Almost immediately a solitary bottle was hurled on to the pitch from the most crowded corner of the ground, swiftly followed by a hail of missiles – bricks, boxes and more bottles, many broken. Within a few minutes of that first bottle being thrown some 3,000 spectators had encroached on the playing area after climbing the tall wire barrier. A handful threatened the two umpires, forcing the England captain, Peter May, after consultation with his opposite number, Gerry Alexander, to lead his team to the safety of the pavilion. Some of the England players carried stumps as they left the field in case they needed to defend themselves and a ricocheting stone hit Geoff Pullar on the elbow. In the radio commentary hut, the BBC's Rex Alston described the appalling scenes that were unfolding before him. 'I've never seen anything like it in my life,' he told listeners. 'The crowd away to my right are behaving like a lot of hooligans.' Unfortunately for Alston the said crowd were tuned in to his commentary on their transistor radios and, on hearing his words of condemnation, they angrily turned towards the derelict commentary box. Alston and his colleagues had to flee as the old box was reduced to a pile of rubble in little more than thirty seconds.

Only fifteen police officers were on duty at the ground when the trouble started and they attempted to control the increasingly aggressive rioters by asking fire chiefs to turn on a water hose. But the pressure was so low that, in the words of one observer, the water 'merely sputtered out in pools at the firemen's feet like an elephant urinating'. The Governor of Trinidad and Tobago Sir Edward Beetham, the Prime Minister Dr Williams, and the Minister of Works Learie Constantine (himself a distinguished former West Indies Test player) all stepped forward in an attempt to restore order but soon had to withdraw. Eventually mounted police reinforcements arrived, supplemented by riot squads wielding tear gas canisters, fire hoses and batons. The invaders slowly dispersed, but not before thirty people had been taken to hospital and another sixty treated on the spot for minor cuts and bruises. Twenty arrests were made. It was dark before the ground was finally cleared and, inevitably, play was abandoned for the day.

Condemnation of the disturbance was swift. Sir Edward Beetham went on radio to apologise on behalf of the people of Trinidad for 'the disgraceful behaviour of a section of the crowd'. Other public figures made similar broadcasts and R W V Robins, the England manager, received a cable from the president of the West Indies Board of Control expressing deep regret. Sir Errol dos Santos, chairman of Queen's Park Cricket Club, offered to abandon the match although he stressed that the demonstration was domestic and not aimed at the England team. This view was supported in the *Daily Telegraph* by E W Swanton who added that neither was the disorder a protest against the run out, 'which was a clear-cut decision'. Instead Swanton blamed crowd congestion and disappointment at the West Indies batting on a blameless pitch. *The Times* went a step further, suggesting that alcohol had fuelled the riot. The newspaper's correspondent wrote of the crowd: 'For safety they were much too tightly packed. They were inadequately patrolled, and inflamed to some extent by rum, which is cheap and plentiful.'

Swanton called it his saddest day in cricket reporting but England, comforted by an increased police presence, said they were happy to continue the match and stressed that relations with the West Indies team remained cordial. When play resumed, the tourists proceeded to press home their advantage and win by 256 runs, the only result in the five-Test rubber.

While England celebrated their victory, a young gardener appeared in court charged with bottle-throwing at the Queen's Park Oval. Handing out a hefty fine, the magistrate told him: 'Your disgraceful act has brought shame on all of us.'

The Great Throwing Debate

1963

Back in the days of Edgar Willsher, throwing was a major issue in cricket, but by the turn of the twentieth century it had been virtually eradicated from the game. However, the problem surprisingly resurfaced fifty years later when a number of international players came under close scrutiny with the result that at least two promising careers came to a premature end.

The first high profile suspect was Surrey and England spinner Tony Lock, whose faster ball landed him in trouble against India in 1952 and in the first Test during the 1953–4 tour of the West Indies. The winter of 1958–9 saw England visit Australia where the locals still harboured doubts about the bowling actions of both Lock and his county and England colleague Peter Loader. But the Australians had four bowlers of their own who were under suspicion – spinners Jimmy Burke and Keith Slater and pacemen Gordon Rorke and Ian Meckiff. The last-named – a left-arm fast bowler from Victoria – was Australia's secret weapon. He took five wickets in the first Test to help Australia to a five-wicket win and followed up with 6–38 in the second Test at Melbourne as England were shot out for 87. England refrained from complaining officially about Meckiff's permanently bent left arm, reasoning that since they had lost the series 4–0 they would merely be dismissed as 'whingeing poms'. However, there were plenty of dark mutterings in the English press. Journalist E M Wellings wrote: 'Meckiff approaches the wicket in the deliberate manner of a bowler who delivers the ball at medium pace. He runs no faster than did Hedley Verity to bowl his slow spinners. And yet the ball leaves his hand at express pace.' Before the game with

Victoria, England captain Peter May noted that Meckiff 'was throwing the ball at a batsman. This seemed an odd way for a bowler to limber up. A few minutes later he was out in the middle bowling to Peter Richardson with exactly the same action.' Australian writers countered that Meckiff's arm had a permanent bend and could not be straightened fully, but the war of words led to relations between the two nations being at their most strained since Bodyline.

In 1960 South Africa toured England. Among their party was fast bowler Geoff Griffin, a player who had been left with a permanent crook in his bowling arm following an accident at school. Griffin had twice been no-balled for throwing while playing for Natal but it was on the England tour that his troubles really started. During the tourists' match with the MCC at Lord's in May he was no-balled by both umpires – once by Frank Lee and twice by John Langridge. At a post-match meeting the umpires said that Griffin's basic action was fair but on occasions he was guilty of throwing. However, later that month he was called eight times against Nottinghamshire. He survived the first Test at Edgbaston intact but endured the ultimate roller-coaster ride on his return visit to Lord's for the second Test. Although he achieved every young bowler's dream of taking a hat-trick on the world's most famous ground, this feat was completely overshadowed by the fact that he was called for throwing eleven times by umpire Frank Lee. Further ignominy was to follow. As the match ended early – England winning by an innings and 73 runs – an exhibition game was arranged but umpire Syd Buller took issue with four of Griffin's first five deliveries and the bowler was reduced to completing the over underarm. The uncompromising Buller even no-balled Griffin's first under-arm delivery because the bowler had failed to inform the batsman of his change of action. The distraught Griffin did not bowl again on the tour and, after failing to correct the flaws in his action, retired from the first-class game, a career finished at 21.

In the wake of the Griffin episode an explanatory note was added to the law regarding throwing. It read: 'A ball shall be deemed to have been thrown if, in the opinion of either umpire, the bowling arm having been bent at the elbow, whether the wrist is backward of the elbow or not, is suddenly straightened immediately prior to the instant of delivery.' This, it was hoped, would clarify the position for umpires and enable them to clamp down on the growing menace of 'chuckers'.

When Australia toured England in 1961 they diplomatically left their suspect bowlers at home, but Ian Meckiff was performing so well in State cricket for Victoria that there was a campaign to have him recalled to the Test team. After all, the only criticism of his action had been in the English press. Then early in 1963 during a Sheffield Shield match in Adelaide he was called for throwing for the first time. Shortly afterwards he was called again, this time in Brisbane. In spite of these setbacks, Australian captain Richie Benaud considered Meckiff's action to be fair and, when his form held up, he was selected for the Test against South Africa at Brisbane starting on 7 December – his first Test appearance for three years.

The selection was nothing if not controversial and the Brisbane crowd waited anxiously to see how umpires Colin Egar and Lou Rowan would receive Meckiff's bowling. The loud applause as Benaud handed the ball to Meckiff evaporated into total silence as the 28-year-old ran in to bowl his first delivery, which passed harmlessly wide of off stump. To huge relief, there was no complaint from square leg umpire Egar, Australia's senior official. It was to prove the lull before the storm because Egar promptly called Meckiff's second delivery a no-ball. When the third ball met a similar fate, Benaud went over from slip to have a word with Meckiff. 'I think we've got a problem here,' said the captain in his typically understated way. 'I think you're right,' replied Meckiff. The fourth ball was deemed fair, but, to the sound of jeering from the crowd, the fifth was called as a throw. Meckiff then produced three good balls in succession before Egar called a fourth no-ball. Meckiff's eight-ball over, which had run to twelve to take into account the no-balls, had lasted eight minutes. It was a personal nightmare.

The crowd wanted Meckiff to be switched to the other end to see whether his action would find favour with umpire Rowan but Benaud opted to remove him from the attack, a decision that was greeted by a chorus of boos. Benaud was barracked for the remainder of the afternoon and at the close of play an embarrassed Meckiff was carried shoulder-high from the pitch by his fans. Australian cricket had found a new antihero. At the evening press conference Benaud explained his move. 'I bowled Meckiff for hundreds of overs before umpires who approved his delivery and I have accepted their decision. Now that an umpire does not accept Meckiff's delivery, I accept that decision, too. I will not bowl him again.' The other villain of the piece in the eyes of the Brisbane public, umpire Egar, commented, 'Somebody had to do something,' adding that he could have called more of Meckiff's deliveries as no-balls but was worried that the over would never have finished. He later admitted: 'I thought the first ball Meckiff bowled was suspect. On the next I took the plunge and called him. I think I heard a pin drop in the outer. It was that electric.'

That night Egar joined several Australian players, including Meckiff, for dinner. Egar told the unassuming father-of-two: 'I'm sorry this had to happen. The second most upset person in the world is me.' The day's events had destroyed Ian Meckiff. He was so upset that he retired immediately from all grades of cricket, even refusing to play social matches.

The Soccer Bribes Scandal

1965

The trial at Nottingham Assizes of ten footballers charged with systematically fixing matches over a period of three years sent shock waves through the footballing world, not least because those found guilty included three of England's best-known players. The names of former Sheffield Wednesday team-mates Peter Swan, Tony Kay and David Layne have passed into soccer's black museum yet the ringleader – a journeyman footballer who plied his trade in the humbler surroundings of places like Swindon and Mansfield – has largely been forgotten. His name was Jimmy Gauld.

By the start of 1960 Gauld's career was going downhill. After failing to make the grade at Charlton or Everton, the Scottish inside-forward had been transferred to Third Division Plymouth Argyle. When Plymouth were promoted, Gauld had been deemed surplus to requirements and in August 1959 he dropped back down to Division Three with Swindon Town. He was 28 and looking for a final payday from the game. Fixed odds betting on football matches was a popular pastime, offering a far more realistic prospect of success than the eight draws required to hit the pools jackpot. There was precious little money to be made from forecasting the results of single matches but multiple bets could yield a handsome profit. After Gauld's Swindon had entertained Mansfield Town in February 1960, a few of the players from both teams had dinner together and discussed the possibility of fixing the results of matches. It was duly arranged for Swindon to lose to Port Vale and for Mansfield to lose to Tranmere Rovers – a result that saved Tranmere from relegation. The fix was carried off successfully and although Gauld's profit from the bets was only modest, it set him thinking about further ventures.

In November 1960 he was transferred to Mansfield but a month later – on 28 December – he broke a leg, an injury that ended his playing career. Now more than ever he needed money.

The results of 21 October 1961 were notable for two shock away wins – Tranmere at York and Bradford City at Mansfield. A spectator at the Mansfield game was so incensed by what he witnessed that afternoon that he voiced his suspicions to the Football League, who simply dismissed it as a case of sour grapes. But bookmakers risked being badly stung by the two results as there had been heavy betting on that particular double. With many of the bets having been placed in Yorkshire in the same surname, the bookies smelled a rat and refused to pay out. They then discovered that although the bets had been spread across some twenty different bookmakers, they had been placed by just a dozen people. The pools firm Littlewoods despatched two of their investigators to interview the twelve. Eleven had no objection to their winnings being withheld, but the twelfth man did. It was Jimmy Gauld and he immediately lodged a formal complaint with the bookmaker Ladbrokes.

The investigators were unable to find any concrete evidence to link Gauld to the match-fixing allegations but Alan Hardaker, secretary of the Football League, decided to interview him anyway on 29 November 1961. Gauld denied any wrongdoing, although he did admit taking part in fixed-odds betting. In what would prove to be an accurate assessment, Hardaker's report said of Gauld: 'The final impression was that he was not telling the truth.'

Hardaker's hopes that the matter would quietly fade away were shattered early in April 1963 when bookmakers were forced to pay out £100,000 on a double covering Derby County's 6–2 victory over Scunthorpe United and Stockport County's 4–1 success against Hartlepools United. Neither result was particularly surprising but the sheer volume of bets on that combination alerted bookmakers, who subsequently informed the League of their suspicions. Hardaker saw no reason to act but three weeks later the *People* newspaper carried a front-page story headlined: SOCCER BRIBE SENSATION. Investigative reporter Mike Gabbert and soccer correspondent Peter Campling revealed that Bristol Rovers goalkeeper Esmond Million had confessed to deliberately letting in two goals during the course of a Third Division relegation battle at Bradford Park Avenue on 20 April 1963. Million, who had signed from Middlesbrough the previous summer, was in financial difficulties having been unable to sell his bungalow in Teesside. So when he received a telephone call offering him £300 to throw the Bradford game, he accepted and met his contact on Doncaster railway station where he was given a down payment of £50. To fulfil the fix, he enlisted the help of team-mate Keith Williams but the plan went awry as Rovers quickly found themselves 2–0 up, one of the goals stemming from a pass by Williams. Million did his best to retrieve the situation, conceding two soft goals, but the opposition's incompetence left the final score at 2–2. However, Million's abject display had not gone unnoticed by Rovers' manager Bert Tann who, in the dressing-room after the game, accused his goalkeeper of conceding the goals on purpose. Million broke down and confessed. Ironically his Teesside bungalow was sold three days later.

Million and Williams, who also admitted his part in the proceedings, were suspended by the club and reported to the League. The following week the *People* named Million's Doncaster station contact – Brian Phillips, captain of Mansfield Town. In July of that year Doncaster magistrates found the pair and a third footballer – Ken Thomson, captain of Hartlepool – guilty of attempted match-fixing. All three were fined and suspended by the League for life. Reasoning that it would prove more difficult to influence the results of three matches at a time than two, the League also banned doubles in fixed odds forecasting so that a treble was now the minimum bet.

Thomson issued a statement to the *People* in which he admitted being paid £200 to lose a game against Exeter City in March 1963. On the same day he had collected £327 in winnings from his bet on the crooked syndicate's double, the other match being a fixed game between Stockport and Crewe Alexandra.

But Thomson was only small fry. Although Phillips had been unmasked as a go-between, even he was clearly not the ringleader of the betting syndicate. As police and reporters alike searched for the mastermind, the name of Jimmy Gauld kept cropping up. He had been incriminated at the Doncaster magistrates' hearing, following which he appeared before Rochdale magistrates to answer six charges of offering bribes to footballers and was fined £10 on each count. A month later he received a cheque from the Football Association for £500 – money he was due from the Professional Footballers' Association insurance fund for injured players. If only the FA had known it was paying the man who was putting the 'fix' into fixed odds.

With the net closing in, Gauld decided to go public and sell his story to the *People* in return for a sum in excess of £7,000. As even his own counsel would later admit, Gauld 'acted as a Judas and betrayed others'. On 11 August 1963 the paper named Gauld as the mastermind. He claimed that his betting ring had earned him up to £1,000 a week and boasted that he virtually had 'a queue of players wanting to join the scheme', which, over its three-year life span, had all but covered the length and breadth of the country, operating from Swindon in the south to Dundee in the north.

Until now the League had the scant consolation of believing that at least the big clubs were untainted, but that optimism proved to be sadly misplaced when, following a winter of further investigations and additional statements from Gauld, the *People* published a story on 12 April 1964 headlined: THE BIGGEST SPORTS SCANDAL OF THE CENTURY. This time three of the best-known names in football were implicated – Peter Swan, Tony Kay and David 'Bronco' Layne. Swan was an outstanding centre half for Sheffield Wednesday with nineteen England caps to his credit; wing half Kay, who had one England cap, had recently been sold by Wednesday to Everton for £55,000; and Layne was Wednesday's free-scoring centre forward, a fans' favourite who took his nickname from the TV western hero Bronco Lane.

The distinguished trio had been enticed into the network of corruption by pure chance. On his day off Layne had attended a midweek match at Mansfield. There he bumped into Gauld who saw the opportunity for a new recruit and persuaded Layne to help fix Wednesday's First Division match at Ipswich on 1 December 1962. A month before the trip to East Anglia, Layne approached Swan and Kay, asking them if they wanted to make some money. Swan subsequently testified: 'He (Layne) said he knew some games which were going to be fixed and he could get me two-to-one odds.' Gauld arranged for three matches to be fixed on 1 December – Ipswich *v* Sheffield Wednesday, Lincoln City *v* Brentford and York City *v* Oldham Athletic – all three designed to end in home wins. That was how the results turned out and Kay, Swan and Layne picked up £100 apiece after Wednesday's 2–0 defeat. That was the only fixed match in which they were involved.

The following week the *People* named six more players, three of whom were never prosecuted, and in May, Gauld was banned for life by the FA. The football authorities had never wanted to admit that bribery was commonplace in the game – partly for fear of attracting adverse publicity in the build-up to the 1966 World Cup finals – but now they had to accept that not everything in the garden was rosy. Indeed, League secretary Hardaker later conceded that for every player who was caught, another twenty escaped unpunished.

Ten players went on trial at Nottingham in January 1965 accused of conspiracy to defraud. Gauld, described by the prosecution as the 'spider in the centre of the web', pleaded guilty to charges relating to the fixing of fourteen English and Scottish League matches covering the period between April 1960 and April 1963. His fellow defendants were Samuel Chapman and Brian Phillips, both former Mansfield captains; York City's John Fountain, a professional since 1949 who had met Gauld after joining Swindon Town in 1957; Richard Beattie (St Mirren); Ken Thomson (ex-Hartlepools United); David Layne, Peter Swan and Tony Kay; and halfback Ron Howells of Walsall and Scunthorpe United.

The court heard that Fountain was the first to join forces with Gauld, followed by Chapman who, on signing for Mansfield from Portsmouth, revealed that he had been in the pay of a bookmaker on the south coast for the past two years.

Gauld had led the *People* journalists to Fountain and incriminating correspondence between the two conspirators was produced, along with a tape recording of a conversation between Gauld and Fountain. On the second day of his trial, Fountain decided to plead guilty.

Beattie (who had made an estimated £600 from the operation), Chapman and Phillips also pleaded guilty but Howells denied all charges relating to the match between Scunthorpe and Derby in April 1963. However, Howells' fate was sealed after the jury were played a tape recording of him telling Gauld: 'We ought to have had a hundred but we only got paid out eighty pounds each.'

Although Thomson admitted having bets against his team, he insisted that he had never thrown a match. But during the game between Hartlepools and Stockport, Thomson was overheard telling a Stockport player not to harass the goalkeeper because the match was fixed. Thomson was found guilty on two counts.

Press interest in the case reached fever pitch when Layne, Swan and Kay stood in the dock. All were expected to plead not guilty but the result was a foregone conclusion from the moment Layne dramatically changed his plea to guilty. Summing up the folly of his client, Kay's counsel said: 'For £100 Kay has finished what is probably one of the greatest careers in football. He is virtually finished in this country and, I am told, in any other. This conviction not only debars him from playing football, but from coaching and getting a manager's job.' Even the judge, Mr Justice Lawton, expressed sympathy with Swan and Kay. 'Swan,' he said, 'had never even seen or spoken to Gauld until they appeared together in the dock.' Of Kay, the judge remarked: 'He was tempted once and fell.' All three were sentenced to four months' imprisonment.

Fountain and Phillips were jailed for fifteen months, Beattie for nine months, and Thomson, Howells and Chapman for six months. Sentencing Gauld to four years in prison, the judge described him as 'an unpleasant rogue'. He went on: 'Over a long period and from one end of this kingdom to another you have befouled professional football and corrupted your friends and acquaintances. You have done it in order to put money into your own pocket. You are responsible for the ruin of footballers of the distinction of Kay and Swan and you have ruined the life of an intelligent man like Thomson.'

Kay later told author Arthur Hopcraft how he was put in charge of training the prison football team and how the football-mad governor used to referee most of the matches. 'We only lost one game out of fourteen,' remembered Kay, 'and that was because the other lot brought their own referee: the game was bent.'

On their release from jail, those who had not been banned by the FA before the trial were all suspended for life, but in 1971 the FA amended the rules, allowing banned players to appeal after seven years. By 1972 most were too old to make a comeback but Swan and Layne did return to Hillsborough in an attempt to resurrect their careers with Sheffield Wednesday. Layne's progress was limited to the reserves but Swan signed a one-year contract with Wednesday before moving to Bury. Then in 1975 he led Matlock Town to victory in the FA Challenge Trophy final at Wembley – an unexpectedly upbeat finale to a career that had appeared dead and buried ten years earlier.

Ali's War of Words

1967

When Muhammad Ali told a reporter, 'I ain't got no quarrel with them Viet Cong,' the self-styled Louisville Lip discovered that he had opened his mouth once too often. Even though his views on the prospect of being drafted to fight in Vietnam were honestly held and admirable in their candour, he was instantly labelled a traitor by American politicians and ultimately stripped of his world heavyweight title.

Of course controversy was nothing new to Ali who, with his arrogant poems and predictions, had always gone where others feared to speak. Then there was the deliberately split glove that spared him from probable defeat at the hands of Henry Cooper, the suspicious title fights with the hitherto fearsome Sonny Liston who twice seemed to give up without much of a struggle, and the adoption of the Muslim faith with its attendant name change from Cassius Clay. Yet Ali had charisma, style and integrity. He raised the art of boxing to new heights. He was a champion in and out of the ring. However, none of this was enough for some Americans who were just waiting for the moment when pride would come before a fall.

The eighteen-year-old Cassius Clay had originally registered in Louisville in 1960. Two years later he was classified 1-A, which meant that he was fully eligible for immediate induction into the armed forces, but in 1964 he took the physical and written exam given to all draftees and failed the fifty-minute aptitude test, registering a score so low that the US army declared his IQ to be just 78. Although humiliated by the experience, he was able to joke with reporters: 'I said I was the greatest, not the smartest.' Accordingly the army reclassified him 1-Y, which gave him deferred status and made him ineligible for active service. Shortly after he became world champion, the army retested him in case he was feigning ignorance. He wasn't.

As the Vietnam War intensified, the military call-up was expanded and early in 1966 the pass mark in the intelligence test was lowered so that fewer candidates would be ruled out. Among those now ensnared in the army's recruitment trap was the world heavyweight champion. At the time Ali was preparing for the third defence of his title, against Ernie Terrell, and his lawyer immediately asked the Louisville draft board either to postpone reclassification or grant Ali a deferral. But on 17 February the request was rejected and Ali was officially reclassified 1-A, fit for combat. The following day he expressed his anger and disbelief to a TV reporter:

> For two years the army told everyone I was a nut and I was ashamed. And now they decide I am a wise man. Now, without ever testing me to see if I am wiser or worser than before, they decide I can go into the army... I can't understand it, out of all the baseball players, all of the football players, all of the basketball players – why seek out me, the world's only heavyweight champion?

The question was almost rhetorical, for Ali was convinced that the answer lay in his decision to embrace Islam and to champion the civil rights movement. With black civil rights activists being called up by local draft boards right across the southern states, he strongly believed that the US government had targeted him specifically. He explained his position in an emotional outburst to a reporter from *Sports Illustrated*:

> Why should they ask me to put on a uniform and go 10,000 miles from home and drop bombs and bullets on brown people in Vietnam while so-called Negro people in Louisville are treated like dogs? If I thought going to war would bring freedom and equality to 22 million of my people, they wouldn't have to draft me. I'd join tomorrow. But I either have to obey the laws of the land or the laws of Allah. I have nothing to lose by standing up and following my beliefs. We've been in jail for 400 years.

Ali's statement that he had no quarrel with the Viet Cong further inflamed the situation. The media labelled him a 'draft dodger' while the Kentucky state legislature, which had honoured him when he won the Olympic gold medal in 1960, now attacked him for discrediting 'all loyal Kentuckians'. In Congress politicians called for a boycott of his upcoming fight with Terrell, scheduled to take place in Chicago on 29 March, and Congressman Frank Clark of Pennsylvania branded Ali 'a complete and total disgrace'.

To be fair to the government, Ali was given several opportunities to accept a commission in the special services branch of any of the armed services, an offer which would have obviated the need to carry a weapon or even see military action, but by then his beliefs were so firmly entrenched that he refused. Instead he announced publicly and defiantly that he would not be drafted. Compromise was not on his agenda.

Ali's stance led to renewed backings for the Terrell fight to be boycotted. When the Illinois State Athletic Commission refused to grant a permit, an alternative venue to Chicago had to be found but as pressure groups began to flex their muscles, Louisville, Bangor (Maine) and Huron (South Dakota) all followed suit. And when Terrell himself pulled out, promoter Bob Arum declared Ali to be 'a dead piece of merchandise'. With one door after another being closed in the United States, the promoters looked towards Canada where a substitute opponent was found in George Chuvalo for what would now be a non-title fight. However, Montreal, Edmonton (Alberta) and Sorel (Quebec) all fought shy of staging the contest after local sponsors withdrew their support. Eventually it took place in Toronto but even there many sponsors backed out amid the ongoing furore surrounding Ali. The result was a hollow victory for the world champion.

In the same month Ali appeared before the Louisville draft board to request exemption as a conscientious objector. When this proved unsuccessful he tried to delay his call-up by asking for a transfer from Louisville to Houston, Texas. As the case dragged on, Ali took time out to fight Terrell in Houston on 6 February 1967. There was no love lost between the two men. Terrell had inherited the World Boxing Association's version of the heavyweight title, of which Ali had been stripped (ostensibly on a technicality), although most of the boxing world still saw the undefeated Ali as the true champion. At 6ft 6in Terrell was considered too tall for military service and was thus classified 1-Y, but he had nevertheless denounced Ali's stance on the draft. Furthermore he had riled Ali at the prefight press conference by repeatedly calling him 'Clay'. A pumped-up Ali responded by taunting Terrell mercilessly in the ring on his way to a comfortable points victory with chants of 'What's my name, fool? What's my name?' It was an awesome display of power and cruelty.

In March Ali's appeal against reclassification failed. A few days later he received his formal induction notice but his lawyers, working overtime, managed to get the call-up postponed until 28 April so that he could fight Zora Folley, whom he duly knocked out in round seven. As the personal attacks on Ali continued, *Ring* magazine declined to nominate a fighter of the year on the grounds that 'Cassius Clay is most emphatically not to be held up as an example to the youngsters of the United States'. Three days before his scheduled induction, Ali's lawyers made one last desperate attempt to save their client by filing a petition in federal court requesting exemption on religious grounds as a minister of Islam, claiming that killing and bearing weapons were against his religious principles. The petition was rejected.

Friend and foe alike were gathered outside the US Customs House in Houston. When his name was called out at the induction, Ali repeatedly refused to step forward and join the other draftees. After the third refusal, he was informed that his inactivity constituted a federal offence and that he would be charged with draft evasion. His response was to issue a statement:

I am proud of the title world heavyweight champion, which I won in the ring in Miami on February 25, 1964. The holder of it should at all times have the courage of his convictions and carry out those convictions, not only in the ring but throughout all phases of his life. It is in light of my own personal convictions that I take my stand in rejecting the call to be inducted into the armed services. I do so with full realisation of its implications and possible consequences. I have searched my conscience and I find I cannot be true to my belief in my religion by accepting such a call.

His forebodings were well founded. The New York State Athletic Commission led the way by suspending his boxing licence. Other states quickly followed. He was tried for draft evasion in Houston on 19 June. The prosecution argued that if Ali escaped the draft, many more black youths would be encouraged to adopt the Muslim faith. The all-white jury took just twenty minutes to find him guilty. He was given the maximum sentence – five years in prison – but was freed on bail pending appeal. He was also stripped of his world title and his passport was confiscated. Unable to fight anywhere in the world, he spent his time in exile touring college campuses to denounce the Vietnam War while waiting for the result of his appeal and could only look on helplessly as lesser boxers took part in elimination bouts for his vacant title. He warned: 'Everybody knows I'm the champion. My ghost will haunt all the arenas.'

With his lawyers continuing to pursue the legal fight, the only time Ali served in jail was ten days in Miami in December 1968 for driving without a valid licence. Regaining his boxing licence was a much lengthier process. Repeated applications for reinstatement to the WBA met with rejection and 38 different states turned down the offer to stage an Ali fight until, in August 1970 – a month after the court of appeals had upheld his conviction – the black-controlled city of Atlanta finally gave Ali a licence to fight. By then Joe Frazier was the official world champion, but Frazier's managers backed out of a confrontation with Ali, claiming a prior engagement with Bob Foster. Instead Ali's first comeback opponent would be Jerry Quarry.

Although Atlanta had been able to take advantage of the absence of a state boxing commission in Georgia, the decision to stage the contest provoked anger in many quarters. Ali was bombarded with hate mail, including a package containing the decapitated body of a black Chihuahua, accompanied by a message that read: 'We know how to handle black draft dodging dogs in Georgia. Stay out of Atlanta!' Another parcel contained a rag doll dressed as a boxer, a rope tied around the doll's neck and the head jerked to the side to depict a lynching. Despite these and more overt death threats, Ali refused to be bowed. He was only in moderate physical shape following his three-year lay-off but he trained hard for the fight and stopped Quarry in three rounds.

His second fight after exile was against Argentina's Oscar Bonavena in New York, that state's athletic commission having been forced to return Ali's licence when it admitted granting licences to ninety fighters convicted of embezzlement, rape and murder – crimes that made Ali's transgression seem positively trivial. The scheduling of the fight for 7 December – Pearl Harbor Day – prompted fresh attempts to have it called off but Ali remained focused on the job in hand and went on to beat Bonavena on a technical knockout. This earned him a shot at Frazier in March against the unusual backdrop of both men claiming to be heavyweight champion of the world. Frazier won on points to inflict Ali's first defeat as a professional. Now he could no longer call himself even the unofficial world champion.

Many thought Ali should have quit boxing after the Frazier fight but he merely upped his training schedule, his determination bolstered by the news that his case was about to come before the Supreme Court. On 28 June 1971 the Supreme Court reversed Ali's conviction and the Justice Department dropped all criminal charges against him. Asked how he felt about the return of his passport and boxing licence, he said: 'I don't really think I'm going to know how that feels until I start to travel, go to foreign countries. Then I'm gonna know I'm free.'

The career of Muhammad Ali would have many more ups and downs, finally reducing him to a frail shadow of his former self. Liston, Patterson, Frazier, Foreman – they were all formidable opponents, but none came bigger or tougher than the US government. That Ali managed to beat the highest power in the land and eventually regain the weight of American public opinion was, in the final analysis, perhaps his most remarkable victory of all.

Pedalling Drugs

1967

Back in 1886 a racing cyclist by the name of Linton died from an overdose of tri-methyl, thus becoming the first recorded drug death in the sport. Linton's untimely demise passed virtually unnoticed, but the same cannot be said of the shock death 81 years later of Tommy Simpson, Britain's finest ever road racing cyclist, during the world's premier cycling event, the Tour de France. For when the autopsy revealed that Simpson had consumed a cocktail of amphetamines designed to push his body through the pain barrier, the outcry forced the cycling authorities to ban such stimulants from the sport.

Born in County Durham and raised in Nottinghamshire, Simpson turned professional in 1959 after winning a bronze medal at the 1956 Olympics as part of the 4,000 metres pursuit team and a silver in the individual pursuit at the 1958 Empire Games. In 1962 he became the first Briton to wear the yellow jersey at the Tour de France, albeit only for a day, before finishing a highly respectable sixth – a result he would never better in five other attempts. Three years later he won the Tour of Lombardy and was crowned World Road Race Champion – a remarkable feat as it followed a horrific fall in the Tour de France when doctors feared they might need to amputate one of his arms. By 1967 Simpson was living in Belgium and had fully recovered from his injury but, after a barren year in 1966, his public profile was slipping. He needed a big win, a last big payday before retirement. At 29, he knew that time was running out in his bid to win the coveted blue riband event of world cycling.

Simpson acquitted himself well over the first twelve stages of that year's Tour de France and was in seventh place overall at the start of the thirteenth stage, from Marseilles to Avignon. The major obstacle to negotiate on the 133-mile stage was the ascent to the summit of Mont Ventoux, some 6,000ft above sea level. The climb was steep and relentless, offering precious little opportunity for riders to gain even a moment's respite, and because the final few miles of road rose above the tops of surrounding trees, there was no protection whatsoever from the wind or the sun, which in July was often frighteningly hot. To make matters worse, the ascent came towards the end of the stage at a time when riders were nearing the point of exhaustion. Simpson did not underestimate the challenge that lay ahead. He had been through it all before. After his first ride up the mountain he had remarked: 'It is like another world up there among the bare rocks and the glaring sun. The white rocks reflect the heat and the dust rises, clinging to your arms, legs and face... It was almost overwhelmingly hot up there; my pants were soaked and heavy with sweat. It was running off me in streams.'

On 13 July 1967 the temperature on the upper slopes of Mont Ventoux was 131 degrees Fahrenheit. It was no place for the weak. Simpson is said to have fortified himself for the awesome climb by stopping off at a bar at the foot of the mountain in company with a handful of fellow riders and downing a large cognac. What made it a lethal cocktail was the fact that various other substances were already circulating around in his bloodstream.

Simpson was part of the main pack desperately trying to rein in the breakaway group. At first the brandy and amphetamines did their work, pushing his body way beyond the normal levels of endurance, but as the heat grew more searing, his legs started to tire. On and on he climbed, ever slower, losing touch with the leaders by the minute. A mile and three-quarters from the summit he suddenly started to wander about the road alarmingly. Television viewers attributed his plight to sunstroke. Refusing all offers of help, he pressed on erratically until he toppled sideways and fell from his machine. When team assistants rushed to his aid, Simpson murmured breathlessly: 'Put me back on my bike.' They were to be his last coherent words. After being lifted back into the saddle, he wobbled on for another half mile before slumping to the ground again, almost unconscious. His fingers could hardly be prised from the handlebars of his bike; his face was yellow. A nurse from the Tour's medical team gave him the kiss of life, followed quickly on the scene by the Tour doctor, Pierre Dumas, who administered oxygen in an attempt to revive Simpson. Realising the gravity of the situation, Dumas radioed for a police helicopter and the comatose Simpson was airlifted to a hospital in Avignon where he died at 5.40 p.m. without regaining consciousness. His mechanic Harry Hall firmly believes that Simpson was already dead before the second fall.

The cycling world was stunned. How could a seemingly healthy sportsman drop dead just like that? In honour of their comrade, the other British riders wore black arm bands to the start line the next day and the eventual winner of the event, Roger Pingeon, became little more than a footnote in cycling history because of the terrible loss of Tommy Simpson. But if the sport's fans and governing body were shocked by his death, they were even more horrified by the results of the autopsy, which revealed the presence of amphetamines in Simpson's blood, urine, stomach and intestines. Three tubes of amphetamines – two of them empty, the third half-full – were found in his jersey pockets and handed to the police. The autopsy report, published on 4 August, stated:

> Death was due to a cardiac collapse which may be put down to exhaustion, in which unfavourable weather conditions, an excessive workload, and the use of medicines of the type discovered on the victim may have played a part. The dose of amphetamine ingested by Simpson could not have led to his death on its own; but on the other hand it could have led him to go beyond the limit of his strength and thus bring on the appearance of certain troubles linked to his exhaustion.

The conclusion was obvious: he had pushed himself too far in his quest for glory.

The following year the International Union of Cycling began banning performance-enhancing substances. On the surface at least, cycling would be squeaky clean.

A memorial to Simpson stands atop Mont Ventoux, a reminder of a great champion but also of a fallen hero. His fierce rival, the Belgian rider Eddy Mercx, once said: 'It's unjust that his name should forever be so indelibly linked with drugs... On the slopes of Ventoux his ambition killed him. His pride had no limits. He never relinquished the belief that he could win the Tour de France.'

The Ignoble Art of
Time-wasting

1967

By tradition Yorkshire cricketers are an uncompromising bunch who grant no favours and expect none in return. Few fitted the stereotype better than Brian Close, a figure hewn from pure Yorkshire granite and who, in comparison, made Geoffrey Boycott look like a veritable pussycat.

Close led by example. Who could forget his defiant stance in 1963 when, battered and bruised, he stood unflinching against a barrage of bouncers from the West Indies' fearsome pace duo of Wes Hall and Charlie Griffith? Close received blow after blow to the ribs, but never once complained. It would have been a sign of weakness. Four years on and he was captain of both county and country, only to lose the England job on a dank August afternoon at Edgbaston when he allowed his competitive nature to spill over into a wretched display of gamesmanship.

Chasing their third County Championship title in five years, Yorkshire were struggling to impose themselves on their hosts. In reply to Yorkshire's 238, Warwickshire had made 242, thus picking up the precious points for a first-innings lead. When Yorkshire were then dismissed for 145 in their second innings, their only hope of salvaging anything from the match appeared to rest in holding out for a draw, for which they would collect two points. With the skies above Birmingham suitably grey and menacing, a draw seemed the most likely outcome, particularly as Warwickshire needed to score 142 to win in just 102 minutes, but, inspired by the swashbuckling John Jameson, the Warwickshire batsmen set about their task with a vengeance and soon had the Yorkshire bowlers on the back foot. Sensing the prospect of even a draw slipping away, Close realised the situation called for desperate measures. Yorkshire went on a go-slow.

The over rate was reduced to a crawl. Yorkshire's three fast bowlers – Fred Trueman, Tony Nicholson and Richard Hutton – took an eternity over each delivery. Field placings were altered, the damp ball wiped incessantly. The skies grew darker and light rain began to fall intermittently, but still Warwickshire bludgeoned their way towards their improbable target. With half an hour remaining Warwickshire still needed 54 runs. Jameson helped reduce the deficit by driving Nicholson over the sightscreen whereupon Close wasted more time by walking in to deliver fresh instructions to his bowler. The blatant delaying tactics incurred the displeasure of umpire Charlie Elliott who had a quiet word with the Yorkshire captain. Close responded by appealing against the rain. This was initially turned down, but Close's prayers were answered when the drizzle got heavier and the players started to walk off. Barely had they reached the pavilion, however, than the rain stopped. The umpires and the batsmen were quickly back out in the middle but Yorkshire lingered in the dressing room for another minute before returning to the fray. A total of four minutes had been lost, leaving Warwickshire just eleven minutes to score the remaining 24 runs.

Trueman managed to stretch the next over to six minutes. It included two no-balls, three bouncers and the wicket of Dennis Amiss. His replacement, A C Smith, was at the crease long before Trueman was ready to continue. With Trueman's over finally completed, Close set about ensuring that only one more over would be possible by summoning Hutton in from the deep to bowl from an end that was new to him. This change, it was decided, necessitated a long, laborious practice run. It was indeed the last over, play ending at 6 p.m. with Warwickshire stranded on 133–5, nine runs short of victory. Yorkshire had bowled just 24 overs in the innings and only two in those last eleven minutes.

The Warwickshire supporters gave vent to their frustration, jeering and booing Close's men as they left the field. Close himself was involved in a verbal altercation with a spectator while Trueman was reportedly attacked by a man with an umbrella. Close needed an escort from the ground but was apparently happy with the two points, which took Yorkshire to the top of the table.

The wrath of the media descended on Close. Michael Melford of the *Daily Telegraph* described Yorkshire's as a 'petty, unworthy performance' while in *The Times* John Woodcock wrote scathingly: 'Without exception, Yorkshire's performance was, of its kind, the least attractive I have seen on a cricket field, and the blame lies, squarely, at the door of England's captain and Yorkshire's... After the match Close left for Northampton to help choose the England side for the next Test. I wished it had been Mike Smith instead. A man capable of condoning and conducting such an operation as Yorkshire's last evening would seem a peculiar choice to take an MCC side to the West Indies on an expedition that demands from its leader a strong sense of sportsmanship and responsibility.'

Close denied the accusations of time-wasting, insisting that he had not ordered his bowlers to go slow. He again demonstrated his ability to fend off dangerous bouncers by defending himself in his book *Close to Cricket*. 'The conditions were such,' he wrote, 'that with a wet ball, a greasy pitch and the run-saving field-setting, a normal over-rate was impossible. Had the fieldsmen not wiped the ball we might have bowled two or three more overs, but wiping and cleaning the ball is accepted in all normal regular day-to-day cricket as being in all fairness to the fielding side.' The counties' Executive Committee (comprising six former county captains) took a different view and found Close entirely responsible for the unsporting behaviour. He was severely censured and told that his tactics 'constituted unfair play and were against the best interests of the game'.

Close vowed that the reprimand would not affect his approach to the England captaincy. He went straight from the meeting to lead England to victory over Pakistan but when it came to the winter tour of the West Indies he was replaced as skipper by the more diplomatic Colin Cowdrey. His 'draw at all costs' attitude had cost him the top job in English cricket. His strength was now perceived as his weakness.

Close remained adamant that he had done nothing wrong but the counties ensured that there would be no repeat of the Edgbaston fiasco by introducing a new law stating that twenty overs had to be bowled in the final hour of championship matches.

Black Power Salute

1968

To the dispassionate outsider, interest in an Olympic medal ceremony is rarely sustained beyond the opening few discordant bars of the first national anthem. But the victory podium after the men's 200 metres final at the 1968 Mexico Olympics staged a drama that overshadowed the race itself as two black athletes, Tommie Smith and John Carlos, used their moment in the world spotlight to wave the civil rights flag defiantly in the face of white America. Although it was a peaceful, dignified demonstration, their black power salute enraged the International Olympic Committee who demanded retribution. The US Olympic Committee responded with rare haste, suspending the pair and throwing them out of the Olympic village. Smith and Carlos became martyrs to the cause.

The possibility of some form of demonstration by disenchanted black American athletes had hung over the Mexico Games from the outset. A feeling that the civil rights movement was not doing enough to eliminate the injustices experienced by black American competitors led to the formation of a splinter group, the Olympic Project for Human Rights (OPHR). Among the group's loudest voices was sociologist Harry Edwards who advocated an all-out boycott of the Olympics. The boycott never materialised but Edwards' oratory impressed a number of athletes, including Smith and Carlos, both students at San Jose State College, California. A further source of discontent was IOC president Avery Brundage, himself no stranger to controversy throughout his long career of officialdom (see the chapter 'Slow Boat to Hamburg', page 104). Brundage had angered black athletes by supporting the admission of apartheid-ridden South Africa to the Olympic movement and had been quoted before the Games as saying that any competitor who demonstrated at Mexico City would be sent home. Brundage's hardline stance resulted in a number of black American athletes – including long jumper Ralph Boston and sprinters Smith, Jim Hines and Charlie Greene – saying that they did not want him officiating at medal ceremonies. To avoid confrontation, it was Lord Exeter who stepped forward on 16 October to present the medals for the men's 200 metres final.

The son of a migrant labourer, 24-year-old Smith had won gold in a world record time of 19.83 seconds. Carlos, 23, from Harlem took bronze behind Peter Norman of Australia. As the only white athlete on the podium, Norman showed his support for the black runners by joining them in wearing OPHR badges. Smith and Carlos had black scarves draped around their necks and wore long black socks with no shoes. Mounting the podium, they kept their hands hidden behind their backs. When the United States national anthem – 'The Star-Spangled Banner' – began to play, Smith and Carlos bowed their heads and brought their hands into view. Smith's right hand and Carlos's left were each covered by a black glove. The pair proceeded to clench their gloved fists and raise them skywards in a black-power salute. Smith later explained the significance of their attire to newsmen: 'I wore a black right-hand glove and Carlos wore the left-hand glove of the same pair. My raised right hand stood for the power in black America. Carlos's raised left hand stood for the unity of black America. Together they formed an arch of unity and power. The black scarf around my neck stood for black pride. The black socks with no shoes stood for black poverty in racist America. The totality of our effort was the regaining of black dignity.'

The ceremony over, the pair dismounted the rostrum and marched towards the stand with their arms still raised. Although England's Roger Bannister described the demonstration as 'a gesture conducted with dignity and poise', white Americans in the crowd felt that their nation had been slighted and began booing. Carlos reacted angrily at a press conference, telling reporters: 'You think of us as animals.

Tommie and I heard them boo tonight and we saw their white faces.' He revealed that they had bowed their heads to express their belief that the words of freedom in the US anthem only applied to white Americans. 'If I win I am an American, not a black American. But if I did something bad then they'd say I was a Negro. We are black and we are proud of being black. Black America will understand what we did tonight.' Carlos added that he wanted to let the world know that black athletes 'were not some kind of workhorse who can perform and then be thrown some peanuts and say good boy, good boy. When Tommie and I got on the stand, we weren't alone. We knew that everyone who was watching at home was upon that stand. We wanted to let the world know the problems about black people, and we did our thing and stepped down. We believe we were right. We'd do it again tomorrow.'

That was precisely what the US Olympic Committee feared. The ejection of Smith and Carlos sent a clear message to any other black athletes planning a protest. The next potential flash point was the men's 400 metres medal presentation where black Americans Lee Evans, Larry James and Ron Freeman took gold, silver and bronze. The trio mounted the podium wearing black berets but stopped short of donning the contentious black gloves.

If Smith and Carlos might have expected the kneejerk reaction of the US Olympic Committee, the venom directed at them on their return home shocked them. They and their families were subjected to death threats and, following widespread criticism of their actions in the press, both men struggled to make a living from the sport as coaches. Carlos lamented: 'Doing my thing made me feel the finest I ever felt in my whole life, but I came home to hate.'

An Innocent Man

1968

Basil Lewis D'Oliveira was among England's most popular cricketers in the late 1960s. A hard-hitting batsman and a deceptively penetrative seam bowler, he wrapped his talents in a modest charm that endeared him to whoever he encountered. His stock was already high before the 1968 controversy that thrust him unwillingly into the world's headlines, but it was the calm, dignified manner in which he kept his head while all around were losing theirs that ensured his place in the game's folklore.

D'Oliveira – or 'Dolly' as he came to be embraced by the British public – was born in Cape Town in October 1931. As a Cape Coloured he was prevented by South Africa's segregation rules from playing with white cricketers but still made a name for himself at a minor level. To further his dreams of playing in England, he wrote to legendary broadcaster John Arlott, whose voice he had heard on the radio. Arlott helped D'Oliveira land a professional placement with Middleton in the Central Lancashire League and he stayed for four seasons. It was that most elegant of English strokemakers, Tom Graveney, who persuaded the unassuming D'Oliveira that he had the talent for county cricket and he spent 1964 qualifying for Graveney's county, Worcestershire, in the process making a century against the touring Australians. His progress was such that in 1966 he made his Test debut and quickly became established as England's premier all-rounder.

But there was a cloud on the horizon. In the winter of 1968 England were due to tour South Africa, a country whose rigid apartheid regime excluded its non-Whites from participating in mainstream international sport. As the first non-White South African to play professional cricket in England, D'Oliveira was very much the focus of attention, but being thrust into the spotlight appeared to have an adverse effect on his form and he struggled for runs on the 1967–8 tour of the West Indies. With Australia the visitors to England in the summer of 1968, clearly his form in that series would decide whether or not he was chosen to tour South Africa. He began well, top scoring with 87 not out in the second innings of the first Test, only to be dropped by the selectors. Although he picked up plenty of wickets in July, runs continued to elude him at county level and it was something of a surprise when he was selected for the fifth Test as a last-minute replacement for Northamptonshire batsman Roger Prideaux, who had to withdraw through illness. Just when it was needed, D'Oliveira produced his finest Test innings, 158, to help England to victory. Surely he had secured his place on the winter tour to his homeland.

The South African government's views on D'Oliveira were unclear. In 1967 the Minister of the Interior had indicated that D'Oliveira would not be welcome as a tourist but Prime Minister Vorster had hinted that visiting mixed teams would be acceptable on condition that the motivation for inclusion of any non-Whites was not political. Nevertheless it was a distinctly grey area. So when D'Oliveira was omitted from the England party, the MCC selectors, under chairman Doug Insole, were immediately accused of bowing to pressure from South Africa, of appeasing a nation that operated despised policies. The MCC countered that the party had been chosen purely on merit, that D'Oliveira's bowling would not be suited to South African wickets and that his batting put him behind both Prideaux and young Keith Fletcher of Essex.

The D'Oliveira Affair dominated the headlines. MPs and anti-apartheid groups protested at his exclusion, MCC members resigned in disgust, and former Test player the Revd David Sheppard headed a faction of angry MCC members who openly challenged the MCC's handling of the situation. With the MCC under siege, a way out of the predicament suddenly presented itself. Warwickshire's Tom Cartwright – a steady seamer in a similar mould to D'Oliveira – was forced to withdraw from the party because of a shoulder injury. D'Oliveira was promptly named as his replacement, a decision at odds with the selectors' stated reasons for leaving him out in the first place. Prime Minister Vorster was incensed. He said the party was 'no longer a cricket team, but a team of troublemakers for South Africa's separate development policies. It is not the MCC team; it is the team of the anti-apartheid movement. We are not prepared to have a team thrust upon us.'

A week later the MCC, having succeeded in antagonising both sides of the apartheid argument in the space of a few days, announced that the tour was cancelled. Common sense and decency had finally prevailed. The D'Oliveira Affair was to hasten South Africa's eventual isolation from international cricket.

While the murky waters of apartheid swirled around his ankles, Basil D'Oliveira stood tall. His exemplary conduct was recognised in 1969 by the award of the OBE and when he retired from the county game a decade later, he was accorded the honour of a standing ovation on every ground. The game of cricket has rarely had a finer ambassador.

Bobby and the Bracelet

1970

To prepare for the high altitude that his footballers would face at the 1970 World Cup in Mexico, England manager Sir Alf Ramsey took the squad on an acclimatising trip to South America. The intention was to play competitive warm-up games in Colombia and Ecuador before flying on to Mexico, better equipped to handle the stamina-sapping atmosphere that they would encounter in the finals. Ramsey was not one of the world's great travellers. Here was a man who felt ill at ease in Scotland. He made no secret of his dislike for, and mistrust of, all things foreign and, following his unhappy experience against Antonio Rattin and Argentina at the 1966 World Cup, South America was pretty much top of his list of places to avoid. Ramsey's natural instinct was to spend as little time as possible on the continent, but even he acknowledged the need for thorough preparation in this instance. As things turned out, he may have wished that he and the players had gone straight from Heathrow to Mexico on the last available plane.

Ramsey was under no illusions as to what might lay in store for the party during their brief sojourn in the Colombian capital, Bogota, and on sightseeing tours the players were warned to avoid street traders and to visit only reputable shops. The squad booked into the city's hotel Tequendama on the afternoon of 18 May and, with an hour to spare before dinner, a number of the players sauntered down to the foyer. Among the establishments located in the foyer was a jewellery shop called Fuego Verde (Green Fire). Bobby Charlton wanted to buy a present for his wife and so he, Bobby Moore and a few others looked in the window to see if there was anything suitable.

Charlton later recounted: 'I saw a ring on display inside the shop. It didn't have a price on it so we decided to go in and see what it cost... The young woman took the ring out of the cabinet and brought it round to us. She had taken it out having first opened a glass door. We discussed the price, or I should say we worked it out, and found that it was too expensive so we left. We had been in the shop five minutes at most.'

With nothing worth buying, the two players then strolled across the hotel foyer to seats barely 20ft from the shop window. Moore said: 'We were just chatting idly. I watched an elderly woman go into the shop, come out again and walk towards us. She asked Bobby and me to step into the shop. We said yes, thinking they had found something to interest Bobby for his wife. As we stood up the woman fumbled with the cushions where we'd been sitting. Still nothing registered. But as we got back inside the shop she said: "There's some jewellery missing."'

Moore and Charlton immediately volunteered to be searched but the offer was rejected and the police were called instead. By now Ramsey had been alerted to the commotion. Ever protective of his players, he saw the preposterous accusation as another example of South American foul play. In his eyes, it was clearly a setup and the affair merely served to reinforce his xenophobia. The players made formal statements to the police and that appeared to be the end of the matter. Two days later England beat Colombia 4–0 before flying on to Ecuador where they defeated their hosts 2–0 on 24 May. The flight from the capital of Ecuador, Quito, to Mexico necessitated a change of planes in Bogota where the England party were surprised to be met by armed police intent on arresting Moore. An international incident was averted only by the intervention of the British Chargé d'Affaires, Keith Morris, who arranged for Moore to be taken 'voluntarily' to a police station to confirm his statement. However, Moore was taken instead to a local courthouse where he was informed that the shop girl, Clara Padilla, had seen him toying with a glass wall cabinet in Fuego Verde – the very cabinet from which a £625 gold bracelet studded with emeralds had allegedly gone missing. For the first time Moore began to lose his customary cool, due in no small part to the fact that his team-mates had been forced to fly on to Mexico without him. He felt abandoned, unaware that Dr Andrew Stephen, chairman of the FA, and Dennis Follows, secretary of the FA, had stayed behind to secure his release. After seven hours of interrogation, Moore was about to be thrown in jail when the result of frantic high-level lobbying enabled him to be placed under house arrest at the hacienda of Alfonso Senior, director of the Colombian Football Federation. Moore's every move was shadowed by two armed guards with whom he became quite friendly during his detention. They at least had faith in him for when, after a heavy night's drinking, they were too hungover to accompany him on his morning run, they made him promise to return. Naturally Moore obliged.

On 27 May, under a quaint Colombian judicial custom, Moore returned to Fuego Verde for a reconstruction at which he came face to face with his accuser, Clara Padilla. The shop owner, Danilo Rojas, was also present as was a dubious new witness who, from a vantage point outside the shop, claimed to have seen Moore take the bracelet. The volatile Padilla kept changing her version of events. Confronted with Moore, she insisted that he had put the bracelet in the left pocket of his England leisure suit whereupon Moore, who was wearing the same suit for the reconstruction, calmly revealed that there was no pocket on the left. At this juncture he burst out laughing. He thought it was all over. It wasn't yet.

The reconstruction had not gone well for the police. Furthermore they had measured the size of Moore's fist to ascertain whether it could have fitted through the hole in the glass cabinet from which the bracelet was stolen, but it was too big. While Judge Dorado debated whether there was sufficient evidence for the case to go to trial, the Colombian newspapers reached their own verdict. Moore's detention was a national disgrace, they chorused.

Meanwhile Britain's opportunist Prime Minister Harold Wilson had entered the equation. With a general election looming, he knew that securing the release of the England captain would be a real vote-winner so he began putting pressure on Foreign Office diplomats to resolve the situation.

Colombia's security service chief was persuaded to visit Judge Dorado to warn him of the ramifications were Moore to be held any longer. On 28 May a Foreign Office official wrote: 'If Mr Moore's case is not settled in the course of today, the Prime Minister would like urgent advice on whether he should himself send a personal message to the President of Colombia, particularly having regard to the growing evidence of delay caused by administrative inefficiency.' The judge bowed to the weight of political and public opinion and ordered Moore's release on condition that he made himself available for further questioning if needed. On 29 May a relieved Moore flew off to Mexico to join the rest of the England party. His World Cup could finally get under way.

While Moore was treated like a hero on his departure from Bogota airport, Padilla and Rojas became hate figures for the Colombian people. In a desperate attempt to save his business from going under, Rojas sacked Padilla but customers continued to boycott the shop and after just six months' trading Fuego Verde closed for good.

Moore put his problems behind him with a typically polished performance at the World Cup and in August Captain Jaime Ramirez of the Colombian secret police published evidence of a plot to frame Moore, hinting that a double of the England captain had been planted to steal the bracelet. Brazil manager Joao Saldanha confided to Moore that he had experienced similar difficulties in Colombia, but had taken the precaution of locking the doors of the shop, calling the police and insisting that he was searched. Despite what appeared to be overwhelming evidence in support of Moore, the case dragged on as Colombian judges continued to discuss whether or not he should be extradited from Britain for trial. Moore was becoming increasingly anxious to clear his name but the Foreign Office – aware that at the time four out of every five Colombian legal cases were never decided – strongly advised him to keep a low profile and refrain from discussing it with the press in the hope that it would all be quietly forgotten. The advice appeared to be sound when, in November 1972, a Colombian judge announced that the charges had been shelved. However, a year later the case was suddenly reopened, only to be dropped finally in December 1975 for lack of evidence. Still awaiting exoneration, Moore was deeply frustrated. 'It wasn't what I was looking for,' he said later. 'I wanted my name cleared... I was innocent and I wanted the world to know I was innocent. It made me sick to my stomach that some people thought I still had that damn bracelet.'

The truth about what happened in that Bogota jewellery shop may never be known. The popular theory is of a South American setup to target the England captain and unsettle the squad prior to the World Cup, but rumours have persisted regarding the presence of a third player inside the shop. In his statements on the matter, Moore said he knew nothing of any third person because he had his back to the door all the time he was in the shop. However, before his death from cancer in 1993, he hinted to journalist Jeff Powell that 'perhaps one of the younger lads with the squad did something foolish, a prank with unfortunate circumstances'. If Bobby Moore had his suspicions, he wasn't saying. His East End upbringing meant that it was a matter of honour not to 'grass'.

There were no winners in the case. Moore had to endure a prolonged whispering campaign; Ramsey came home from the World Cup with his tactical reputation in shreds but his hatred of foreigners intact; and Colombian justice was shown to be a contradiction in terms. Even Prime Minister Wilson's calculated plan to garner popular support backfired as he surprisingly lost the general election to Edward Heath, aka Sailor Ted. In the minds of the British public sailing clearly held a bigger appeal than soccer in the summer of 1970.

V for Victory

1971

At the start of the 1970s the world of British men's showjumping was one dominated by cut-glass accents, innate breeding and impeccable manners. But in the midst of this old-boy network one man stood out like a sore thumb – Harvey Smith, a blunt Yorkshireman who called a spade a shovel and appeared not to give a damn what anyone thought of him. To some he was a major source of irritation; to others he was like a breath of fresh air in a stuffy sport. To the press boys he represented good copy. He even had his own column in the *Sun*.

Showjumping had to battle for every inch of column space on the back pages of the tabloids in the face of stiff competition from higher profile sports but in August 1971 Smith's latest controversial outburst propelled it on to the front pages of the broadsheets. The occasion was the high spot of the outdoor showjumping season, the WD and HO Wills Derby at Hickstead in Sussex. Riding Mattie Brown, Smith was attempting to become the first person to win the Derby in successive years. While the public were rooting for another victory for the most popular rider of the day, many within the sport privately hoped that the trophy might end up in more restrained hands. Among those who had not always seen eye to eye with the forthright Smith was Douglas Bunn, owner of Hickstead, chairman of the show, and vice-chairman of the British Show Jumping Association. They were like chalk and cheese, Smith cast in the role of naughty schoolboy to Bunn's officious headmaster.

The day of the Derby – 15 August – began badly for Smith who arrived at Hickstead without the Derby Cup. Protesting

---

170

that no one – meaning Bunn – had asked him to bring the trophy, he hastily arranged for it to be put on a train and it eventually arrived just in time for the presentation. Nevertheless the atmosphere between the two men was frostier than usual. Fired up by his perceived shabby treatment, Smith rode Mattie Brown to a historic victory in a jump-off and as he completed his winning round he turned towards the directors' box where Bunn was sitting and delivered a two-fingered gesture in their general direction. The crowd roared with laughter; the directors sat stony-faced.

Afterwards Bunn presented the trophy to Smith, saying only 'well done', and the victor drove home to Yorkshire that night, leaving the cup behind for engraving. As Smith headed north he was blissfully unaware that moves were afoot to disqualify him and withhold the first prize of £2,000. The directors of Hickstead met within four hours of the finish and sent Smith a telegram stating that he had been disqualified from first place because of a 'disgusting gesture' and that all prize money was forfeit. The telegram was signed by Bunn in his capacity as chairman of the show. Smith had been found guilty in his absence without even so much as a trial.

Smith received the grim tidings from a man who was on his way to milk his cows. When he arrived home and saw the telegram, for once in his life he was rendered almost speechless. He quickly regained his composure and started to fight his corner, insisting that the 'disgusting gesture' was nothing more than a Churchillian victory salute, although television viewers could plainly see that Smith's palm was facing inwards instead of outwards. 'It was a straightforward V for victory,' Smith maintained. 'Churchill used it throughout the war. They tell me whenever I win a big class that I never smile; now they take me the wrong way.' Expressing his anger at the disqualification, he went on: 'This competition was judged under international rules, and there is no way they can do such a thing after a competition has been won. If a football player scores a legitimate goal and then punches the referee on the nose they do not disallow the goal.' The British Show Jumping Association countered by claiming that the disqualification was made under a local Hickstead rule on incivility, which stated that any kind of discourtesy to any judge would entail disqualification.

Bunn and his colleagues were on shaky ground. Public support was overwhelmingly on Smith's side. In *The Times* even Bernard Levin pleaded for mercy. Faced with accusations that they had overstepped their powers and lost their sense of humour, the directors reinstated Smith's win two days later pending an inquiry. In doing so, Bunn acknowledged that the directors of Hickstead 'acted wrongly in making their decision concerning Harvey Smith in not first asking him to appear before them'. The inquiry was set for 23 September.

Smith stuck manfully to his defence and turned up for the hearing at the British Show Jumping Association headquarters in London carrying a huge file of photographs depicting Churchill giving V signs in the same manner as he himself had done at Hickstead. After hearing evidence from witnesses and watching TV film of the incident, the stewards cleared Smith of misconduct and officially reinstated his Derby win. In their statement the stewards decided 'that after completing the winning round in the Wills Jumping Derby Mr Smith did make a gesture which he should have realised might have been considered offensive. Nevertheless, they were satisfied that this did not amount to a contravention of the rules.' Afterwards Smith, who was adamant that the gesture had not been meant offensively nor been aimed at anyone in particular, apologised to Bunn and the pair shook hands. He also announced that he would be giving £150 of his prize money to a charity for disabled riders.

The episode did nothing to diminish Smith's popularity, in fact quite the opposite. Despite his protestations of innocence, the general perception was that he had stuck two fingers up at pompous officialdom and got away with it, thus acquiring heroic status in the mould of Dick Turpin or Robin Hood. Nor would his deed ever be forgotten as 'giving a Harvey Smith' proceeded to enter the English language and eclipse even Churchill's imaginative use of two fingers.

Medical Negligence

1972

The swimming competition at the 1972 Munich Olympics is remembered almost exclusively for the amazing seven gold medals of Mark Spitz. Yet in those tempestuous Games another American swimmer – his name largely forgotten outside his own country – made all the wrong kind of headlines. He was a sixteen-year-old freestyler from San Rafael, California, named Rick DeMont and he became the first American since Jim Thorpe (sixty years earlier) to be stripped of his gold medal.

Allergic to wheat and fur, DeMont had been taking medication for asthma since the age of four. On qualifying for the US Olympic team, he was asked to complete a standard medical form in which he clearly stated that he was asthmatic and that, in addition to receiving weekly shots for his allergies, he was taking medicines called Marax and Actifed. While other countries checked such information for any possible banned drugs and recommended acceptable substitutes, the US Olympic Committee's Medical Commission all but ignored it, simply telling the athletes not to take any drugs within 48 hours of competition unless they had cleared it with a doctor. Thus DeMont was oblivious to the fact that each little pill of Maraz contained a banned IOC substance, ephedrine.

The night before the men's 400 metres freestyle, DeMont woke up wheezing between one and two o'clock and, to alleviate the symptoms, he took a tablet of Marax. Some six hours later he took another Marax pill and at noon qualified comfortably for the final. Since his prescription stated that he should take one tablet every six hours, he probably took another Marax some time before the final, which started at 6.40 p.m.

After a slow first 200 metres, DeMont scythed through the field in the second half of the race, eventually pipping Australia's Brad Cooper for gold by just one hundredth of a second. At sixteen, Rick DeMont was on top of the world, the new Olympic champion.

After the race DeMont, Cooper and bronze medallist Steve Genter (USA) undertook routine dope tests. No immediate problem surfaced and the medal ceremony went ahead as planned.

Two days later, on 3 September, DeMont began his quest for a second gold – in the 1,500 metres freestyle, an event in which he was the world record holder. Again he qualified easily for the final, which was scheduled to take place the following morning. As the packed Schwimhalle waited for the start, a loudspeaker announcement proclaimed that DeMont had been eliminated from the 1,500 metres on the recommendation of the Medical Commission of the IOC. While a baffled DeMont sat forlornly in the stands, it was revealed that his post-400 metres final urine test had shown traces of ephedrine. The IOC stripped him of his victory, handed him a lifelong suspension and gave his gold medal to Cooper.

DeMont was shattered. He was guilty of nothing more than ignorance, never having made any attempt to conceal the fact that he was taking Marax. Indeed, when US team officials entered his room at the Olympic village to confiscate his drugs, the bottle of Marax was plainly visible. Instead of standing by their swimmer and explaining that he was the victim of an oversight, the US Olympic Committee effectively washed its hands of him. With the team physicians severely reprimanded for their incompetence by the IOC, they went looking for a scapegoat. They blamed the swimming coaches, DeMont's family doctor, even DeMont himself, claiming that the USOC had never been notified that he was asthmatic or been informed about the amount or type of medication that he was taking. It amounted to a cover-up in the finest American tradition.

For years DeMont lived with the whispers and sneers that he was a cheat until in 1996 he decided to take positive action to clear his name by filing a lawsuit against the US Olympic Committee, claiming that it had mishandled his medical disclosure. Five long years later the US Olympic Committee finally admitted that it had erred in its handling of DeMont's medical information at the 1972 Olympics, although the settlement stopped short of an apology.

So after 29 years Rick DeMont was cleared of any deliberate wrongdoing and his achievements were belatedly recognised by the US Olympic Committee. It was certainly a victory but one which is unlikely ever to earn him the gold medal he probably deserves. 'I think no one really wanted to admit they were responsible,' he said in 2001 while working as assistant swimming coach at the University of Arizona. 'It was easier to hang a sixteen-year-old kid out to dry than to tell the truth.'

Countdown to Confusion

1972

In the history of basketball there has never been a finish to a game quite like the one between the United States and the Soviet Union in Munich on 10 September 1972. It was the Olympic final and the US went into the clash with an aura of invincibility, having never lost in Olympic competition – a period spanning no fewer than 62 games. The start was put back to 11.45 p.m. to accommodate US television, where millions of people tuned in expecting to witness another glorious chapter in the story of American basketball. Instead they could only look on shell-shocked as the Soviets snatched victory in a chaotic last three seconds that left the American team and officials convinced that they had been robbed of gold.

Flying in the face of the form book, the Soviets led from the outset and with five minutes remaining still held a 44–36 advantage. The Americans then stepped up a gear, steadily closing the gap, but with just six seconds left they still trailed by one point. The odds were still on a Soviet victory until their star player, Aleksandr Belov, blundered by conceding possession to Doug Collins whose progress was deliberately impeded by Zurab Sakandelidze. Collins duly converted the two free throws to put the US ahead for the first time in the game, 50–49, with only three seconds to play. It was then, against a deafening crescendo from the crowd, that all hell started to break loose.

Following the free throws, the Soviets failed to score, leaving jubilant US players and fans to swarm on to the court in celebration of what they thought was America's eighth consecutive basketball gold. However, their joy was cut short when it became apparent that head referee Renato Righetto of Brazil had spotted a commotion at the scorer's table and called an administrative time-out with one second remaining. The USSR coach, Vladimir Kondrashkin, claimed that he had called a time-out after Collins' first shot but that the call had been drowned in the sea of noise. To add to the confusion, the time out horn had been sounded as Collins made his second throw and some mistook this for the final horn to signal the end of the game. Both Righetto and timekeeper André Chopard believed that one second remained but at this stage Britain's R William Jones, secretary-general of the International Amateur Basketball Federation, intervened and ordered the clock to be set back to three seconds, the point at which the Soviet official had originally called a time out.

The court was cleared and play resumed. Kondrashkin introduced Ivan Edeshko but the switch seemed in vain when a Soviet long shot fell short and the three seconds passed without any further score. Once again the Americans celebrated at the sound of the horn, only to discover that the timekeeper had not been ready when play had restarted. Consequently the three seconds had to be played again. The drama was unbearable.

This time Edeshko hurled the ball the length of the court to Belov who muscled his way past Jim Forbes and Kevin Joyce to score a simple basket. The final horn sounded. At the third attempt the Soviets had snatched an improbable victory, 51–50.

The Americans immediately launched a formal protest but after studying television footage of those fateful last three seconds, the jury rejected the appeal. Seen by Americans as the villain of the piece, Jones explained: 'The whole trouble started when someone at the scorer's table sounded the buzzer too late for a time out requested by the Russians. The Americans have to learn how to lose, even when they think they are right.'

Not for the first or last time in sporting history, the Americans were utterly graceless in defeat. In what one columnist described as 'a sorry display of poor sportsmanship', the

American team and coaches refused to appear at the awards ceremony or to accept their silver medals. US Olympic basketball committee chairman Bill Summers complained: 'We do not feel like accepting the silver because we feel we are worth the gold.'

To this day the 1972 basketball silver medals remain unclaimed in an Olympic vault in Switzerland.

Pitch Sabotage

1975

In 1974 a policeman was shot during an armed robbery on an Electricity Board office in Ilford, Essex. For his part in the crime George Davis, a 34-year-old East End minicab driver, was sentenced to twenty years in jail – a decision that sparked fury from Davis's family and friends who insisted that he was innocent. They launched an intense publicity campaign to draw attention to Davis's plight. There was a march to Downing Street, cars were rammed into the gates of Buckingham Palace and influential national newspapers, a banner was draped across the dome of St Paul's Cathedral, and campaigners chained themselves to Wren's Monument in Central London. Right across the country buildings and walls were daubed with the phrase 'G Davis is Innocent'. So persistent was the crusade for freedom that even those with no knowledge of the case could not help wondering whether there had perhaps been a miscarriage of justice. However, after a year of canvassing the campaign had singularly failed to attract the support of the people that mattered, leading the friends of George Davis to the conclusion that a major publicity stunt – more audacious than anything that had gone before – was needed to turn the tide in their favour.

The principal sporting event in England during the summer of 1975 was the visit of the Australian cricket team. Led by Ian Chappell, the Australians held the Ashes and were one up in a four-Test series going into the third Test at Headingley in August. In reply to England's 288, the tourists had slumped to 135 all out, spinner Phil Edmonds taking 5–28 on his Test debut. England had then cemented their advantage with a second innings total of 291, leaving Australia facing the colossal task of scoring 445 to win. Nevertheless they made a good fist of it and at close of play on Monday evening – with just one day remaining – they had reached 220–3 with Rick McCosker unbeaten on 95.

At 6.50 on the morning of that final day – 19 August – Headingley's head groundsman, George Cawthray, pulled back the covers and discovered to his horror that the Leeds wicket had been deliberately sabotaged during the night. Three-inch deep holes had been gouged out of the wicket and filled with oil, roughly on a spot where the ball would pitch. All around the ground, walls were daubed with slogans proclaiming 'G Davis Is Innocent'. It did not take Sherlock Holmes to work out who was responsible.

At nine o'clock the two captains, Chappell and Tony Greig, inspected the damage in company with the umpires. Groundsman Cawthray thought he could repair the holes but the oil spillage was altogether more serious. It was suggested that play could be resumed on an adjoining wicket of similar wear. With the distinct possibility of squaring the series, Greig was all in favour but not surprisingly Chappell (his team on the back foot) vetoed the plan and the match was abandoned. As it turned out, rain set in before lunch to ensure that the game would have finished in a draw anyway, so the only real casualty was McCosker who was deprived of his maiden Test century.

The four individuals behind the wrecking of the third Test – Peter Chappell (definitely no relation), Colin Dean, Richard Ramsey and Geraldine Hughes – revealed how they had dug up the pitch using knives and forks stolen from a motorway service station and had purchased a gallon of oil from the same location. They said they had sabotaged the wicket because the campaign had so far failed to obtain an official inquiry into Davis's conviction.

While the quartet served short jail sentences for their act of vandalism, they no doubt felt their deeds were fully justified by the news that the police had finally agreed to review the identification evidence at Davis's trial. In May 1976, amid much rejoicing from Davis's supporters, Home Secretary Roy Jenkins announced that Davis should be freed. Jenkins said that he had decided to show mercy on the grounds that the shift in the balance of evidence in the case was such that it would be wrong for Davis to remain in jail.

That might have been the last the world heard of George Davis except for the fact that less than eighteen months later – in September 1977 – he was caught red-handed as part of a six-man gang who robbed the Bank of Cyprus in North London. He pleaded guilty and was sentenced to fifteen years. This time there was no campaign to free him...

Wired for Sound

1976

Red Army Major Boris Onishenko, a 38-year-old teacher from Kiev in the Ukraine, went into the 1976 Montreal Olympics as one of the most respected modern pentathletes in the world. An international since 1966, he had won a silver medal in Munich four years earlier and was a former individual world champion, the man everybody had to beat. Yet he exited Canada in disgrace with banner headlines around the world denouncing him as 'Disonishenko'.

Modern pentathlon is a five-discipline event comprising riding, fencing, shooting, swimming and running. The second day of competition in the team event was the fencing tournament in which the favourites from the USSR met Great Britain. Fencing in the pentathlon is a sudden death affair (metaphorically rather than literally) with the first hit in each bout winning. Although the likelihood was that Montreal would be his final Olympic appearance as he was lined up to become coach of the Soviet pentathlon team, Onishenko was still, at his advanced age, the star performer and represented a formidable opponent for the British fencers. As if meeting a swordsman of Onishenko's stature was not intimidating enough, Britain's Adrian Parker felt that the fates were conspiring against him when the automatic light registered a hit for the Ukrainian even though he did not appear to have touched his opponent. Veteran Jim Fox, who watched the contest and knew that Parker thought he had been robbed, was the next Briton to be drawn against Onishenko and when he too lost a hit without being touched, he made an official protest.

As soon as Fox challenged the touch, Onishenko said: 'No, no, Jimmy, there was no hit. I will change the weapon.' But Fox, believing that it was short-circuiting, insisted that it go to weapon control for detailed examination and referee Guido Malacarne duly ordered Onishenko to surrender his épée. Onishenko pretended not to understand and hurried away to where his colleagues had already brought out another épée to exchange with his own. Malacarne prevented the swap and demanded that the Russians hand him the correct weapon, whereupon a heated argument broke out. Fortunately, from the moment of protest, the referee had made a point of keeping a close eye on the faulty weapon, thereby thwarting any attempt at subsequent Soviet subterfuge.

The offending épée was taken away, leaving Onishenko to fight on with another sword, but soon word filtered back that he had been disqualified. In what one official described as an act of 'blatant cheating', the sword had been wired with a concealed push-button circuit breaker so that Onishenko could trigger the electronic scoring system with his hand and register a hit whenever he wanted. The device was so sophisticated that it was impossible to detect without dismantling the weapon.

Onishenko's immediate reaction was to deny that the rigged sword was his yet it had been made for a left-hander such as himself and the rest of the Soviet team, including the reserve, were all right-handed. Under rules laid down by the International Fencing Federation, all competitors' weapons were checked on arrival at the Olympics and re-examined before each fight. Each team had its own armourer whose job it was to submit the various épées, sabres and foils to an inspecting committee prior to use in the competition, but Onishenko had managed to cheat the system. The rules of the sport were subsequently amended, with grips that could hide wires or switches being banned.

Onishenko's protestations of innocence fell on deaf ears and the entire Soviet team were disqualified although the other two members were allowed to compete in the individual team competition. Britain went on to win the team gold.

For Fox the success was tinged with sadness over the Onishenko affair. 'Why did he do it, he of all people?' he asked reporters. 'He's been such a great sportsman for ten years. The pressure's getting too much, the political pressure. People are so desperate to win now. Onishenko was expecting promotion to lieutenant colonel soon, and this was his last chance to win the gold. Perhaps he needed it too much. Poor old Boris, now his life is ruined.'

Speculation grew regarding the length of time Onishenko had been cheating, particularly when it became apparent that his fencing scores had shown a marked improvement since 1970. A Soviet team official said: 'It is a very sad matter and he will probably be stripped of all his medals and honours back home.'

If there was one thing the Soviets despised more than one of their countrymen cheating at sport, it was when they were *caught* cheating at sport. Onishenko knew he could expect no mercy. He had brought shame on his people and would be hustled out of Canada as quickly as possible before any more awkward questions could be asked. Within hours of his disqualification, he was taken quietly from his room at the Olympic village and driven to the airport in a private car. He was never again seen outside the USSR.

Back home he was indeed stripped of his medals and discharged from the army but, with the help of an uncle in high places, he was able to secure a post as manager of a large swimming complex in Kiev. Rumour has it that in 1991 he was found drowned in the very same pool, assassinated by the KGB. Others claim to have spoken to him since by telephone, but nobody can be entirely certain of the pentathlete's precise fate. Whatever the truth, Boris Onishenko represented a murky episode in the history of Soviet sport – one that the authorities would prefer to forget.

Kerry Packer's Flying Circus

1977

It was the silent revolution that shook cricket to its very foundations. In May 1977 it was announced that 35 of the world's leading cricketers had secretly signed up with the Kerry Packer organisation to play a series of matches that would run in direct competition with official Tests over the next three years. The backlash was felt far and wide, nowhere more so than in England when it emerged that Packer's chief recruiting officer was none other than the England captain, Tony Greig.

So who was this Kerry Packer, the man accused of threatening the whole future of the game? The head of Australian television station Channel 9, Packer had been trying to obtain sole rights to Test cricket, only to be consistently thwarted by the Australian Cricket Board who preferred to sell nonexclusive rights to the Australian Broadcasting Commission for considerably less money. It was an old pals' act that worked fine for the ACB and ABC but did not adequately reward the most marketable aspect of the product – the players. Times were changing. Players, particularly in Australia, were demanding a larger slice of the cake. Money talked – and nobody's money talked louder than Packer's.

The 35 rebels who had joined the Packer Circus, as it became known, were drawn from five countries and included all but four of the Australian team that was currently touring England. The ACB allowed Greg Chappell to continue as Australian captain for the 1977 Ashes tour even though he had signed up with Packer, and England, too, fielded their Packer players . . . with one notable exception. Tony Greig was seen as the villain of the piece, a traitor, a Judas, who, because of his South African birth, was now no longer considered truly English. He was vilified in the press and quickly sacked as England captain, to be replaced by Mike Brearley, a man who could have stepped straight out of a vicar's tea party. John Woodcock of *The Times* had little sympathy for the deposed Greig. He wrote: 'Disloyalty, such as that shown by Greig in involving himself and two more of England's leading players, Knott and Underwood, in a scheme which drastically reduces their availability for England, deserves what punishment it gets.' Greig protested that he had only been acting in the best interests of English cricket, but his pleas fell on deaf ears.

With 54 days of international cricket planned by Packer – including five-day Tests and one-day matches – the threat to official tours and Test series was all too obvious. In July the International Cricket Conference took decisive action. It refused to grant first-class status to the Packer matches and ruled that anyone who appeared in them would automatically become ineligible to play official Test cricket. Individual countries were also urged to apply similar sanctions at domestic level, but the ICC's move backfired when the Packer Organisation took the Conference to court on the grounds that it was guilty of restraint of trade and was also advocating players to break their contracts.

The court case in London lasted almost seven weeks, at the end of which Mr Justice Slade, in a 60,000-word judgement, found in favour of the Packer rebels. He declared: 'A professional cricketer needs to make his living as much as any other professional man. It is straining the concept of loyalty too far for the authorities to expect him to enter into a self-denying ordinance not to play cricket for a private promoter during the winter months merely because the matches promoted could detract from the future profits of the authorities, who were not themselves willing or in a position to offer him employment over the winter or guarantee him employment in the future.' The ICC was also ordered to pay costs of £250,000.

Despite the introduction of such exciting innovations as night games and restrictions on defensive fields at the start of matches, the Packer series – fought out between teams representing Australia, the West Indies and the Rest of the World – struggled initially to win public support. By contrast the official Test series in which Australia beat India 3–2 attracted large crowds and high TV ratings. And although Mr Justice Slade had prohibited any widespread ban on the Packer rebels, divisions still existed in the various camps. When the West Indies dropped some Packer players on the eve of the third Test against Australia, Clive Lloyd, the West Indies skipper, resigned in protest, a mass walkout ensued, and a new team had to be hastily assembled. Meanwhile England had not picked any Packer players for the tour of Pakistan as they would not be available for all the matches. So when Packer suddenly released three Pakistan stars for the decisive Test, England threatened not to play. An embarrassing situation was avoided only by the nonselection of the trio.

After a disappointing start, the pendulum began to swing Packer's way. The Australian public lapped up Channel 9's gimmicky presentation and, with the official Australian team being humbled by Brearley's England, many fans switched their allegiance to Packer's World Series Cricket. Faced with a decline in revenue, the Australian Cricket Board caved in and decided to seek peace with Packer as soon as the ABC contract expired. In April 1979 the ACB concluded a lucrative deal with Packer, that, by giving him pretty much everything he had wanted in the first place, awarded him a controlling voice in the future of world cricket. Critics accused the ACB of selling out, especially when it cancelled a proposed tour by India in favour of a triangular series involving England, Australia and the West Indies. Now it was Packer who called the shots regarding clothing, the rules and even the choice of tourists. The purists were appalled.

However, marketing and sponsorship were here to stay. To some, cricket may have sold its soul but it had really only moved with the commercial times, bringing itself into line with sports such as soccer, tennis and golf, where players were properly rewarded for their talents. Kerry Packer did not exactly endear himself to the establishment but without him cricket might still be waiting to be dragged kicking and screaming into the modern world.

An Ingenious Apparatus

1978

It was Jacques Anquetil, one of the legendary heroes of the Tour de France, who once remarked: 'You don't ride the Tour on mineral water.' Whatever it was that crack Belgian cyclist Michel Pollentier rode the 1978 Tour on, he was so intent on concealing it from official dope-testers that he rigged up an elaborate network of tubing which enabled him to pass someone else's urine. He deserved to succeed, if only for the sheer audacity of the scheme, but, as is so often the case in sport, you don't always get what you deserve.

The 27-year-old Pollentier was no stranger to positive testing, having been caught twice before – on the Tour of Piedmont in 1974 and on the Tour of Belgium in 1977. According to those closest to him, Pollentier had taken a mild adrenalin stimulant, alupin – a common drug, sold over the counter in Belgium – to help with his breathing during the 1978 Tour. However, his previous experiences had made him so wary of the dope-testing control caravans lurking menacingly at the end of each stage that he went to extraordinary lengths to cheat the system.

It had all looked so rosy for Pollentier as he raced away with the sixteenth stage of the Tour, from St Etienne to the skiing village of L'Alpe d'Huez, to take over the race leader's yellow jersey. It was a tortuous climb yet Pollentier had come home alone, unchallenged, in a class of his own. As his team manager, Fred de Bruyne, commented: 'I had followed Pollentier throughout his long breakaway, five metres behind, all the way up the L'Alpe d'Huez climb. It was a fantastic athletic exploit and I cried like a child as I was so full of joy.' Within a few hours those emotions would change dramatically.

Crossing the finish line, Pollentier totally ignored the doping caravan parked nearby and headed straight to his room at the Hotel Castillan half a mile away. De Bruyne assumed he must have forgotten about the control amid the excitement of victory. Now wearing a long-sleeved jersey (for reasons that would soon become obvious), Pollentier suddenly appeared at the test centre an hour after the stage had ended. He eventually emerged smiling nearly three hours later, telling increasingly interested reporters that everything was fine. He even returned to his hotel to drink champagne with his manager and assembled journalists. But a further hour later, Jean Court, President of the International Jury of Race Commissioners, and Felix Levitan, Director of the Tour, sensationally announced that Pollentier had been found guilty of serious violations at the doping control.

Gradually the truth of what had occurred inside the caravan began to emerge. Asked to fill a bottle with urine, Pollentier had alerted officials' suspicions by, as one report described it, 'pumping his elbow in and out as if playing a set of bagpipes'. He was then instructed to lift his jumper and did so to reveal a contraption of tubes and pipes that stretched from his armpits to his shorts. To the doctor's amazement, he found a small rubber bulb filled with drug-free urine strapped beneath Pollentier's arm. A tube then ran from the bag to an area immediately below Pollentier's penis where a plastic pipe concealed in his shorts gave the impression that the urine he was passing was his own. It was when the device had started to malfunction during the test that Pollentier had resorted to pumping his arm furiously. If it wasn't such a grave breach of regulations, it would have been laughable.

It transpired that Pollentier had gone to his hotel straight after the stage solely to attach his new plumbing system, which, in the finest traditions of *Blue Peter*, was one he'd made earlier. As all hell broke loose, Pollentier bleated that it was the slackness of previous controls on the Tour that had encouraged him to take such a risk. It was even whispered that he had been made a scapegoat simply for being Belgian. When sanity was restored, Pollentier had the grace to apologise for 'sullying the standing of the Tour'. His punishment was to be disqualified from the Tour, fined 5,000 Swiss francs and suspended from all international racing for two months.

Encouraged by thousands of letters of support he received from cycling fans across the world, Pollentier returned to the saddle before finally retiring in 1984. Sadly the doping scandal of the 1998 Tour de France indicates that today there are still precious few cyclists riding the Tour on mineral water.

Over the Moon

1979

British football was in need of cheering up in 1979. Scotland's inept performance at the previous year's World Cup had made Ally MacLeod and co. a laughing stock, their comical catalogue of catastrophes capped by Willie Johnston being sent home in disgrace from Argentina for failing a dope test. Few will forget Johnston's graphic description of the moment when he, Kenny Dalglish and the Scots' Peruvian tormentor, Teofilio Cubillas, gave their sample. 'We all pissed in the bottle,' remarked Johnston ruefully, 'and theirs was a lot clearer than mine.' Oh how we English pissed ourselves... until we remembered that we hadn't actually qualified for the World Cup. Even the Scottish fans saw the funny side. 'Pep pills?' they queried in chorus. 'We thought they were tranquillisers.'

So with the national game on both sides of the border in need of resuscitation, everyone needed a moment of light relief that did not have dark undertones. Step forward Sammy Nelson.

Arsenal's Northern Ireland international left-back was a great favourite with the Highbury crowd on account of his wholehearted defending and aggressive attacking play. There were certainly more gifted players in the side – Pat Jennings, Liam Brady, Frank Stapleton – but then again there was also Willie Young. And anyway what Nelson lacked in flair, he compensated for with sheer boundless enthusiasm. On 3 April 1979 Arsenal were entertaining Coventry City in front of a crowd of around 30,000. Having already reached the FA Cup Final, Arsenal were expected to dispose of the Midlanders without too much fuss, even though City were enjoying one of their more fruitful seasons in the First Division – i.e. one that

191

didn't entail a last-day battle against relegation. But it all turned sour in the 33rd minute when Nelson deflected a shot into his own net to put the visitors into a shock lead. The Gunners rallied strongly in the second half in a desperate attempt to salvage something from the game, but had to wait until a quarter of an hour from the end when Nelson atoned for his earlier blunder by equalising with a splendid drive. Highbury breathed a collective sigh of relief, no one being more delighted than Nelson who celebrated by turning his back, dropping his shorts and mooning in front of the jubilant North Bank. Referee Clive Thomas didn't see the incident but there were plenty who did!

The match ended 1–1 but the following day's newspaper reports centred around what Arsenal manager Terry Neill described as Nelson's 'moment of madness'. Nelson himself was suitably contrite, while the press suggested that his gesture was in response to the barracking he had received from the North Bank following his own goal, although that version of events is disputed by the majority of those at the game. Arsenal reacted quickly, suspending him for two games and fining him two weeks' wages. The Football Association then fined him £750 and tacked on a further two-match suspension, which, to Nelson's relief, cleared him to play in the Cup Final. Bert Millichip, chairman of the FA commission, said: 'I think the player was very lucky. If it had not been for the excellent character report submitted by his manager, the penalty would have been more severe.'

So Nelson was able to help Arsenal beat Manchester United 3–2 in a final with a memorable climax. For the remainder of his career he was always remembered for the mooning incident – a genuinely spontaneous celebration in stark contrast to the tediously choreographed goal routines that litter the game today.

Australia's Underhand Tactics

1981

Once upon a time there were three brothers – Ian, Greg and Trevor. Ian and Greg have gone down in Australian cricketing folklore as outstanding batsmen and inspirational captains of their country, whereas Trevor is solely remembered for outrageously bowling the last ball underarm to deny New Zealand the chance of a tie in a World Series final. Yet ironically the demoniacal plan was not Trevor's idea at all but Greg's, which goes to show that the memory can be alarmingly selective when it comes to sporting heroes. History often forgives and forgets the flaws of the great, preferring to heap the blame on someone else altogether – in this instance Trevor, the least talented of the three Chappell brothers.

The World Series final of 1981 was to be decided by the best of five 50-over matches. Australia were clear favourites but had surprisingly lost the first game by 78 runs before rallying to win the second by seven wickets. The third encounter took place at the Melbourne Cricket Ground on 1 February. Batting first, Australia made a total of 235–4, due in no small part to an innings of ninety from their captain Greg Chappell. In a foretaste of the controversy to come, Chappell survived a skied catch to mid-wicket on 52. New Zealand fielder Martin Snedden claimed a brilliant diving catch but Chappell refused to accept it and the umpires, who subsequently admitted that they had missed the incident because they were watching the crease at their respective ends for possible short runs, gave him not out. In reply New Zealand, helped by a century from Bruce Edgar, reached 221–6 at the start of the final over and thus needed fifteen to win from those last six balls. It was a tall order, all the more so because Edgar was stranded at the non-striker's end. Greg Chappell had originally intended to bowl the last over himself but having taken early wickets (he finished with three), he opted to bowl out his allotted ten overs. So in his hour of need he turned to his brother Trevor.

Richard Hadlee hit Trevor's first delivery for four but was then out lbw to the second, leaving eleven to win from four balls. Wicketkeeper Ian Smith struck the third and fourth for two apiece, only to be bowled while swinging at the fifth. Thus New Zealand needed six off the final ball to tie the game. The incoming batsman was tail-ender Brian McKechnie, a burly All Black rugby player who, while technically not the most gifted wielder of the willow, possessed the necessary physique for a short sharp slog and would not be fazed by the pressure. Seeing McKechnie stride purposefully to the wicket, Greg suddenly became nervous, thinking to himself: 'If anyone can hit one over the fence, this bloke can.'

McKechnie, who had been told by his team-mates as he left the pavilion not to worry about getting his eye in, had already decided on his strategy. Anticipating a yorker, he proposed to step outside leg stump, charge down the wicket and hammer the ball back over Trevor's head in the direction of the shortest boundary. It sounded simple on paper but his best-laid plans were about to be wrecked. Australian wicketkeeper and vice-captain Rod Marsh had just advised Trevor to bowl more of the same when Greg sauntered over to his brother and asked: 'How are you at bowling your underarms?'

Underarm bowling was still permissible in Australian one-day games (although it was swiftly banned after this episode) and Trevor was evidently impressed with the suggestion. He later revealed: 'It didn't enter my mind to say no. I actually didn't consider it to be a yes/no type of question. It was the captain of my team asking me to do something that was, at the time anyway, within the rules of the game. It seemed like a good idea.'

Having secured Trevor's approval, Greg then informed umpire Don Weser that the final ball would be bowled underarm. Weser rolled his eyes in amazement and duly approached McKechnie who thought he was being reminded that this was the last ball of the match. On being told of Greg's plan, McKechnie growled 'You've got to be joking!' and dropped his bat in disbelief. Even Marsh, that most formidable of competitors, shook his head and called to Trevor: 'No, mate, don't do it.' Trevor simply shrugged his shoulders and nodded in the direction of Greg to indicate that he was just obeying orders.

Off a two-step walk-up, taking care to avoid a no-ball, Trevor Chappell sent down a slow grubber. As the crowd roared its collective disapproval, McKechnie weighed up his choices. There was no point in hitting a four and he had no wish to suffer the ignominy of taking a swing and being bowled, so he quietly blocked the ball before hurling his bat to the ground in disgust and standing arms akimbo, glaring at the offending bowler. 'I couldn't believe they'd stoop so low,' said McKechnie afterwards. As he made his way towards the pavilion, the undefeated Edgar raised two fingers in the general direction of anybody on the field with the surname Chappell.

Back in the New Zealand dressing room the scene was one of uproar. Skipper Geoff Howarth marched on to the field in his socks to remonstrate with the umpires, only to be informed that the underarm delivery was perfectly legal. Soft-drink cans and paper cups were thrown at the Australian team as they sprinted off but even in the sanctuary of their dressing room there was no celebration of their six-run win. Instead there was a stony silence. Marsh later apologised privately to Howarth.

However, the furore that followed was very public. On Channel Nine, Richie Benaud called Greg Chappell 'gutless', adding: 'There are 50,000 people here at the MCG today. I would hazard a guess that you might find three or at the very most four who wouldn't have a sinking feeling in their stomach at the moment over that last delivery.' Greg stoically defended his actions at the post-match press conference on the basis that 'if it is written in the rules of the game it is fair play.' Not surprisingly the New Zealanders saw it differently and threatened to bowl all fifty overs underarm in the next match. Kiwi Prime Minister Robert Muldoon labelled Chappell's decision an act of cowardice and even his Australian counterpart, Malcolm Fraser, felt that Greg had made an error of judgement. The New Zealand Cricket Council chairman,

Robert Vance, suggested that the Australian Cricket Board should cancel the result whereupon the ACB felt obliged to state its own position in a strongly worded statement. It read:

> The Board deplores Greg Chappell's action and has advised him of the Board's strong feelings on this matter and of his responsibilities as Australia's captain to uphold the spirit of the game at all times. We acknowledge that his action was within the laws of the game, but that it was totally contrary to the spirit in which cricket has been, and should be, played.

If Greg hoped the fuss might die down overnight he was wrong. The *Sydney Morning Herald* wrote: 'One ball dents Australia's image as a sporting nation.' His own brother Ian was equally critical in his newspaper column, writing: 'Fair dinkum, Greg, how much pride do you sacrifice to win $35,000?' Other former players were quick to add their condemnation. Tony Greig, that paragon of cricketing virtue, called for the captain's sacking while Keith Miller said that one-day cricket had died and that Greg Chappell should be buried with it.

Callers to a Sydney radio station demanded that the Australian ambassador to New Zealand be recalled as a mark of national shame and in Wellington a flag above the office of an Australian insurance firm flew at half-mast. Qantas capitalised on the situation by running a newspaper advertisement offering cut-price air fares to New Zealand. The advert showed a photograph of the infamous underarm delivery with the caption: 'New Zealand $299 return. Once again the opposition will accuse us of cheating.'

Meanwhile the man at the centre of the storm was under media siege in his Melbourne hotel. On the evening of 2 February Greg was persuaded by the ACB to issue a conciliatory statement, in which he said: 'I have always played cricket within the rules of the game. I took a decision yesterday which, whilst within the laws of cricket, in the cool light of day I recognise as not being within the spirit of the game. The decision was made whilst I was under pressure and in the heat of the moment. I regret the decision. It is something I would not do again.' By way of mitigation he later explained that after an exhausting schedule of five Tests and ten lead-up games in the World Series, he had been anxious not to extend the finals longer than necessary and had therefore resolved to despatch New Zealand as quickly as possible.

Greg knew he had blundered and when he went out to inspect the Sydney pitch before the fourth match in the series, he carried a white handkerchief in his pocket to wave in case he got a hostile reception from the crowd. Australia duly won that game without fuss to seal a 3–1 series win. And who was named Man of the Series? Greg Chappell.

Exonerated of his crass gamesmanship within a few days, it is hardly surprising that time has largely forgiven Greg Chappell. But Trevor Chappell remains a trivia quiz favourite. Wasn't he the guy that disgracefully bowled underarm against New Zealand?

The Bombing of Eden Park

1981

Relations between the rugby-playing nations of New Zealand and South Africa had long given cause for concern. When the Springboks first toured New Zealand in 1921 they played a team of Maoris who were billed as 'New Zealand Natives', but a bad-tempered match at Napier, which ended in a narrow 9–8 victory for the tourists, prompted C W F Blackett, a member of the South African party, to send an angry cable back to his homeland. Part of it read: 'It was bad enough having to play a team officially designated New Zealand Natives, but the spectacle of thousands of Europeans frantically cheering on a band of coloured men to defeat members of their own race was too much for the Springboks who were, frankly, disgusted.' Intent on avoiding a repeat performance, the South Africans informed the 1928 All Blacks that no Maori players would be acceptable on the tour. Consequently men of the calibre of young fullback George Nepia were not selected for the trip. The first rumblings of apartheid were being felt in sport.

For a country with a record of harmonious race relations, it was alarming that New Zealand should have allowed itself to be dictated to in such a fashion – and even more so that it should maintain links with South Africa even when apartheid in the republic became an open policy. While the rest of the world cut off sporting links with South Africa, the ironically named All Blacks went ahead with a 1976 tour – a decision that led to the boycott of the Montreal Olympics by African nations.

When it was announced that the Springboks would be visiting in 1981, the rugby-mad New Zealanders were caught between a rock and a hard place. For while they adored their sport – and a meeting between the All Blacks and the Springboks was always a special occasion – the ethical dilemma caused consciences to be severely examined. Prime Minister Robert Muldoon was in favour of the tour proceeding, trotting out the age-old argument that politics has no place in sport, but the All Blacks' captain, Graham Mourie, stirred up the opposition by declaring himself unavailable for selection. Mourie explained: 'The first consideration was apartheid and whether it was right or wrong. The second issue was the tour itself and whether it would be good for New Zealand rugby, and thirdly whether it was going to be good for New Zealand as a country. I knew it was going to be bad on all three counts.'

Although All Black centre Bruce Robertson also opted out of the series on moral grounds, the controversial 56-day tour went ahead but each Springbok match was marred by protests. When the game against Waikato at Hamilton was cancelled after protesters occupied the pitch and refused to move, irate rugby fans hurled bottles and bricks at the demonstrators. New Zealand was becoming a nation divided. Soon barbed wire was erected around the perimeter of grounds to keep the protesters out and riot police stepped up their presence. It was starting to turn uglier than the average Number Eight forward.

Matters came to a head at the third Test, staged at Eden Park, Auckland, on 12 September. Upwards of 60,000 anti-apartheid demonstrators marched through Auckland on the morning of the game and the atmosphere inside and outside the ground was decidedly tense, police struggling to keep the rival factions apart. Then with the match under way a Cessna light aircraft, hired from a local club, made a series of runs above the ground, dropping flour bombs, nets, carpet tacks, smoke canisters and some burning material on to the pitch below. One flour bomb scored a direct hit on All Black prop Gary Knight, knocking him over. As the bombing runs continued, police in another plane gave chase. By now all eyes were on the action in the skies rather than that on the pitch, the 49,000 crowd becoming increasingly fearful that the protesters' plane might crash into the stands. The pilot swooped lower and lower, at one point heading straight for a goalpost before climbing steeply to safety at the very last minute. Horrified spectators threw beer cans at the plane but the pilot – a man named Marx – made as many as 62 runs before finally landing, at which point he was arrested. Ironically the only injuries sustained inside the ground were caused by the beer can missiles falling back on to the heads of the crowd.

In the streets outside, the situation was more serious as protesters, some said to be armed with acid-filled eggs and Molotov cocktails, fought running battles with riot police and rugby fans. A total of 45 people, including 32 police officers, required hospital treatment, many injured by flying stones. Eventually 148 people were arrested, among them the pilot, Marx, who was jailed for six months.

As for the match, New Zealand won 25–22 to clinch the series by two games to one but the 'Barbed Wire Tour', as it became known, left a bitter aftertaste. The question of maintaining sporting links with South Africa was placed firmly under the microscope once more, with New Zealand rugby now experiencing the same sense of shame felt by Australia's cricketers earlier in the year. The upshot was that the official All Blacks' visit to South Africa in 1986 was cancelled after the courts ruled that such a tour would violate New Zealand's constitution by denying Maoris the same rights as white New Zealanders. Nevertheless a rebel Cavaliers' tour, featuring most of the All Blacks, did take place. They would not be denied their rugby.

Erica Uncovered

1982

When 25-year-old Australian Michael O'Brien streaked at the England–France rugby international in April 1974, the Twickenham crowd reckoned it was the biggest helmet they had ever seen. It belonged to a Metropolitan Police officer who had removed his headgear and strategically positioned it so as to conceal the evidence. O'Brien became a celebrity for fifteen minutes and started a trend for streaking at major sporting events.

The following year Michael Angelow (no relation to the Renaissance artist) risked life and limb by running naked on to Lord's Cricket Ground and straddling the stumps. 'One ball left,' proclaimed the commentator.

But while male streakers merely served to remind us how cold British summers are, Erica Roe warmed the hearts of thousands of rugby fans when she stripped to the waist and bounced across Twickenham one afternoon in January 1982.

The 24-year-old bookshop assistant from Petersfield, Hampshire, was attending the match against Australia with her elder sister Sally and a large group of boisterous friends. On arrival they headed straight for the beer tent and by the time the game got under way, Roe was, as she later put it, 'definitely tipsy'. Having moved down to the front, she and her friend, Sarah Bennett, became bored. 'We thought we should do something,' recalled Roe, 'and within seconds had decided, "Let's streak". It was an impulse thing. We threw our clothes off. I handed my bra to some people behind me – and my packet of Marlboro. Half-time arrived, and off I went.'

Millions of TV viewers saw Roe's forty-inch chest career across the turf, closely followed by the rest of her body and a number of policemen. The players could hardly believe their eyes. England scrum half Steve Smith turned to captain Bill Beaumont and said: 'Hey, skipper, there's a bird just run on the pitch and she's wearing your bum on her chest!'

'I remember running like hell,' said Roe, 'knowing I was being pursued and looking back for Sarah, who didn't join me. I heard all this screaming and thought, "I have to get off, the second half is starting." But I quickly realised the roar was for me. Then of course I behaved like an egotistical bitch, put my arms in the air and went, "Yes! Hi!" That was fun. Then I turned back to try and get Sarah out, which is why I was caught.'

Overhauled after a Keystone Cops-type chase, Roe was led off the pitch with a police officer placing his helmet over her chest to protect her modesty. Given Ms Roe's generous proportions it would have required the intervention of several officers for the cover-up to have been wholly effective.

Meanwhile her father Peter, a farm manager, and two brothers had been watching the match on television. At half-time Peter Roe got up to make a cup of coffee and in his absence one of the sons called out: 'Pa! Pa! A woman just ran across the pitch who looked like Erica!' But they all assumed it must have been someone else and resumed watching the match. Shortly afterwards Mr Roe was informed by the police that his daughter had been involved in some form of incident but was not familiar with the precise details... until he watched the nine o'clock news. 'To my astonishment,' he told reporters proudly, 'there was a picture of a streaker on television. And there she was, on the box. It was a lovely picture. She had her arms out like the Pope.' That was where any similarity with the pontiff most definitely ended. By way of explanation, Mr Roe added: 'She spent her childhood in Africa where such things are not regarded with any disfavour. It is seen as being perfectly natural.'

Ms Roe was not charged but her boss, Frank Westwood, sacked her for repeatedly taking time off (she was supposed to have been working at the bookshop that day). However, he relented after seeing how much business she was suddenly bringing to his little emporium. Over the next three years she made around £8,000 from personal appearances. She was offered a £250-a-day job modelling double-breasted jackets for the Harry Fenton chain of menswear shops – a role previously filled by Kevin Keegan. She was later voted number 71 in a newspaper poll of the hundred greatest sporting moments but surely the biggest accolade came when Berwick farmer Bob Maxwell named his cow Erica because she had delivered 238,000 pints of milk from her enormous udders.

Roe, who described herself as 'a short, fat little dumpling with big boobs who wasn't very attractive in clothes', compared streaking in front of a big crowd to 'a moment of feeling what it's like to be in The Rolling Stones or Genesis, up there on the stage'. She went on: 'I sincerely hope streaking will continue to be a carefree, nonviolent, to heck-with-it all show of a little genuine madness.'

Erica Roe now lives as an organic farmer in Portugal, but a crop of young wannabes have burst forth to carry on the tradition with the result that streaking at top sporting events has become every bit as commonplace – and just as monotonous – as the Mexican wave. The past twenty years have thrown up publicity-craving streakers at Wimbledon, the Derby and even the National Indoor Bowls Championships … although for some reason they seem unwilling to trespass on the world of bullfighting. The British Open Golf Championship appears to be a great favourite with female streakers. When one cavorted across the fairway at St Andrews in 2000, a sage remarked that Tiger Woods had done well to avoid that particular bit of rough.

The Flockton Grey Switch

1982

When a two-year-old called Flockton Grey romped to a twenty-length victory in the Knighton Auction Stakes at Leicester on Monday 29 March 1982, three things aroused the suspicions of Jockey Club investigator George Edmundson. Firstly, it was a huge distance for any two-year-old to win by so early in the flat season, particularly a 10–1 shot; secondly, the horse's trainer, Stephen Wiles, had enjoyed little success previously; and thirdly, Edmundson had heard that a lot of money had been bet on the horse that afternoon, both at Ayr racecourse and in betting shops across Yorkshire. Edmundson voiced his suspicions to the police and in 1984 three Humberside men appeared in court accused of plotting a betting coup involving the substitution of an older racehorse for a two-year-old.

The mastermind behind the scheme was millionaire businessman, big-time gambler and part-time racehorse owner Kenneth Richardson. Nicknamed 'Rag Tag Richie', 47-year-old Richardson was a self-made man whose East Riding Paper Sack Company was the fourth largest paper-sack company in Britain, giving him the trappings of a luxury home in Driffield, complete with swimming pool and an adjoining stud and stables that housed a string of fifty horses. However, under Jockey Club rules he was not permitted to run horses, having been declared bankrupt in the wake of a collapsed business venture in 1960. Among the horses at Richardson's stables were two almost identical grey geldings – a three-year-old by the name of Good Hand and an unnamed, unraced two-year-old. Good Hand had been bought by Richardson's right-hand man, company director Colin Mathison, from Malton trainer

Nigel Tinkler. It had run three times as a two-year-old and, although it had yet to win a race, had never finished out of the first four. The form was clearly good enough to win a modest race at Leicester, particularly against a field of younger horses. Richardson's miscalculation was in not realising exactly how good the horse was.

Richardson sent the unraced two-year-old to Stephen Wiles who trained at Flockton, near Wakefield. Wiles was keen to make a name for himself but found that all of his attempts to prepare the horse for the racecourse were thwarted by Richardson. In the meantime Richardson entered Good Hand in the Leicester race under the name of a two-year-old, Flockton Grey, having tricked a vet into providing the necessary identification papers. Presented with the documents of a two-year-old, the vet had failed to spot that the horse before him was, in fact, a similar-looking three-year-old. Wiles later testified that when 'Flockton Grey' arrived at Leicester racecourse shortly before the Knighton Auction Stakes it was only the second time he had ever seen the horse, the first being when it was officially named at his yard in the presence of the vet.

On the night before the Leicester race the horse's jockey, Kevin Darley, received a telephone call from an anonymous Yorkshireman advising him that the going would be better on the far side. Darley said later: 'The caller did not explain why he was telephoning and I never heard from him again. I looked at the ground on the day of the race and I took his advice.' It was sound judgement and Darley admitted his amazement when he looked around half a furlong from the winning post to find himself way ahead of the rest of the runners. Therein lay the start of Richardson's problems. For his 'ringer' was way too fast. Instead of winning by a few lengths, Good Hand had annihilated the opposition to such an extent that the stewards immediately ordered an inquiry and advised bookmakers not to pay out on the horse listed as 'Flockton Grey'. This was bad news for Richardson who had arranged for associates to place bets in Hull, York, Driffield and Ayr totalling £2,000. Before too many questions could be asked, the winning horse was driven away from the racecourse with the same indecent haste with which it had arrived and, indeed, run.

As the police began to investigate, they showed veterinary experts a photograph of the winner taken with its mouth open. The experts confirmed that the animal had the teeth of a three-year-old. For months the police then tried to discover the true identity and whereabouts of the horse masquerading as Flockton Grey. Finally in December of that year the fraud squad revealed that the horse in question had been found in a secluded field at Glaisdale, near Whitby, where it had been kept by a woman for the previous eight months. The game was up.

Richardson, his racing manager Mathison and horse box driver Peter Boddy stood trial at York Crown Court in May 1984. The court heard a positive identification of the rogue horse as Good Hand from former National Hunt jockey Colin Tinkler (brother of Nigel) who had trained Good Hand as a foal and recognised a tell-tale scar on the animal. Despite a typically eloquent defence from George Carman, QC, Richardson was fined £20,000 and given a nine-month suspended jail sentence for conspiring to defraud bookmakers and the betting public. Mathison was fined £3,000 and Boddy was given a 12-month conditional discharge. Passing sentence, Judge Bennett said: 'This offence was serious because the actions you took undermined the integrity of racing, which is enjoyed by millions.' There ends the bizarre story of Flockton Grey, the horse that, according to the form book, won a race at Leicester but in truth never set hoof on a racecourse.

But that is not quite the end of the story of Kenneth Richardson. Some years later he re-emerged as the self-styled benefactor of struggling football club Doncaster Rovers. In the early hours of 29 June 1995 fire broke out in the main stand of the club's ramshackle Belle Vue ground, causing £100,000 worth of damage. A mobile phone left at the scene by the hired arsonist implicated Richardson. In 1999 Richardson was found guilty of conspiracy to burn down his own club's stand and sentenced to four years in jail. The fire was thought to be an attempt to force Doncaster Council into offering the club a better site.

The Kidnapping of Shergar

1983

In the frantic days that followed the kidnapping of Derby winner Shergar from the Aga Khan's Ballymany Stud, the Irish police received a succession of calls from someone who said he was sure that the horse was no more than two miles from Ballymany. 'How can you be so sure?' asked the police eventually. 'Sure he'd never get more than a mile and six furlongs,' replied the caller before hanging up.

That was the dichotomy with the mysterious disappearance of Shergar – it was a sad affair but it inspired no end of jokes and ensured that the wonder horse was destined to be remembered as the equine equivalent of Lord Lucan.

The subject of books, documentaries and even a feature film, Shergar has become the stuff of legend. Indeed, the myths surrounding his demise have all but obscured his brief but glorious career during which he won six of his eight races and earned £436,000 for his connections. Bred in Ireland and owned by the Aga Khan, Shergar became the most impressive Derby winner in history when trotting up by ten lengths in the 1981 Epsom classic. Shortly afterwards he won the Irish Derby and when he was retired to stud in September of that year, 34 syndication shares were sold for £250,000 apiece. The facts did not have to be exaggerated much for Shergar to be labelled the £10 million superhorse.

The period when these investors could expect a huge return on their money was the five-month breeding season between mid-February and mid-July, a period that could net over £3 million in stud fee nominations. It was no coincidence that Shergar was snatched just a week before the start of the 1983 breeding season, the kidnappers reasoning that the horse's owners would want to settle the matter as quickly as possible so that Shergar could be returned to his box and continue making money.

Ballymany Stud was situated to the southwest of Dublin. Just after 8.30 p.m. on the evening of Tuesday 8 February a masked, armed gang burst in and held stud groom Jimmy Fitzgerald and his family at gunpoint. One of the gang announced coldly: 'We've come for Shergar.'

The gang took Fitzgerald to the stallion house and asked him which of the two horses was Shergar. They knew anyway but just wanted to test Fitzgerald so that they could be sure he was not about to trick them. While the horse was loaded up, Fitzgerald was forced into the back of a van and driven around for forty minutes before being dumped outside a Chinese restaurant in Kilcock, 24 miles away. He was ordered to phone his boss – stud manager Ghislain Drion – but not the authorities. The kidnappers warned: 'There'll be no police or the horse is dead.'

The groom did as he was told and Drion immediately notified the office of the Aga Khan who adopted a hard line and issued instructions that no ransom should be paid. Instead the Irish police were called in. Using the codename 'King Neptune', the kidnappers first made contact on the afternoon of Wednesday 9 February, demanding a contact number for Drion in Paris. They then rang the Paris number on the Thursday evening where a trained negotiator asked for proof that they still had the horse. Another call to Paris on the Friday evening demanded that someone unconnected with the stud and using the alias 'Johnny Logan' should take £2 million to Dublin's Crofton Airport Hotel at nine o'clock the following morning.

The kidnappers' choice of Ireland's Eurovision Song Contest winner as an alias to be used at the ransom drop introduced an unintentional note of farce to the proceedings. With no group claiming responsibility for the abduction, the rumour mill was working overtime. The IRA were clear favourites but lively outsiders included the Mafia, Colonel Gadaffi of Libya and that trusty standby, the Ayatollah Khomeini. Pan's People were quoted at 500–1. A succession of hoax calls – including a ransom demand of £1.5 million made to an Irish radio station – merely added to the confusion. Wild stories appeared in print. Shergar's ear had been sent to the Garda; Shergar had been spirited off to a stud in the Middle East; Shergar's sperm was being sold on the black market among wealthy Arabs. Given the lack of concrete information, anything was possible.

While the Aga Khan was unwilling to pay up, the Irish Bloodstock Breeders' Association did offer an unspecified amount for the safe return of Shergar two days after the kidnap. Having spent decades building up the lucrative bloodstock industry and encouraging top breeders to Ireland, the IBBA did not want it ruined overnight.

The kidnappers failed to keep the Saturday morning rendezvous at the Crofton Airport Hotel but made two more calls that day. The first said that proof that Shergar was still alive could be obtained at the Rosnaree Hotel on the main Dublin–Belfast road, so a detective hurried to the hotel and picked up an envelope marked for Johnny Logan. Inside was a Polaroid of Shergar with a hand pointing to the Friday edition of the *Irish News*. The second call was made to Paris at 10.40 p.m. The negotiator asked for further proof that Shergar was alive and well whereupon the kidnapper lost his patience. 'If you are not satisfied, that's it,' he raged and then hung up. That was the last that was heard from the kidnappers. It is thought that within minutes of the call ending a bullet was put through the head of the unfortunate Shergar.

While speculation continued regarding Shergar's fate, the stud syndicate's insurers refused to pay out without positive proof that the horse was dead. In 1996 an Irish laboratory tried to match two hairs taken from Shergar by souvenir-hunting veterinary students on a stable visit to the body of a horse that had been found. They did not match. Then in 2000, scientists examined a skull containing two bullet holes, which had been found wrapped in cloth on a footpath in Tralee, 200 miles from the Ballymany Stud, but tests showed that the skull belonged to a much younger horse.

The most hopeful lead occurred in 1998 with the publication of the autobiography of Sean O'Callaghan, a convicted IRA murderer who had turned police informer. He claimed that the kidnap plot was hatched in prison by a former bookmaker's clerk and Republican veteran assigned to raise money for IRA weapon purchases. According to O'Callaghan, a man who 'once worked with horses' was hired to handle Shergar after the kidnapping but he proved ill-equipped to deal with a highly strung, thoroughbred stallion. 'The horse threw himself into a frenzy in the horsebox,' wrote O'Callaghan, 'damaging a leg and proving impossible for the team to control... He was killed within days even though the IRA kept up the pretence that he was alive.'

It was further claimed that Shergar was buried in woodland some 100 miles from Ballymany but, to date, no evidence has been unearthed to conclude one of the most enduring mysteries of the twentieth century.

The Killer Punch

1983

On the night of 16 June 1983, New York's Madison Square Garden was packed to the rafters with boxing fans eagerly anticipating another chapter in the remarkable career of Roberto Duran. Having already held world titles in both the lightweight and welterweight divisions, the 32-year-old Panamanian was going for a hat trick against reigning light middleweight champion Davey Moore. The grand entrance of Muhammad Ali, who made his way to a ringside seat to the accompanying chants of 'Ah-Lee! Ah-Lee!', set the tone for the evening and when Duran scored a technical knockout against Moore to capture a third world title, the sellout crowd cheered till they were hoarse even though the beaten boxer was fighting in his home city. Yet it was a supporting fight on the same bill that would soon be making the headlines – a welterweight contest between Luis Resto and Billy Collins Jnr.

Born in a small town in Puerto Rico, Resto moved to New York City with his mother and six siblings at the age of nine. He was a troubled youth and, after smashing his teacher in the face with an elbow, he spent six months in a Bronx hospital for the mentally disturbed. On being released, he packed groceries until channelling his energies and aggression into boxing. He won two New York Golden Gloves titles and in 1976 competed in the Olympic trials before turning professional. He briefly made the top ten at his weight but although he picked up the notable scalps of Domingo Ayala and Robert Sawyer and regularly sparred with Duran, he could never quite compete with the best. When it came to a bout against a world-class opponent, Resto was invariably found wanting. By the summer of 1983 he was 28. With his best days behind him, he had been consigned to the ranks of useful, journeyman fighters. His biggest failing was the lack of a decent knockout punch. He had a reputation as a light hitter – nimble enough around the ring but not particularly dangerous. In view of what would take place in the Collins fight, the assessment was ironic in the extreme.

Resto was not expected to make much of a mark on 21-year-old Collins, unbeaten in his fourteen professional fights and tipped to become a future champion. But at the end of the bout it was Collins whose face was battered and bruised – a hideous mass of purple welts. His eyes were virtually shut, his nose was broken and his cheeks grotesquely swollen. He had taken a fearful beating from one of the sport's least feared punchers. Immediately after the final bell, Billy Collins Snr, who worked his son's corner, sportingly shook Resto's right glove, saying 'Good fight'. But as he did so, Collins' father made a startling discovery.

'Hey!' he yelled. 'All of the padding is out of the damn gloves. It's all out.'

A speechless Resto looked across the ring for help from his trainer-manager, Carlos 'Panama' Lewis.

'Commissioner... Commissioner!' continued Collins. 'No padding... There's no damn padding.'

The padding had been removed from each of Resto's gloves with the result that Collins had been receiving hammer blows from bare fists. 'It felt like I was getting hit by an ashtray,' he said afterwards. The damage was all too plain to see on his pulped face.

Acting upon the protest of Collins Snr, John Squeri, chief inspector of the New York State Athletic Commission, took the gloves from Resto's dressing room despite the objections of Lewis. The gloves were placed in a cardboard box and handed to commission chairman Jack Prenderville who in turn gave them to Jack Graham, another member of the commission. According to an article in *Inside Sports* magazine, Graham left the gloves in the trunk of his car before taking them to the manufacturer, Everlast, for inspection. From there, the gloves made their way to an upstate police laboratory where, four days after the fight, tests revealed that a three-quarter inch hole had been cut into the lower palm side of each glove through which the padding had been deliberately removed. On hearing this, the commission stripped Resto of his victory and changed the result of the fight to 'no contest'.

Confronted with the evidence, Lewis denied any wrongdoing and claimed that he was the victim of a witch-hunt. His activities had aroused suspicion before. Only the previous year he had been suspected of improper behaviour while working in Aaron Pryor's corner during a light welterweight fight with Alexis Arguello. Pryor had looked out on his feet in round thirteen when, back in the corner, television microphones picked up Lewis asking one of his seconds for a special bottle – 'the one I mixed'. Pryor suddenly came out for round fourteen with a remarkable burst of energy and quickly stopped Arguello. Back in his dressing room after the fight, Pryor was seen doubled up in pain, rolling around on the floor. There were mixed reports about what was in the bottle, but Lewis denied it was anything illegal. Pryor was not subjected to a urine test and the bottle disappeared. But this time there would be no way out.

In 1986 Lewis was convicted of second-degree assault, criminal possession of a dangerous weapon (Resto's gloves), conspiracy and tampering with a sports contest. He served $2\frac{1}{2}$ years of a six-year sentence. Resto was also convicted of the first three charges and served $2\frac{1}{2}$ years of a three-year sentence. Both men were banned from boxing for life.

Resto still maintains his innocence, claiming that the gloves were switched some time between the end of the fight and their arrival at the police laboratory. 'The gloves felt the same as always,' he told *Boxing Monthly* in March 2000. 'There were no holes. Before the fight (referee) Tony Perez felt the gloves and didn't feel anything wrong. If the padding was out, when you hit somebody, you'd feel pain. You'd break your hands. My hands were fine. And if I knew the gloves had been tampered with, why would I have gone to Collins' corner after the fight?'

However, there are few listeners to Resto's conspiracy theory, partly because of what happened subsequently to Billy Collins. The young boxer with the world apparently at his feet had taken such a terrible beating at Resto's ungloved hands that he never fought again. His vision permanently blurred – the result of a torn iris – he became increasingly drunk and depressed and nine months after the fight he drove his car off the road in Antioch, Tennessee. He landed in a creek and died upon impact. His father was convinced that he committed suicide. Of Lewis and Resto, he said simply: 'They killed my son.'

A Helping Hand From the Gallery

1983

The British media has a reputation for building people up to stardom and then knocking them down when they reach the top, whether they are actors, singers or sportsmen. It all boils down to our love of the gallant loser as opposed to the clinically successful champion, which explains why Henry Cooper is still more revered than Lennox Lewis and Colin Montgomerie is more popular on this side of the Atlantic than Nick Faldo. In America winning is everything; in Britain it can be the kiss of death.

Faldo has never had a particularly amicable relationship with the media, who have failed to warm to his single-minded approach. He has trodden on more toes than John Prescott at a Labour Party dance while a few ill-judged comments have done little to build bridges with his detractors. In his victory speech at the end of the 1992 Open he famously thanked the media 'from the heart of my bottom'. It was Faldo's idea of a joke; it was the tabloids' idea of a declaration of war. Thus it has been with great delight that they have chronicled his divorces, professional fallouts and the occasion when his young girlfriend, feisty twenty-year-old American golf student Brenda Cepelak, took a sand wedge to Faldo's Porsche following the break-up of their relationship. Faldo was rumoured to be furious – saying she should have used an eight iron.

Neither has Faldo gone out of his way to endear himself to his fellow players. Commenting on the lack of conversation during a typical Faldo round, American Mark Calcavecchia once said: 'Playing with Nick Faldo is like playing by yourself – only slower.'

Much of the ill-feeling towards Faldo can be traced back to 6 October 1983 when he was competing in the World Matchplay Championship at Wentworth. His first-round opponent was Australia's Graham Marsh (brother of cricketer Rodney). The match was played over 36 holes and, having squared things at the 33rd, Faldo pulled his second shot at the par-four 34th, sending the ball scuttling through the green. Before his supporters could express their disappointment, the ball suddenly reappeared three or four seconds later on the green, having clearly been tossed back on to the fringe by someone in the gallery. It was a despicable exhibition of patriotism, one that clearly had no place on the golf course, but unfortunately match referee Bill McCrea did not see the incident. And when the marshal on the spot told him there was no indication that the ball had been thrown back, but was merely the recipient of a lucky ricochet, Faldo was able to continue. Furthermore since it was ruled that the ball had not stopped moving, he was entitled to play it from where it lay. Sections of the crowd let their feelings be known by booing the Englishman but, totally unruffled, he kept his composure and got down in two. Marsh, however, was less fortunate and three-putted – the only time in the entire match that he had done so – to lose the hole. To make matters worse, some British supporters cheered as Marsh missed his short putt to halve the hole.

Faldo went on to win the next hole to clinch a 2&1 victory, whereupon the courteous Marsh congratulated him on his success. Afterwards a number of spectators were so incensed by Marsh's treatment that they apologised to him but he decided against launching a formal appeal. One of the crowd marshals took matters further by manhandling Faldo and calling him a cheat. That marshal was duly sacked; the one who had erroneously advised the referee went unpunished.

In the wake of the unsavoury affair, Faldo was roundly attacked by the tabloid press for not conceding Marsh's second putt. Faldo saw no reason to apologise. 'What I did was right,' he insisted. 'I came up to the green innocent. Why should I have given him a three-foot putt when I hadn't seen what had happened?'

Fair enough, but the episode served to reinforce the views of those who believed that Faldo was prepared to win at all costs. And not every Briton wept tears of sorrow when he lost in the final to Greg Norman.

There's Something About Mary

1984

As a schoolgirl in Bloemfontein, South Africa, Zola Budd pasted a cut-out picture above her bed of her idol, American athlete Mary Decker. A few years later, after the controversy of the 3,000 metres final at the 1984 Los Angeles Olympics, nobody would have blamed her if she had started sticking pins in it.

The Budd/Decker spat provided one of the most memorable images of the eighties – America's sweetheart sitting sobbing beside the track while the eighteen-year-old Budd, barefoot and bewildered, continued on her way to a crescendo of booing from the partisan home crowd. It was an unequal contest: the shy little Zola pitted against proud Mary, yet in the final reckoning it was David who tripped up Goliath...albeit unwittingly.

That the two ever came to be on collision course is remarkable in itself given their different paths to the top. Having broken her first record at thirteen, Budd had abandoned her university education to concentrate on athletic training and in January 1984 she ran 5,000 metres in 15 minutes 1.8 seconds – seven seconds faster than Decker's existing world record. However, her achievement could not be recognised as South Africa was banned from international sporting events because of its policy of apartheid. Determined to compete somehow at that summer's Olympics, and encouraged by her father, she decided to apply for British citizenship on the grounds that she had a British grandfather. With the *Daily Mail* taking up her case, she was granted an instant British passport and fast-tracked into their Olympic team – a cynical and shameful bid to secure a medal. The manner in which she had conveniently and suddenly become British caused considerable disquiet. Budd herself behaved like a rabbit trapped in the headlights of unwanted publicity, answering questions curtly in her clipped tones. The British public scarcely warmed to her – that is, until she put Mary Decker out of the Olympics.

By the time of the 1984 Games, the Golden Girl of US athletics was 26. She had missed out on the 1976 Olympics through injury and the 1980 Moscow Games because of the US boycott. Now on home soil the American public had decided that 1984 would be Decker's year. They loved her not only for her talent – she had won both the 1,500 and 3,000 metres at the 1983 World Championships in Helsinki – but also for her determination in pursuit of victory. At a 1983 track meeting in New York she had pushed Puerto Rican runner Angelita Lind to the ground when Lind, who was about to be lapped, failed to move to the outside to allow Decker to pass in comfort. Nothing, it seemed, was permitted to come between Mary Decker and winning.

Decker started as clear favourite for the 3,000 metres in Los Angeles. Despite the unseemly haste with which she had been introduced to the British Olympic team, the frail figure of Zola Budd was still very much an unknown quantity, competing in what would be her first major international competition. Prior to the race the athletes showed their running spikes to an official to ensure that they conformed to specifications. Since she always ran barefoot, Budd was left in a dilemma. She later recalled: 'I just picked up my feet and showed them to him, white plasters on my toes and all. The poor man nearly cracked up laughing, but what else could I have done? Everybody else had spikes and I had to show him something.' It was the only moment of light relief on what would prove to be a traumatic day for Budd.

Both Budd and Decker liked to run from the front. For the first half of the race Budd allowed the American to set the pace but then, with no sprint finish to speak of, she thought about making a long run for home. However, shaking off the world champion was no easy matter and at 1,700 metres Decker was literally right on her heels. Budd was about half a stride in front when Decker, running on the inside, hit one of the Briton's legs. The collision caused Decker to lose her momentum briefly but she put on a spurt so that five strides later she was once more almost level when Budd inched over towards the inside lane. They collided again and Budd, jolted by the impact, shot out her left leg for balance whereupon Decker's right foot spiked Budd's left heel, causing the American to crash heavily to the ground. As she fell, she ripped the wax paper number from Budd's back.

Budd looked back concernedly to survey the carnage and saw Decker lying in a crumpled heap by the side of the track. She was still there, sobbing inconsolably, when the leaders passed a lap later. Although Budd continued, her will was sapped by the hostility of the 85,000 crowd who, deprived of an American victory, vented their anger on the supposed villain of the piece. With tears streaming down her face, Budd trailed in seventh.

Afterwards she went over to offer Decker her hand but the American snapped: 'Don't bother.' Decker was then carried from the stadium nursing a hip injury. There was no danger of the incident being underplayed.

The Americans wanted blood – Budd's blood – and were sated when she was disqualified for infringing Rule 141 of the International Amateur Athletic Federation rule book, which states: 'Any competitor jostling, running across or obstructing another competitor so as to impede his or her progress shall be liable to disqualification.'

Budd protested her innocence, claiming that Decker had tripped herself. The view was supported by an independent witness, Romania's Maricica Puica, who went on to take gold. 'It was Mary's fault,' said Puica. 'She was the girl behind and should have seen the way forward.' The jury of appeal agreed and, after viewing videotapes, overturned the disqualification. Budd was reinstated.

Decker remained unmoved by the jury's decision. 'I hold Zola responsible for what happened,' she snarled. 'She tried to cut in without being in front. I tried not to push her, and I fell. Looking back, I probably should have pushed her.' After all, it would not have been the first time Decker had resorted to such measures. The less enlightened members of the American public reflected Decker's bitterness, subjecting Budd to a string of death threats.

Then a strange thing happened. The girl who had been dismissed by many Britons as a charmless mercenary suddenly became 'our Zola' as we took exception to the bullying and bad sportsmanship. She could have become a great British heroine – the perennial underdog – but seemed to possess neither the personality nor the desire to do so. For example, not for one moment did she consider that prime requisite for British sporting popularity – an appearance in pantomime.

While Decker, fully recovered from her injury, was setting a new world mile standard in 1985, Budd ran a bit in races of secondary importance and set a couple of meaningless records before being suspended in 1988 for attending (but not competing in) a cross-country event in South Africa. Angry and disillusioned, she promptly returned to her family in South Africa, thus abandoning her dream of achieving Olympic glory for Britain. Her exit marked the end of a sorry chapter in the history of British athletics, one that was made all the more reprehensible by Budd's persistent refusal to condemn apartheid.

Even today as a wife and mother, Zola Budd is haunted by that day in 1984 and memories of Mary Decker. 'It was like your worst nightmare coming true,' she says. 'Mary says she's forgiven me, but she still blames me.'

The Golfer Who Cheated

1985

Scottish golfer David Robertson was hailed as a star of the future in 1972 when, at the age of fifteen, he became one of the youngest players in history to qualify for the British Open. A former British boys' and youth champion, he became the first player ever to represent Scotland in the same year at boys', youth and senior level and in 1974 the young man from Dunbar took the inevitable step of turning professional. Yet a career that had promised so much eventually foundered in 1985 when Robertson was handed a record PGA ban for cheating during qualification for that year's Open.

Accusations of malpractice were nothing new to Robertson. He had been disqualified twice in his amateur days, once for wrongly marking his card in the Scottish boys' strokeplay championship, and once for improperly marking his ball in an East of Scotland Alliance meeting. Then in 1977, as a professional, he was 'given permission to withdraw' from the Portuguese Open after his playing partner had accused him of dropping a second ball in the rough. But it was another eight years before the cloud of controversy that had always hung over Robertson finally engulfed him.

The 28-year-old Scot was taking part in the first day of the Open qualifying competition on the Prince's course at Sandwich, Kent, alongside playing partners Simon Middleham of Haydock Park and Alvin Odom from the USA. On the tenth hole Robertson's caddie suddenly retired, reportedly because of concerns over the manner in which Robertson had been marking his ball on the green. A new caddie took his place but on the fourteenth Middleham and Odom summoned Royal and Ancient official Graeme Simmers to protest about Robertson's antics. After a lengthy discussion Simmers disqualified Robertson for not replacing his ball in the correct position on the green and ordered him to leave the course.

Witness statements suggested that he had sometimes moved the ball by as much as twenty feet. He apparently pulled off the deception by arriving at the green first, pretending to mark his ball, but merely picking it up and then carrying his marker on his putter around the green and dropping it much nearer the hole.

In August Robertson, who denied the allegations of cheating, attended a meeting of the Professional Golfers' Association's executive committee at The Belfry where he was recommended for expulsion. The committee said the circumstances surrounding his disqualification on 14 July had 'constituted a serious breach of the association's code of ethics'. After considering written statements from his playing partners and their caddies, the PGA announced: 'We were satisfied that Robertson had incorrectly replaced his ball on the green on more than one occasion during the round.'

Robertson was banned from the PGA European tour for twenty years and fined £5,000 – the severest punishment in the history of golf. He also lost his attachment to Musselburgh Golf Club, near Edinburgh. Still maintaining his innocence, he launched an appeal, which, somewhat bizarrely, he failed to attend. In his absence the PGA scrapped the fine but increased the ban from twenty years to life.

After seven years as a golfing pariah, Robertson successfully reapplied for his amateur status and played in some amateur events in the Lothian region.

The Hand of God

1986

Four years after the Falklands conflict and the sinking of the *Belgrano*, Argentina gained revenge over England thanks to their own 'pocket battleship', Diego Maradona. The England players knew in advance what to expect from the dazzling feet of Maradona but had not anticipated the part that his left hand would play in the destiny of the 1986 World Cup. For the goal he palmed over the head of the onrushing Peter Shilton to help Argentina into the semifinals ranks alongside Geoff Hurst's second strike in the 1966 final as the most contentious goal in the history of the tournament. However, with Maradona's effort there is no debate about the legality of the goal. Even the player himself has admitted, albeit belatedly, that he handled the ball. England were cleverly, but blatantly, robbed, leaving manager Bobby Robson to reflect that there is never a Russian linesman around when you need one.

By the Mexico World Cup Maradona was already a superstar, having been transferred three times for a world record fee, the most recent in 1984 taking him to Italian club Napoli for £6.9 million. England arrived in Mexico with cautious optimism, which quickly evaporated following a 1–0 defeat to Portugal and a dismal goalless draw with Morocco during which Bryan Robson dislocated his shoulder and the normally mild-mannered Ray Wilkins was sent off for throwing the ball at the Paraguayan referee. It was like Mother Theresa putting the boot in. Just when all looked lost and England were in danger of catching the early flight home that Scotland always book in advance, Gary Lineker conjured up a hat trick to destroy Poland. He then came up with two more in the second-round game against Paraguay to set up a mouthwatering quarterfinal with Argentina – the first meeting between the two countries since the Falklands War. It would take place on 22 June in Mexico City's Aztec Stadium.

From the moment the quarterfinalists were known, the Argentinian press hyped the game as revenge for the Falklands, putting Maradona on a par with General José San Martin, the nineteenth century revolutionary who helped liberate the country from its colonial shackles. Goalkeeper Nery Pumpido proclaimed: 'To beat the English would represent a double satisfaction for everything that happened in the Malvinas.' However, the respective governments were keen to play down the historical significance of the game and sent out a clear message to all concerned: 'Don't mention the war!' Argentina coach Carlos Bilardo received his warning in a personal phone call from his country's president Raul Alfonsin. Bobby Robson just wanted to concentrate on the football. Even Maradona offered conciliatory words in the prematch build-up, saying that 'when we go on the field it is the game of football that matters and not who won the war'.

Addressing his players before the match, Robson reminded them what Maradona was capable of but told them not to dwell on his importance. In his diary, Robson related how England would deal with the threat posed by the little man. 'We would crowd him, push him across the field. We would keep our back four in position, not lose our shape and not dive in.'

For the first half the plan worked well, Maradona and his team-mates being kept at bay with comparative ease. Then seven minutes into the second period Maradona tried to play a one-two with Jorge Valdano around the edge of the England penalty area. The return pass was intercepted by Steve Hodge but his clearance sliced into the air back towards his own goal. Caught on his heels and by surprise, Shilton was a shade slow off his line but at 6ft tall still looked favourite to punch the ball clear ahead of the 5ft 4in Maradona who had commendably kept on running, refusing to accept it as a lost cause. As Shilton lunged forward, the leaping Maradona, lifting his left arm slightly above his face, flicked the ball over the keeper's head and into the net. From some angles it looked like a clean header, but others showed it to be a clear-cut handball.

Shilton and a couple of his defenders immediately protested to the Tunisian referee Ali Bennaceur who was well placed to spot any infringement. Bennaceur waved them away without even bothering to consult his Bulgarian linesman, Bogdan Dotschev. From his vantage point in the England dugout Robson could scarcely believe what he was seeing. Under no doubt whatsoever that Maradona had palmed the ball into the net, he was fully expecting the referee to disallow the goal. It was only a few seconds later when he saw the official running back towards the centre circle that Robson turned to his assistant Don Howe and gasped: 'He's only gone and given it!'

England were still reeling when four minutes later Maradona scored a second goal that was as sublime as the first had been ridiculous. Picking up the ball from just inside his own half he waltzed past five England players on a mazy run before dummying a mesmerised Shilton and planting the ball into the unguarded net. Shell-shocked England eventually rallied late on with the introduction of John Barnes, who delivered a perfect cross from the left for Lineker to head home from close range. A couple of minutes later Barnes sent over another hanging cross that had Lineker's name written all over it, but just as England's ace marksman was about to apply the finishing touch, an Argentinian defender materialised from nowhere to smuggle the ball to safety. That was England's last chance, their World Cup dreams over for another four years.

Inevitably the post-match inquest centred on Maradona's opening goal. Many of the England players were unaware that he had palmed it into the net until they watched television replays of the incident. Terry Butcher actually asked him whether he had handled it, but Maradona simply smiled and pointed to his head. A little later in an interview Maradona said that if there had been a hand involved, it must have been the hand of God. The phrase would stick. No longer the diplomat, he added: 'That was a final for us. Much more than winning a match, it was about knocking out the English.'

One English player who did see Maradona's subterfuge was Glenn Hoddle. 'I have seen that done in Sunday morning matches at the local park,' said Hoddle, 'and the players there have never got away with it.' Hoddle did concede that Maradona had disguised it cunningly, flicking his head at the same time that he palmed the ball.

Bobby Robson was in shaking of the head mode, a scene to be repeated after Chris Waddle blasted his penalty into the stratosphere four years later. 'Of course I'm not happy that Maradona punched in their first goal,' he lamented, 'especially since I knew it would be crucial. I wish Lineker could have done the same for us near the end, but he wouldn't have thought of that, would he?' Bookmakers William Hill were equally appalled and volunteered to refund all stake money to customers who had bet on a draw. A spokesman said: 'We were stunned when their first goal, a blatant handball, was allowed. We feel that the moral result should have been 1–1.' When bookmakers start behaving generously and talking of morals, it gives an indication of the scale of atrocity that Maradona had committed. On a more predictable note, certain organs north of the border voted Maradona Scottish Player of the Year.

Of course Argentina went on to win the World Cup by defeating West Germany in a final that English fans wanted both teams to lose. Maradona's status as national hero took a knock in 1991 when he was charged with the consumption and distribution of cocaine, as a result of which he was banned from all competitions for fifteen months. At the 1994 World Cup, shortly after opening fire with an air rifle on a group of journalists, he again tested positive for drugs and was thrown out of the tournament, duly receiving another fifteen-month ban. He claimed the banned substances were part of a cold medication.

He remains unrepentant about the 'Hand of God'. In 2001 he told Channel 4's *Football Stories*:

> I was happy, I am happy and I will always be happy with the goal I scored with my hand. All I can do is offer the English a thousand apologies, but I'd do it again. As a boy of five or ten I used to score goals with my hands in the minor leagues and I continued to do it when I played in the First Division.
>
> In Argentina, a carterista is a pickpocket. They get on a crowded bus, bump into people and steal their wallets. That's

what I did to the English – I stole their wallet without them realising. Argentinians are proud because no one saw me. They identify with that.

In his team talk before the 1986 quarter-final, Bobby Robson had warned his players that Maradona could change a game in five minutes. It was a shame he had to take Robson at his word.

When Mike Met Shakoor

1987

Relations on the cricket field between England and Pakistan were decidedly strained in 1987. Trouble had been simmering for months until it finally boiled over in an ugly altercation between England captain Mike Gatting and Pakistani umpire Shakoor Rana at the second Test in Faisalabad. As the most acrimonious England tour since 'Bodyline' threatened to provoke a diplomatic crisis between the two countries, the Foreign Office intervened and lent heavily on the Test and County Cricket Board to ensure that a peace of sorts was restored.

The two teams saw a lot of each other that year. In the summer Pakistan toured England and won the five-test series 1–0. But the principal talking point was the constant criticism by Pakistan's outspoken manager, Hasib Ahsan, of experienced umpire David Constant, which eventually resulted in a request for the Englishman to stand down. With some justification the TCCB stood by their man but the intransigence did little to foster harmony between the two sides. For the most part the authoritative Imran Khan kept his more excitable players in check but when Imran was absent from the field during the Old Trafford Test and Javed Miandad took control, Pakistan discipline appeared to suffer. When the tourists' over rate dropped to eleven an hour, England manager Mickey Stewart voiced his displeasure. His comments were answered in kind by Hasib Ahsan who considered it 'objectionable' that Stewart should publicly accuse Pakistan of spoiling the image of cricket. The touchpaper had been lit.

By the time of the World Cup, which took place in India and Pakistan in November, Javed Miandad had taken over the captaincy following Imran's retirement. With a reputation of something of a firebrand, Javed was like a red rag to the bull that was Mike Gatting. It was not a question of *whether* trouble would break out between the two but *when*. Sure enough when Javed was given out lbw, there was an altercation. Javed claimed that Gatting had sworn at him – an accusation which Gatting denied – and, according to reports, went to take a swing at the English captain. The incident was quickly defused but the bad blood persisted.

Immediately after the World Cup England embarked on a three-test series in Pakistan. They did so without three of their senior players – David Gower, Allan Lamb and Ian Botham. While the absence of Botham, who had been fined £1,000 by the TCCB in 1984 for joking that Pakistan was an ideal place to send your mother-in-law on holiday, was hardly a blow to cordial relations between the two sides, at least that trio had experience of touring Pakistan and knew of the problems that could arise from biased umpiring.

The First test in Lahore was riddled with umpiring errors as leg-spinner Abdul Qadir, with figures of thirteen for 101, helped his team to an innings victory, but the worst incident was the refusal of England opener Chris Broad to leave the wicket after being given out caught behind in the second innings. Broad might have expected a hefty fine for his petulance but instead he received nothing more than a mild reprimand. Furthermore tour manager Peter Lush then issued a statement to the press in which he was critical of the standard of umpiring in the match. Appearing distinctly ungracious in defeat, Gatting warmed to Lush's theme with a diatribe of his own. Bemoaning the fact that England had not been allowed to compete on an even basis, Gatting complained:

> When we come to Pakistan, the umpiring always seems to be the same. I've never seen it as blatant as this. I warned the younger players beforehand what they could expect, but until you've experienced it you can't comprehend how the game is played out here. If I were the opposition, I wouldn't be very happy about the way they had won. Still, to them a win is a win – that's all that seems to matter.

Gatting claimed that nine of the twenty England wickets to fall had been to wrong decisions, all but one by the same umpire, Shakeel Khan, standing in only his fifth Test. He called for more experienced umpires to stand in the remaining matches, adding ominously with regard to the second Test: 'If the umpiring is the same as here, it doesn't matter what we do – we can't win.'

Pakistan's response was to call up one of their most experienced – and controversial – umpires, Shakoor Rana, for the second Test, which was due to begin in Faisalabad on 7 December. Rana's litany of dubious decisions had in the past provoked Australian fast bowler Jeff Thomson to kick over the stumps, Indian batsman Anshuman Gaekwad to confront the entire Pakistan team, and New Zealand to walk off the field. This last incident occurred at Karachi in 1984–5 when Rana rejected the Kiwis' appeal for caught-behind against Javed Miandad. So it is fair to say that Rana would not exactly have been England's first choice of umpire.

The first two days of the Test actually went England's way, although the TV microphone placed behind the middle stump revealed that all was not sweetness and light out in the middle. When a bat-pad catch against a Pakistan batsman was turned down, Gatting was heard to moan, 'One rule for one and one rule for another', followed by Bill Athey muttering: 'The sooner we get out of this f***ing country the better.' In reply to England's total of 292, Pakistan had struggled to 106–5 nearing close of play on the second day. Since Pakistan were on the rack, Gatting was keen to fit in one more over. It was then that it all kicked off.

With spinner Eddie Hemmings bowling, Gatting decided to bring David Capel up from deep square leg and informed the batsman, Salim Malik, that this was what he was doing. Seeing Capel moving in too close, Gatting then gestured for him to stay back, saving one. Hemmings hesitated in his run-up, went back and started again, but no sooner had he delivered the ball than Rana, standing at square leg, called out 'Stop, stop!' In the mistaken belief that Gatting was changing the field behind Malik's back, Rana accused the England captain of 'unfair play' and said: 'You're cheating.' An incredulous Gatting replied: 'I'm allowed to move my fielders where I want, and in any case I wasn't moving him, I was only stopping him. As far as I'm concerned it has always been up to the non-striking batsman to keep the striker informed of field changes behind him, and in any case I'd already told Salim myself.' Gatting added that since Rana was the square leg umpire anyway, there was no need for him to interfere. Instead, suggested Gatting, he should go back to square leg, keep quiet, and allow the players to get on with the game. Rana did not take kindly to this advice and apparently repeated the cheating accusation whereupon Gatting reacted angrily, resulting in an eyeball-to-eyeball, finger jabbing confrontation that had no place on the cricket field.

After Gatting had been ushered away by Athey, Rana announced that he was reporting Gatting 'for using foul and abusive language. No captain has spoken to me like that before.' Rana also threatened to stand down from the remainder of the Test unless Gatting apologised. To his credit Gatting, who had been wrongly accused of cheating in the first place, said he was prepared to apologise if Rana did too, but the umpire refused. England took the field on the third day but Pakistan chose to stay in the pavilion in support of Rana who was still waiting for his apology. Whether they would have demonstrated such solidarity had they been in a winning position is open to question.

The future of the entire tour was now in jeopardy and some observers – including respected former Test star Tom Graveney – called for the England players to return home immediately. However, the Foreign Office pressured the TCCB to find a solution to the impasse and on the rest day Peter Lush drove to Lahore to see the president of the Board of Control for Cricket in Pakistan, Lieutenant-General Safdar Butt. The latter was not optimistic. 'The series might be called off,' he predicted, 'because there is no point playing the game of cricket if this is the feeling to prevail between the umpires and one of the sides.' Eventually the TCCB ordered a reluctant Gatting to make an apology, which he did with a scribbled note on a scrap of paper. With Rana's honour satisfied, the match resumed a day late but petered out into a tame draw.

The incident led to renewed calls for neutral umpires to stand in Test matches. Ironically it was a move that had long been advocated by Pakistan but not by the TCCB.

After expressing his disappointment in Gatting's behaviour, TCCB chairman Raman Subba Row made the surprising decision to award each member of the England party a hardship bonus of £1,000. To many onlookers it appeared that they were being rewarded for helping to drag the good name of English cricket into the gutter.

Having ridden that particular storm, Gatting's downfall as England captain came six months later somewhat closer to home. In June 1998 it was reported that on the night before going in to bat against the West Indies at Trent Bridge, Gatting had invited a barmaid to his hotel room for a drink to celebrate his 31st birthday. Gatting denied any sexual impropriety but admitted that he had behaved 'irresponsibly'. Peter May, chairman of the TCCB selectors, announced that Gatting was being stripped of the England captaincy for the next Test because he had damaged the image of the game and of the England team. May added: 'We like to think it is the greatest honour in the game to play for England.'

Where the entire Pakistan nation had failed, a Nottinghamshire barmaid had succeeded – in bringing an end to Mike Gatting's reign as England captain.

A Korean Sit-in

1988

One of the best fights in the boxing competition at the 1988 Seoul Olympics took place after the bout had finished when irate South Korean officials invaded the ring and attacked the referee. And it was another hour before the ring could finally be cleared as the beaten boxer staged a sit-in to protest at the points decision that had gone against him.

South Korean boxers enjoyed a good sit-in. Back in 1964 at the Tokyo Olympics Choh Dong-kih took root after being disqualified in the first round of the flyweight competition. Displaying the stubbornness associated with his name, he sat down in the ring and fought off all attempts by officials to drag him out. In desperation they resorted to bribery, promising to order a review of the referee's decision if the boxer would only leave the ring. Dong-kih accepted the carrot and abandoned his sit-in after 51 long minutes.

At the 1984 Los Angeles Olympics the South Koreans felt that the judging was heavily biased against their boxers, in particular when US welterweight Jerry Page was given the nod over Kim Dong-kil. Four years later, now that they were hosting the Games, the Koreans went about settling a few old scores. American light middleweight Roy Jones clearly outboxed South Korea's Park Si-hun but was adjudged to have been beaten on points and, as more and more fights ended in controversial decisions, accusations of corruption and bias became rife. Whenever a South Korean lost, it seemed to herald a wave of protests. Trouble flared when light-flyweight Oh Kwang-soo lost a marginal verdict to Michael Carbajal of the United States and then the following day Korean bantamweight Byun Jong-il faced Alexander Hristov of Bulgaria.

From the outset New Zealand referee Keith Walker struggled to control proceedings. After warning Byun on three occasions to stop using his head as a battering ram, Walker eventually lost patience and ordered the judges to deduct a point from the Korean's score. And when Byun repeated the offence in the final round, Walker signalled for the deduction of a second point. Those two penalties cost Byun the fight.

As soon as the verdict was announced, an incensed Korean trainer, Lee Heung-soo, waded into the ring and hit referee Walker on the back, thus provoking a mini riot. Other Koreans, apparently under the misapprehension that Walker had also refereed the Carbajal–Kwang-soo fight, joined in the pursuit of the hapless official who had to be rescued from the onslaught by his fellow referees. Fending off the attackers and a hail of chairs that were being thrown into the ring, they handed Walker over to security guards so that he could be escorted safely from the arena. This proved a major miscalculation as the guards were every bit as angry with the verdict as the coaches and trainers. One guard aimed a kick at Walker's head while the Chief of Security, after first taking the precaution of removing his uniform, chased Walker around the arena. When quizzed later, he proclaimed: 'I acted instinctively for the love of my fatherland.'

Meanwhile the fracas continued, the Koreans venting their spleen on Emil Jetchev, the Bulgarian president of the Referees' Committee of the International Amateur Boxing Association. When a Korean coach attempted to smash Jetchev on the head with a plastic box, the blow was intercepted by an American judge, Stan Hamilton, who had to receive medical treatment for a badly cut hand.

With order finally restored, the beaten Byun sat down to stage a silent protest in the centre of the ring. The lights were turned out – presumably in the hope that he was scared of the dark – but Byun's lonely vigil continued. After 35 minutes a squatters' rights campaigner gave him a chair and Byun sat there in comfort for another half-hour, comfortably breaking Choh's Olympic sit-in record. At last, 67 minutes after he had started, Byun decided that he had made his point but before leaving the ring he bowed graciously to the near-empty auditorium. In the aftermath five Korean boxing officials were suspended, the president of the Korean Olympic Committee resigned and the South Korean government issued a formal apology to New Zealand.

As for referee Walker, he caught the first flight home. Ironically, earlier in the tournament he had been pilloried by Irish officials for failing to penalise Korean welterweight Song Kyung-sup for head-butting. Who'd be a boxing referee in South Korea?

The Shaming of Ben Johnson

1988

When Ben Johnson sprinted to victory in the Olympic men's 100 metres final in a world record time of 9.79 seconds, Canada was celebrating its first track-and-field gold medal for 56 years. Amid scenes of great rejoicing, the *Toronto Star* carried the banner headline: BEN JOHNSON – A NATIONAL TREASURE. Two days later Olympic officials walked into Johnson's room and walked out with the gold medal. He had tested positive for steroid use and was sensationally stripped of his title – the most dramatic disqualification since drug testing had been instigated in 1968. Once again Johnson was headline news across the world, but this time for all the wrong reasons. The national treasure had become a national disgrace.

The Ben Johnson story began in Falmouth, Jamaica, in 1961. A small shy boy, he developed a stammer at the age of twelve as a result of constantly mimicking his older brother's speech impediment. At fourteen, he moved with his family to Toronto where, following a sudden teenage growth spurt, he began to show an aptitude for sprinting and came under the watchful eye of crack coach Charlie Francis. Competing in the 1980 Pan-American Junior Championships, Johnson gained his first view of a sight with which he would become all too familiar over the next five years – the heels of Carl Lewis. Johnson was so obsessed with Lewis that in the 1984 Olympic final he deliberately false-started in an attempt to unnerve the American. The plan didn't work. Lewis took gold; Johnson had to settle for bronze. In fact it was not until 1985 that, after seven consecutive defeats, Johnson finally got the better of his great rival.

In that same year Johnson gave an interview to Canada's *Athletics* magazine, which would acquire extra significance in view of events to come. Insisting that no drugs would ever pass into his body, he said: 'Drugs are both demeaning and despicable and when people are caught they should be thrown out of the sport for good.'

Johnson's hypocrisy was breathtaking. As early as 1981 Francis had persuaded him to take anabolic steroids on the grounds that everyone else was doing so. Afraid of being left behind, Johnson went along with Francis's prescription for success. By 1986 Johnson had got the measure of Lewis and was being hailed as the fastest man on earth. Bursting out of the blocks with phenomenal pace and power, he racked up five straight victories over Lewis, culminating in the 1987 World Championships in Rome where he set a new world record of 9.83 seconds. Lewis could only finish second – a full tenth of a second behind – and afterwards launched a tirade against athletes who took performance-enhancing drugs. No names were mentioned, but it was clearly a thinly veiled attack on Johnson. Lewis was by no means the first to voice suspicions about the Canadian who was nicknamed 'Benoid' by other athletes on account of his yellow-tinged eyes and highly sculptured muscles – both signs of steroid use. However, Francis was always quick to remind the accusers that Johnson had passed countless drug tests.

At the start of 1988 Johnson appeared to be in pole position to take the Olympic title in Seoul, but then a series of injuries severely hampered his preparation. When he returned to competition in the summer, he suffered an alarming dip in form and twice trailed in third behind Lewis who was now installed as the Olympic favourite.

At Seoul Lewis cruised into the final almost without breaking sweat. Johnson, too, seemed to have suddenly rediscovered his zest and earned his place among the elite with a convincing semifinal run. The final took place on 24 September. Johnson got off to his usual blistering start and this time Lewis was unable to overhaul him. The gold and the glory were Johnson's. Not wishing to be accused of sour grapes again, Lewis kept his counsel about Johnson's performance.

An hour after his win, the new Olympic champion and toast of Canada entered the doping control area for the mandatory test on the first four finishers. Struggling to produce a urine sample, he was obliged to drink three beers and some liquid from a flask that he had left in a bag during the race. Two days later the Canadian team received a letter from the IOC medical commission informing them that Johnson's first test had proved positive. Three hours later his second sample was also found to be positive. A Canadian team official said that when Johnson was given the news he 'appeared to be in a complete state of shock. It was like he didn't know what was going on around him. He was just not able to speak.'

At 3.30 the following morning Canadian Olympic chief Carol Anne Letheren visited Johnson to collect his gold medal. 'We love you,' she told him, 'but you're guilty.' Seven hours later Johnson's disqualification was confirmed by the IOC. The International Amateur Athletics Federation annulled his world record and he was suspended from competition for two years. Johnson denied using steroids, Francis claiming that someone must have spiked the athlete's drink while it lay unattended in the flask. He even hinted that the Lewis camp might have been responsible.

Britain's Linford Chrstie, who was promoted to second by Johnson's exclusion, expressed sympathy for the Canadian. 'It's not a nice way to win a medal,' said Christie. 'There's a certain sadness about it. It's a very sad day for athletics as a whole.' (Ironically, Christie himself received a two-year ban after testing positive for the anabolic steroid nandrolene in 1999). However, British distance runner Eamonn Martin took a different view. 'This sort of thing brings shame on his country and on the whole world of sport. Despite all the suspicious rumours flying about Ben, I kept an open mind. Now we know they weren't rumours. It's a good thing they have caught someone at the top. We are better off without him.'

While Johnson reeled from the prospect of losing millions of dollars in endorsements and sponsorship fees, the Canadian government ordered an official inquiry into the use of banned substances. Johnson's doctor, Jamie Astaphan, revealed the full details of the athlete's history of steroid use, which apparently included an injection 26 days before the Olympic final. That injection contained a compound used to fatten cattle before they are sent to market. Johnson himself appeared before the inquiry in June 1989 and finally admitted to having taken steroids. Three months later the IAAF stripped Johnson of his 1987 world record even though he had passed the drug test in Rome.

After serving his suspension, Johnson returned to competition in 1991 but two years later he tested positive again at a Montreal track event and was banned for life by the IAAF. Reduced to appearing as a novelty act, in 1999 he ran against two racehorses and a stock car in a charity event in Charlottetown, Prince Edward Island, finishing third when the car became bogged down in the mud.

Ben Johnson could well have been an Olympic champion without the use of drugs. But he will never know. These days he cuts a forlorn figure as he reflects: 'It kind of feels sad to think how fast I could have gone.'

Clough Gets Rough

1989

There was no sitting on the fence with regard to Brian Clough. You either loved him for his brash, outspoken arrogance or you hated him for the same reasons. The red three-quarters of Nottingham revered him for his achievements in taking a relatively modest club such as Forest to European Cup glory, as a result of which he became second only to Robin Hood in terms of the city's affection.

The only thing that was predictable about Clough was his unpredictability. Players, staff and journalists never knew what to expect from one day to the next. He liked it that way. It kept everyone on their toes. He was a man of contradictions – a firm disciplinarian who would suddenly allow the players to let their hair down on the eve of a cup final, a man who would sign a player (Trevor Francis) for a record fee of £1 million and then make him clean his own boots and those of his team-mates before consigning him to the third team for his Forest debut. One constant, however, was his distaste for antisocial behaviour in others. He was the first manager to make a stand on swearing among supporters and, as two Forest fans discovered to their cost in January 1989, he was none too keen on pitch invasions either – no matter how good-natured they were.

Forest had just beaten Queen's Park Rangers 5–2 at the City Ground to reach the semifinals of the League Cup. As Clough rose from the dugout, he found his way blocked by fans leaping about in scenes of wild celebration. Later comparing it to having uninvited guests burst into his kitchen, he reacted angrily and gave a couple of the trespassers a sharp clip around the ear. In his autobiography he wrote: 'I was bloody furious that they had "come over the wall" and that I was having difficulty getting past them... I detest seeing fans on the pitch, or on the edges of it, and I simply struck out. I clipped or belted two or three of them who just happened to be nearest to me as I made for the tunnel.' Unfortunately for Clough, television cameras captured the incident.

He had hit one fan with such force that when he did make it to the dressing room he needed treatment from the club physio for an injured wrist. He then joined assistant manager Ronnie Fenton in his office and told him: 'I've just hit a couple of supporters who ran on to the pitch. I think I've really done it now.'

One of the young victims of Clough's novel interpretation of the striker's role said: 'He was just swinging round like a madman. He just thumped me on the back of the head – I thought it was a QPR fan. I couldn't believe it when I turned round and saw it was Brian Clough.'

Clough decided to nip the incident in the bud by going to chairman Maurice Roworth to apologise. He also offered his resignation but must have known that he was on safe ground. After all, it was Roworth who, when Clough led the club to relegation a few years later, made no mention of the demotion in his end-of-season appraisal but instead congratulated Clough on winning the youth league. Sure enough Roworth backed his manager to the hilt when the news broke the following day, pointing out that the fans had no permission to be on the pitch and that ninety per cent of callers to a local radio station were in favour of Clough's actions. Asked whether Clough deserved to get the sack, Roworth replied: 'Sack? No way, he's got us into another semifinal.'

Clough also issued a public apology, calling the incident 'regrettable' but insisting that he acted with the best of intentions. 'I was concerned about a possible confrontation between our supporters and theirs,' he explained. 'It is a very frightening situation when you have 300 people running on to a football field. I just wanted to help the police clear the pitch as quickly as possible.'

Clough was inundated with letters of support, including one from Labour Party leader Neil Kinnock and one from a chief superintendent in Sheffield. Kinnock wrote: 'Anyone who has ever seethed at hooliganism and pitch invasion will understand why you did what you did on the spur of the moment.' Not everyone took such a charitable view. Some considered that it was another example of Clough being way too big for his boots, one scribe suggesting that the incident was a case of 'the shit hitting the fan'.

Clough knew the value of good publicity and soon afterwards kissed and made up with two of the errant fans on local television. The police issued him with an official warning over his behaviour and, after he had promised the FA that he would try very hard to control himself in future, he escaped with a touchline ban and a £5,000 fine. He could have raised that by taking back his empties.

The entire episode summed up his love-hate relationship with so many people, including his former assistant Peter Taylor. One minute they were an inseparable team, the next Clough was refusing to speak to him. It was the same with the fans – hitting them one day, kissing them the next. In more ways than one, there were no half measures with Brian Clough.

The Aga Saga

1989

Prince Karim Aga Khan IV – better known as the Aga Khan – is one of the most successful owner/breeders in the world. Back in 1989 his family had been associated with the British racing scene for 68 years in what was a mutually beneficial arrangement. He had ninety horses in training in England at the time, with Michael Stoute and Luca Cumani at Newmarket, and had won three Derbies with the ill-fated Shergar (1981), Shahrastani (1986) and Kahyasi (1988). The fillies' classic, the Oaks, had repeatedly eluded him but it seemed that the jinx had been broken when the Stoute-trained Aliysa, starting at 10–11 favourite, passed the winning post at the end of the 1989 race three lengths ahead of Snow Bride. Naturally a man of the Aga's experience never took anything for granted – there was always the danger that an unexpected stewards' inquiry might turn victory into defeat within twenty minutes – but even he did not expect his horse to be disqualified from first place 528 days later.

In July 1989 – a month after the Oaks – it was revealed that the routine post-race test conducted on Aliysa showed traces of camphor in the horse's urine. The use of camphor, an old-fashioned remedy employed for dealing with respiratory infections and for treating sprains and strains, had concerned the authorities the previous year when two trainers, Jack Berry and Gerald Ham, had their horses Meine Vonne Lady and Glen Lodge disqualified after winning races at Haydock Park and Devon and Exeter respectively. A notice subsequently appeared in the *Racing Calendar* in November 1988 warning trainers about the use of camphor, which is a prohibited substance under the Rules of Racing. When news broke of Aliysa's positive test, Stoute professed himself 'amazed and baffled' while a Newmarket veterinary surgeon, asked to assess the advantage that a horse could gain from being treated with camphor, said bluntly: 'I can't think it has any beneficial effects.' Nevertheless the Jockey Club in its wisdom had deemed it a banned substance and were thus duty-bound to pursue the matter to a conclusion.

The Aga Khan had successfully challenged positive tests for illegal medication in his racehorses on two previous occasions, notably in 1981 when Vayrann was disqualified from first place in the Champion Stakes after testing positive for an anabolic steroid. Now he and Stoute hired eminent Canadian scientists to prepare their case. In November 1990 the scientists argued that the source of 3-hydroxycamphor discovered in Aliysa's post-race urine test was not camphor at all but borneol, a substance contained in foodstuffs or the wood-shavings used for stable bedding. This evidence conflicted with that of the Horseracing Forensic Laboratory, who had conducted the test on Aliysa's sample. Using more sophisticated tests than the HFL, the Aga's experts poured scorn on the methods of their British counterparts, claiming they were hopelessly outdated. But the Jockey Club was standing by the HFL findings.

Since Aliysa had been guarded round the clock before the Oaks, there was no possibility that any camphor could have been administered deliberately, and indeed none of the lengthy Jockey Club investigations were able to offer any clue as to the source of the traces of 3-hydroxycamphor. Although the evidence against owner and trainer was inconclusive – reflected in Stoute's £200 fine – the Jockey Club decided to disqualify Aliysa and promote Snow Bride to first place. Aliysa thus became the first English classic winner to be thrown out for drug-related offences.

It was not simply the loss of the £108,500 prize money that rankled with the Aga; it was what he perceived as the incompetence and unfairness of the Jockey Club whose procedures, he said, were so designed that 'you are guilty until proven innocent'. Describing the drug testing of racehorses in Britain as an amateur system run by amateurs, the Aga Khan announced that he would be withdrawing all of his horses from training or racing in Britain until the Jockey Club reviewed its methods 'because I don't think it is possible to race under scientific conditions which are unsound'. Instead his string was sent to France, Ireland and the United States – a massive blow to Newmarket and to British racing in general. 'It was not a decision taken lightly,' he added, 'and it is not a decision taken happily. But I have to weigh that against the level of risk that I would be running if I continued with the present scientific circumstances as they have been demonstrated since the Vayrann case.'

In July 1991 he attempted to overturn the ruling but the High Court ruled that Jockey Club decisions were not susceptible to judicial review. So he took the case to the Court of Appeal, only to receive the same answer. British horseracing remained the loser until 1998 when the Aga Khan finally forgave the Jockey Club and sent his horses back to Newmarket.

The Hurricane Whips Up a Storm

1990

Every sport has its black sheep but the assorted misdemeanours of Irish snooker player Alex 'Hurricane' Higgins were worthy of an entire flock. Throughout a career that had more ups and downs than the Footsie, the self-styled People's Champion experienced numerous brushes with officialdom and fellow professionals alike. On more occasions than he probably deserved his temperamental outbursts and wayward behaviour were forgiven by those willing to make allowances in order to accommodate his undoubted talent and drawing power. That was the price you sometimes have to pay for genius, they reasoned. But in March 1990 he finally overstepped the boundaries of human decency with an attack on fellow Irishman Dennis Taylor that was as unwarranted as it was vitriolic.

Higgins and Taylor came from opposite sides of the divide in Northern Ireland. Higgins was a Protestant from Belfast, Taylor a Catholic from Coalisland. They were also contrasting characters – Higgins wild, undisciplined and mercurial; Taylor genial, polite and a great ambassador for the sport. They had known each other for years and when the young Higgins first came over to England in 1968, it was Taylor who took him under his wing, finding him somewhere to live and generally doing his best to help him find his feet. As Higgins turned increasingly to drink in later years, finding his feet would sometimes represent a formidable challenge.

By 1990 Higgins's best years were behind him. The World Championship triumph of 1982 was but a distant memory for the 41-year-old, although he had recently managed to fight his way back into the elite top sixteen following a ban. However, his private life was in turmoil and when his ex-wife Lynn refused to allow him into the house with presents for their children, he responded by hurling a skateboard through the window and was subsequently fined £50 for criminal damage. A few weeks later Higgins was part of the three-man Northern Ireland team competing in the World Team Cup at Bournemouth where his colleagues were Dennis Taylor (captain) and the inexperienced Tommy Murphy.

Higgins was clearly up for the fight but there were deep signs of unrest in the camp when, after helping the Irish to a place in the final against Canada, he told the press: 'If I'm not captain tomorrow, I'm not playing.' Persuaded eventually to turn out for the final, Higgins became more irrational than usual when he insisted on holding the prematch team meeting in the women's toilets. When asked why, he replied: 'Because we might be overheard in the men's.' The trouble with Higgins was that nobody could be sure whether or not he was joking, so Taylor and Murphy decided to indulge him. Then in the afternoon session Higgins demanded to stay on against Alain Robidoux when Taylor should have taken over. Higgins lost both frames to leave Northern Ireland trailing 6–2 at the interval. Taylor later remarked wearily: 'It was glory-hunting as usual because this meant he (Higgins) could play more frames in the evening. I am supposed to be the captain, but we let Alex have his own way just for a bit of peace and quiet.'

The Irish went on to lose 9–5 but at his post-match press conference, Higgins alluded to a major row that had taken place backstage during the interval. Taylor, who was in line for the £6,000 high-break prize, had allegedly said he would refuse to split the money with Higgins because the latter had made it clear in the past that he would keep any such winnings for himself. Higgins now blasted Taylor before the press: 'In my estimation,' he raged, 'Dennis Taylor is not a snooker person. He is a money person. The more he gets, the more he wants. He will never be sated. He puts money before country. He belongs back in Coalisland. He is not fit to wear this badge, the red hand of Ulster.'

Stung by the remarks, Taylor responded by criticising Higgins for his comments after the semifinal when, in front of witnesses, he had told Murphy he 'played like a c**t'. That, said Taylor, visibly shaking, 'was a good way to get him into shape for the final'. Taylor went on to reveal that in the course of their backstage row during the final Higgins had viciously insulted the memory of Taylor's late mother Annie (who had died in 1984) and had issued a chilling threat. Higgins had snarled: 'I come from the Shankill and you come from Coalisland. The next time you're in Northern Ireland I'll have you shot.'

A mix of fury and distress, Taylor, who had always made a point of steering clear of Northern Ireland politics, concluded: 'I was literally shaking when I went out to play tonight. I wanted to win this for Tommy, but everything was shaking.'

Higgins immediately denied the comment, saying: 'I never mentioned the Shankill. What I said was that I'd blow his brains out if I had a gun.' Taylor replied that he wished he'd had a tape recorder but in any case he had a reliable witness to the threat in the form of John Spencer, chairman of the World Professional Billiards and Snooker Association. Higgins was forced to backtrack and issued an apology through his manager Doug Perry 'for remarks made to Dennis, said in the heat of the moment'. Higgins added, presumably by way of justification: 'In this tournament I was not playing for Alex Higgins or financial gain – my heart was in doing my very best for my country.'

Even those who had tolerated some of Higgins's past excesses were appalled that he could threaten to have a fellow professional shot. In the *Sunday Times*, Clive Everton wrote of Higgins: 'He claims a child's licence to say the most hurtful things he can think of; and seeks adult refuge in alcohol and denial of unpalatable realities.'

Taylor was singularly unimpressed by the Higgins apology and the bad blood between the two men added extra spice to their quarterfinal meeting at the Irish Benson's tournament in Kildare the following week. In the ultimate grudge match, Taylor, who went on to win 5–2, briefly shook hands with Higgins at the start but refused to look him in the eye. At the post-match press conference Higgins was, as they say, 'tired and emotional'.

A month later he was in trouble again after suddenly punching press officer Colin Randle in the stomach following defeat at the Embassy World Championships in Sheffield. In a rambling, largely incoherent speech, Higgins then announced his retirement. 'I'd just had enough,' he said later. 'They were treating me like a dancing bear.' A dancing bear with a permanently sore head.

No sooner had Higgins started to think twice about retiring than the WPBSA handed him an enforced lay-off. He was banned for a year, stripped of 25 ranking points and ordered to pay £5,000 costs for the Taylor row and for the assault on Randle. The WPBSA did consider a life ban but 'concluded that the interests of snooker did not require Higgins to be expelled from the association'. The suspension would cost him over £100,000 in prize money. Naturally Higgins felt he had been harshly treated. 'I feel it is a very severe price I have to pay but I shall just have to live with it. I have to take it like a man.' He said he would eke out a living by playing exhibition matches to 'display my exceptional snooker talent to my loyal fans all over the world'.

Perhaps the most remarkable aspect of the whole Alex Higgins story was that he still had any. For as a bodyguard told one female fan: 'We're not here to look after Alex, we're here to protect the public from him.'

Gower's Flight of Fancy

1991

The England cricket team's tour of Australia in the winter of 1990–1 saw them plunge the sort of depths normally reserved for visitors to the *Titanic*. The first two Tests ended in crushing defeats – by ten and eight wickets respectively – and a draw in the third was sufficient for Australia to retain the Ashes. The battered tourists eventually returned home with a record of just one win in their eleven-match itinerary. Ironically that solitary victory came against Queensland in a match that was overshadowed by what turned out to be an imaginative but rather expensive prank.

David Gower liked to live dangerously and ruffle the feathers of authority. England's most elegant and gifted batsman of the past thirty years had aroused management anxiety a few years earlier when he and team-mate Allan Lamb sat in a bobsleigh on the famous Cresta Run. But at least the England hierarchy were aware of that one; his impromptu fly-past at Carrara took them completely by surprise.

Australia had already retained the Ashes when England flew from Albury to Carrara in the third week of January to play Queensland between the third and fourth Tests. The languid left-hander was notorious for growing bored with the long periods of inactivity on tour and with England in a good position at lunch on the third day, he and his old partner-in-crime Lamb discussed the possibility of livening up proceedings. It was very much a spur-of-the-moment decision. Gower had noticed that there was an airfield nearby and, during the lunch interval, proposed hiring a couple of planes that afternoon for a flight with a local instructor. Vice-captain Lamb was unable to take part because he was still batting but John Morris, with a century already under his belt, overheard and persuaded Gower to take him as his co-pilot. Morris was on his first tour and, as Gower subsequently acknowledged, 'probably thought that any escapade being talked over between senior player and vice-captain could not have been too far over the top'. Gower thought about asking captain Graham Gooch for permission to visit the airfield. 'But I knew he would have been unhappy with us flying, and as that was the entire point of the exercise, I decided that it was best not to mention it at all.'

And so while Lamb and Robin Smith – the latter nearing a century – resumed the England innings after lunch, Gower and Morris headed for the airfield. Morris confirmed afterwards: 'It was never meant to be a prank with any malice involved. We just thought a bit of light-hearted fun would help lift spirits.'

The pair had to wait a while for a flight and, after checking that Lamb and Smith were still batting, they took to the skies in the passenger seats of two 1939 Tiger Moth planes, hired at £27 apiece. After circling the ground a couple of times, Gower persuaded his pilot to dip down between the 200ft-high flood-light pylons and waggle the wings to salute Smith's century. Lamb had told Smith about the lunchtime conversation and the two batsmen, convulsed with laughter, now pretended to shoot down the passing planes with their bats.

Unbeknown to Gower, one of the pilots had alerted the local newspaper before taking off and on landing at the end of their fifteen-minute flight the two Englishmen were asked to pose for photographs in 'Biggles' leather flying helmets and goggles. Gower had not intended to publicise the stunt but was happy to oblige as a favour to the pilot.

Back at the ground, Gower was collared by a suspicious Gooch who inquired: 'That wasn't you up there, by any chance?' Gower feigned innocence with that faintly angelic look that made it impossible to disbelieve him. His secret remained intact until the evening press conference when a journalist asked about the two boys in the planes. Tour manager Peter Lush knew nothing about it and while team manager Mickey Stewart had seen the fly-past he though they were joyriders. When told who the occupants were, Stewart said: 'Are you serious? Two of mine?'

Gower had gone out for dinner but on his return he found no fewer than three urgently scribbled notes from Lush pushed under the door of his hotel room. The following morning he and Morris faced the music. Lush, Stewart and Gooch were all in favour of sending the pair home but Lamb who, according to Gower, 'was turned to the wall trying hard not to wet himself', pointed out the folly of such a punishment, not least because it would leave the side's batting understrength for the remainder of the tour.

So Gower and Morris were instead fined the maximum penalty of £1,000. Announcing the fines, Lush said that he and Gooch considered the incident 'immature, ill-judged and ill-timed'. Lush added that he was especially disappointed that Gower, as a senior member of the party, had failed to set a better example, and that one of the younger players (Morris) should have suffered as a result. Furthermore, continued Lush, the publicity had 'detracted from one of England's best performances on the field'.

Both players apologised, Gower recognising that perhaps he should have thought things through but still not understanding what all the fuss was about. 'It was pure fun,' he said recently. 'The fact they took it so seriously was a huge misjudgement – the most misguided reaction I've ever known from an England management.'

Wisden was sympathetic towards Gower's plight. 'For all their dereliction of duty in leaving without permission a game in which they were playing it was a harsh penalty for an essentially light-hearted prank, reflecting all too accurately the joyless nature of the tour.'

But Gower's heaviest punishment was still to come. Despite finishing second to Gooch in the Test averages for that tour with 45.22, he was dropped from the team. There can be little doubt that the unauthorised flight in Carrara contributed greatly to his nonselection. He was briefly recalled in June 1992 but when overlooked again he decided to quit the international arena that he had graced with such style.

So it proved a costly episode in every respect. 'It's certainly more expensive than flying from Brisbane to

Adelaide,' mused Gower when informed of his pecuniary punishment. 'If I had known what the fine would be, it might have made me think a bit more.'

Indian Mutiny

1991

Just a week after David Gower's Tiger Moth prank, cricket was again making the wrong sort of headlines when scenes of unprecedented violence broke out on the field during the final of the Duleep Trophy, India's premier tournament.

The five-day final was contested between the North Zone, captained by Kapil Dev, and the West Zone, led by fellow Test star Ravi Shastri, at the neutral venue of Jamshedpur in the East Zone. Batting first, North Zone compiled a massive 729–9 declared with 33-year-old Raman Lamba, who had played in four Tests for his country, top scoring with 180. West Zone replied with 561 and in their second innings the North had reached 59–0 with a quarter of an hour to go before tea on the final day. The match seemed to be drifting towards a tame draw when it suddenly exploded in what *Wisden* described as a 'violent action, senseless yet far from unprovoked' that 'will be remembered as the most shameful moment in the history of Indian cricket'.

The seeds of unrest had been sown earlier in the game when North Zone fast bowler Manoj Prabhakar, who later claimed he was acting on his captain's instructions, bowled a bouncer at tail-ender Rashid Patel. So as the North Zone openers came out to bat for a second time, Patel was fired up for revenge. The left-arm quickie had already taken a hammering in the first innings from Lamba, who, incidentally, by virtue of his Irish wife had played for Ireland against Sussex in the previous year's NatWest Trophy. Now Lamba started taunting him about his ineptitude, causing Patel to unleash a succession of hostile bouncers and beamers by way of retaliation. Eventually

Patel delivered another fearsome bouncer from way beyond the popping crease. Ramba drew away from the wicket and remonstrated with the bowler, accusing him of deliberately overstepping the mark in an attempt to cause personal injury. At this point Patel pulled out a stump and charged down the wicket towards Lamba. Non-striker Ajay Jadeja, who had followed Patel up the pitch to warn his team-mate of the impending assault, took the first blow on his elbow. Then Patel, waving the stump as a weapon, set off in pursuit of Lamba, chasing him all the way to third man. Lamba only managed to avoid serious injury by using his bat as a shield to fend off the repeated blows.

The savagery on the pitch was immediately reflected in the crowd, stones being thrown on to the playing area, and covers and any other inflammable material being set alight. The match was abandoned with North Zone being declared the winners on account of their first innings lead.

Madhav Rao Scindia, president of the Board of Control for Cricket in India, described the incident as 'outrageous, shameful and shocking'. He added: 'Such reprehensible actions...smear the fair name of the game. Nobody is above the game and those who violate cricket's spirit have no right to be part of this sport.' Bishen Bedi, India's tour manager to England in 1990, blamed the scenes on indiscipline among senior players and accused umpires V K Ramaswamy and Sabroto Banerjee of lacking courage. Bedi stated: 'No punishment is big enough for such a dastardly act.'

The Indian cricket board wasted no time in holding an inquiry. A three-man disciplinary committee met in Delhi and quizzed five players – Patel, Shastri and Kiran More of the West Zone and Lamba and Prabhakar of the North Zone. They also asked the umpires to explain why the match had been allowed to become so ill disciplined. The results of the inquiry were announced on 25 February. Twenty-six-year-old Patel, who had played one Test for India back in 1988, was banned from all cricket under the board's control until March 1992, a remarkably lenient sentence in view of the crime. Lamba was banned until December 1991. Shastri and More were reprimanded and told that their conduct had not been of the standard expected from senior players, while Prabhakar was warned as to his future conduct.

In a tragic footnote to this sorry episode Raman Lamba was killed during a club match in Bangladesh in 1998 after taking a fatal blow to the head while fielding at short leg.

The Grand National Fiasco

1993

The name of Esha Ness has become as much a part of Aintree folklore as that of Devon Loch. For the royal runner's misfortune in 1956 was mirrored 37 years later by Jenny Pitman's 50–1 outsider who passed the post in first place, only for the race to be declared void. It was the year that the world's most famous steeplechase was reduced to a shambles amid false starts, flag waving, non-flag waving, and angry recriminations. It was the year when it was not jockeys or trainers but humble recall man Ken Evans who suddenly became a topic of barroom conversation. It was the year that produced the Grand National that never was.

The 1993 National should have been a proud day for 64-year-old Captain Keith Brown who was starting the race for the fifth and final time, but it was to turn into a nightmare played out in front of millions on the worldwide TV stage. A total of £75 million had been bet on the great race but the first signs of a troublesome afternoon ahead occurred when, with the 39 runners milling around at the start, a group of animal rights protestors planted themselves in front of the first fence. His attention drawn to the demonstration, Captain Brown ordered the jockeys to 'take a turn' while police removed the trespassers. This caused a delay of some ten minutes by which time a number of the horses were becoming fractious. When the field did finally come into line, the starting tape was limp rather than taut and went up so slowly that it caught under the hooves of some of the horses. Captain Brown immediately waved his red flag to signal a false start and recall man Evans, who was positioned 100 yards further down the course to warn jockeys of any false start, claimed that he then flourished his flag to send the runners back (his version of events was subsequently disputed). Whatever, the horses that had set off were all pulled up before reaching the first fence.

With steady rain falling, horses and jockeys were growing increasingly restless. Captain Brown called them into line again but once more the tape failed to rise properly, almost strangling Richard Dunwoody on Won't Be Gone Long, who was consequently unable to go anywhere. Realising that the start was faulty, eight more jockeys quickly pulled up their mounts but the remaining thirty runners raced away in earnest. The recall man was conspicuous only by his absence, Evans later claiming that because the Captain's flag did not unfurl properly on the second occasion it had not been visible from his vantage point. As the field pressed on, an attempt was made to call a halt to the race at The Chair but the jockeys thought that the officials running along the course wielding traffic cones were more protestors. A handful of riders pulled up at halfway but nine went the full four and a quarter miles.

At the end of two arduous circuits, jockey John White thought he had achieved the highlight of his career on board Esha Ness ... but his joy was short-lived, the race being ruled void as Captain Brown had signalled a false start. Describing it as a 'nightmare experience', White revealed:

> It wasn't until I saw fellow jockey Dean Gallagher standing on the ground past the finish and he shouted that there had been a false start, that I realised anything was wrong. Afterwards I was numb with shock. Valet John Buckingham tried to get me to weigh in, which gave me another flash of hope, but the Aintree officials wouldn't let me sit on the scales. On the first false start I saw a chap with a white flag. I had not gone twenty yards and I pulled up knowing it was a false start. But when we jumped off the second time I didn't see any flag.

Asked by a TV interviewer why he had not realised there were a lot of horses missing, White laughed and replied: 'Ever ridden in a National? You don't have time to count horses.'

Jockey Peter Scudamore, another of those who had been oblivious to the second false start, said: 'The first time we all heard him (Captain Brown) say false start; the second time nobody heard a thing. I did not know a thing until I saw people waving after I had jumped The Chair. Then, when I had gone a full circuit, I saw trainer Martin Pipe waving at me. I thought, "if he's telling me to stop, it's right".'

The *Sunday Times* described it as 'arguably the greatest debacle in sporting history'.

Meanwhile Jenny Pitman was in floods of tears, Captain Brown was nearly accosted on his way to the weighing room and Evans needed a police escort to protect him from irate punters. Trainer David Elsworth called it 'a disaster and a great tragedy for the race'. Fellow trainer John Upson was more forthright, saying: 'It is an absolute disgrace that the world's number one National Hunt race is run like this. It would not happen in a point-to-point field in Ireland! All of the top jockeys say they saw no signs of flags whatsoever.'

After studying television coverage of the fiasco, the official inquiry pointed the finger of blame at flagman Evans, Captain Brown and the 'outdated' starting procedures. Having heard conflicting evidence, the inquiry concluded that Evans had failed to do his job on the day and had not raised his flag at either false start. He was further criticised for standing only 100 yards from the start, giving him a matter of seconds to get out of the way of advancing horses. Captain Brown was criticised for having allowed the runners to get too close to the starting tape, which stretched more than 65 yards across the track. The report said: 'We have no doubt that the proximity of the horses to the start line this year was a major contributory factor to the two false starts. He (Brown) is in control of the start and must be responsible for its proper and effective conduct.' Captain Brown had recommended that the width of the start be reduced after the 1991 race when the tape had also risen too slowly, but Aintree had rejected the idea. The report added that the starting gate was obsolete and should not have been used. 'Responsibility for its continued use,' said the report, 'has to be shared by the Jockey Club and by the Aintree executive.'

By the time of the 1994 National the starting tapes had been changed so that instead of going up vertically, they rose at a 45-

degree angle away from the horses. Hopefully there will never be a repeat of the day when British jump racing became a laughing stock.

The Fall of Olympique Marseille

1993

Bernard Tapie is France's answer to Jeffrey Archer. Politician, sportsman, felon, he's been them all. He even wrote a bestselling book in jail – just like our Jeffrey – and shares with the Bard of Weston-super-Mare that remarkable ability to bounce back from every adversity. In fact in terms of durability, Archer is strictly Ryman League to Tapie's Premiership. For the Frenchman has done so much more besides. He started out as a singer before reinventing himself in the 1980s as a venture capitalist. He then briefly hosted his own talk show, *Ambitions*, on French TV, sailed the Atlantic in record-breaking time, served as his country's Minister of Urban Affairs and owned football club Olympique Marseille. Add to that actor, radio host and rap star and you will have some idea of the versatile French phenomenon that is Bernard Tapie.

However, to most people this side of the English Channel, he is known for one thing only – masterminding the bribes scandal that saw Olympique Marseille banned from Europe, stripped of their European Cup win and their French League title and demoted to the Second Division. For a club that had been crowned French champions for five successive years, it was an astonishing fall from grace.

Like Lord Archer, Tapie was not everyone's cup of tea. His successes in the fields of politics, business and sport had antagonised a number of people who were eager to shoot him down. In the spring of 1993 he provided them with all the ammunition they needed.

In May of that year Olympique Marseille were closing in on another League title and a European Champions Cup final.

No French club had ever lifted a European trophy and their meeting with AC Milan in Munich was keenly anticipated. However, on 20 May, six days before the final, Marseille faced a tricky League match at Valenciennes, which they needed to win to maintain their position at the head of the table. It was an equally important game for Valenciennes who, seventeenth in the table, were staring relegation in the face. A crowd of over 18,000 packed into Valenciennes' compact ground and saw Allen Boksic put the visitors ahead in the first half with what would turn out to be the only goal of the game. Bizarrely at half-time the referee was locked in earnest discussions with the home team.

On course for the League, Marseille completed the first half of their double with a 1–0 victory over AC Milan thanks to a Basile Boli header. Briefly at least, the biggest club in France were also the most popular. Then three days later they wrapped up the League by defeating Paris St Germain 3–1. But storm clouds were gathering on the horizon. The daily sports paper *L'Equipe* carried allegations made by Valenciennes sweeper Jacques Glassmann regarding the match with Marseille. 'They wanted to buy us off,' said Glassmann. 'I was offered 200,000 francs if I didn't try too hard, and I'm not the only one: approaches were also made to Jorge Burruchaga and Christophe Robert.'

The National Football League president Noël le Graët immediately promised a full investigation, insisting: 'If there has been any attempt to alter the course of the League results, I can assure you that Marseille will not be appearing in Europe next season.'

On 24 June Valenciennes midfielder Robert was arrested. He claimed that prior to the game he and Glassmann had been phoned in their hotel room (in the presence of the Argentinian Burruchaga) by Marseille midfielder Jean-Jacques Eydelie. Robert said that Eydelie then passed the phone to Marseille's general manager, Jean-Pierre Bernès, who arranged for Robert to be paid 250,000 francs (about £30,000) on the agreement that Valenciennes would take it easy during the match. Robert revealed that his wife, Marie-Claire, collected the money from Eydelie in the car park of

Marseille's team hotel. Investigators duly found 250,000 francs in an envelope hidden in the garden of Robert's aunt at Périgueux. Mme Robert also confessed and she and her husband were charged before being released on bail.

When Eydelie was charged three days later with offering bribes, Marseille fans complained about a conspiracy against their club and particular its president Bernard Tapie. Some supporters felt so strongly that they threatened to blow up the offices of the French Football Federation.

On 1 July Burruchaga was charged with receiving bribes and on the same day Marseille's preseason training camp high up in the Pyrenees was raided by twenty police officers just as the players were about to have lunch. The entire first team were taken away for questioning. The club offices were also raided, police seizing files, opening safes and rummaging through dustbins in the search for vital evidence.

Bernès was the next to be charged – a move that the authorities hoped would lead them to Tapie – but the general manager denied everything. Fortunately there were others who were not prepared to remain silent, including Valenciennes coach Boro Primorac who made a statement incriminating Tapie. Primorac said that at a meeting in Tapie's Paris office on 17 June the Marseille president had suggested that in return for 'carrying the can for this business' Primorac would receive a payoff and the post of coach at Martigues, a Second Division club some thirty miles from Marseilles. Presented with the allegations, Tapie came up with an alibi for the time of the supposed meeting – a story supported by socialist minister Jack Mellick and his parliamentary secretary, Corinne Krajewski. Tapie was proving an elusive quarry.

Jean-Jacques Eydelie could hold his nerve no longer, however. Remanded in custody since being charged, he finally cracked on 12 July and wrote a letter to the examining magistrate, Judge Bernard Beffy, requesting a fresh interview. Fearing that his family would become embroiled in the scandal, he admitted everything he knew. Bernès was made of stronger stuff and continued to deny any involvement, although he did relinquish his post at Olympique Marseille on 26 July.

As some of Tapie's supporters began to desert him, the police tried to break down the wall of silence surrounding the club president. It was no easy task and it was not until December 1994 that Tapie and Bernès were summoned to appear before the Valenciennes Criminal Court in connection with the offering of bribes.

The trial started the following March with a sensation. Bernès changed his story and admitted attempted bribery but insisted that it was carried out at the behest of Tapie. Bernès testified that Marseille had spent £1.2 million a year on incentives for opponents to throw matches, some of it going to buy referees. He claimed that even the 1993 European Cup final against AC Milan was fixed.

With the noose tightening around Tapie's neck, Corinne Krajewski, who had originally backed Mellick's alibi for Tapie, changed her testimony, too. Within days Mellick was arrested and, retracting his earlier statements, admitted that he had not seen Tapie on 17 June 1993. Mellick subsequently received a six-month suspended sentence for having suborned Krajewski.

Meanwhile Gennadi Kostylev, coach of CSKA Moscow, claimed that his players had been offered money to go easy against Marseille in the 1992 European Cup. Marseille had beaten CSKA 6–0 at home, drawing 1–1 in Moscow.

As the full scale of Tapie's bribery network became evident, stiff sentences were handed out to club and individuals. While Marseille fans adjusted to the loss of their titles and the prospect of Second Division football, Tapie was sentenced to two years in prison, with sixteen months suspended, fined 20,000 francs and rendered ineligible for public office for three years. Bernès was sentenced to eighteen months suspended and fined 15,000 francs while Eydelie received a one-year suspended sentence and a fine of 10,000 francs. Burruchaga and the Roberts were sentenced to six months suspended and each fined 5,000 francs.

There was never any possibility that Bernard Tapie would drift quietly into obscurity. While serving his eight-month jail sentence he penned his autobiography and on his release recorded a chart-topping song, 'C'Est Beau La Vie' ('It's a Beautiful Life'), with French rap artist Doc Gyneco in which

he joked about his experience. Soon he had his own breakfast
show on Radio Monte Carlo – *Allo Bernard* – and as an actor
appeared in a stage version of *One Flew Over the Cuckoo's Nest*,
playing the role made famous by Jack Nicholson. He was also
the subject of a film, *Who is Bernard Tapie?*

Things were looking up on the football front, too. In 1999
the Council of State refused a request from the French
Football Federation to suspend indefinitely Tapie's licence to
run a football club. Consequently his unique talents were not
lost to the game forever and sure enough in 2001, in a
turnaround that was incredible even by his own standards, he
resurfaced as sporting manager of his old club, Olympique
Marseille. Top that, Jeffrey.

Kneecapping Nancy

1994

We expect better from ice-skaters. Tales of skulduggery on the rugby field or the soccer pitch barely merit the raising of an eyebrow but ice-skating always seemed such a genteel pastime, populated by clean-cut folk who were dedicated to their art and enjoyed a shared love of tinny music. True, the sport lost much of its appeal when the stony-faced, fur-clad judges who used to step on to the ice and hold up cards to mark the performance were replaced by an electronic scoreboard, but we could still admire the upright carriage and impeccable manners of the skaters themselves. We always imagined that away from the ice Torvill and Dean devoted all their energies to helping old ladies across the road. Then along came Tonya Harding, the bad girl of ice-skating, the woman who added 'iron bar' to the sport's vocabulary alongside 'triple salchow' and 'double axel'.

Harding was the rough diamond among the sequinned dresses. She smoked cigarettes, drove trucks, played pool and was fiercely competitive but she skated like an angel. Born in Portland, Oregon, she began skating as a toddler, won her first national title in 1991 at the age of twenty and had the distinction of being the first American woman to perform a triple axel jump in competition. Her great rival – both on the domestic and international stage – was Olympic bronze medallist Nancy Kerrigan from Stoneham, Massachusetts.

January and February of 1994 were big months for Harding and Kerrigan, with the US Figure Skating Championships in Detroit followed by the Winter Olympics in Lillehammer, Norway. Both skaters had trained long and hard for the events, the Detroit competition serving as a trial for the Olympics, only the top two finishers being selected for Lillehammer. There was a great deal at stake and although Kerrigan was the reigning national champion, Harding was in typically bullish mood on her way to Detroit, telling reporters: 'I'm going to go there and kick some butt.' Again, it was not a turn of phrase usually associated with Jayne Torvill.

Two days later, on the afternoon of 6 January, 24-year-old Kerrigan was practising on a rink adjacent to the main arena in Detroit. At the end of the session she walked behind a curtain separating the rink from a hallway leading to the locker rooms and stopped momentarily to talk to a reporter. Suddenly a man ran by, whacked Kerrigan on the right knee with a metal baton and fled before he could be identified. Kerrigan crumpled to the ground in agony and was forced to withdraw from the competition. In her absence, Harding won to book a place at the Olympics.

As the FBI began investigating the attack, a Portland minister, Eugene Saunders, revealed that he had heard three men discussing a 'hit'. The three were Harding's bodyguard, Shawn Eckardt, her ex-husband, Jeff Gillooly, and a friend Shane Stant. Although Harding and Gillooly were divorced the previous August after three and a half years of marriage, they had since reconciled. Eckardt quickly confessed to the FBI, also implicating two friends, Stant and Derrick B Smith, Gillooly and, most significantly of all, Tonya Harding. According to Eckardt, Harding made two telephone calls to the Tony Kent Arena in South Dennis, near Boston, Massachusetts, to try to determine Kerrigan's practice schedule. He named Gillooly as the man behind the conspiracy. Pleading her own innocence, Harding swiftly announced that she and Gillooly were separating again. She said: 'I believe during this crucial time of preparation for the Olympics that I must concentrate my attention on my training.'

Following Gillooly's arrest and with speculation growing by the minute regarding her personal involvement in the attack, Harding issued a statement in which she admitted failing to report things she knew about the assault on Kerrigan. She said:

> I had no prior knowledge of the planned assault on Nancy Kerrigan. I am responsible, however, for failing to report things I

learned about the assault when I returned home from the Nationals (on 10 January). Within the next few days, I learned that some persons close to me were involved in the assault. I am embarrassed and ashamed to think that anyone close to me could be involved. I have a great deal of respect for Nancy.

Harding concluded the statement by begging to be allowed to compete in the Olympics:

Despite my mistakes and rough edges, I have done nothing to violate the standards of excellence and sportsmanship that are expected in an Olympic athlete. I have devoted my entire life to one objective: winning an Olympic gold medal for my country. This is my last chance.

On 1 February Gillooly pleaded guilty to one count of racketeering in connection with the Kerrigan assault in exchange for a two-year jail sentence. Damningly, he also alleged that Harding had approved the attack on her rival. He claimed that on 28 December 1993 Harding met him following a rendezvous with Eckardt and Smith. Gillooly said he left the final decision about injuring Kerrigan up to Harding whereupon she had allegedly replied: 'Okay, let's do it.' He went on to detail how Harding had tried to pinpoint where and when Kerrigan practised and how she had provided Eckardt with a magazine photo of Kerrigan so that Stant, who had been hired to carry out the actual attack, would target the right person.

Feeling the pressure in the wake of Gillooly's allegations, Harding fell while practising the following day – an incident seized upon by press and television. Worse was to follow when a restaurant owner in Portland discovered Gillooly and Harding's rubbish in his bin. The FBI revealed that among the contents were notes apparently written by Harding, including the phone number of Kerrigan's practice arena.

Each new revelation threatened Harding's Olympic place but her lawyers managed to delay planned hearings so that she could skate in Lillehammer . . . where she lined up alongside Kerrigan, who had thankfully made a quick recovery and been given special dispensation to compete by the selectors. The Olympic showdown between Kerrigan and Harding captivated the nation. It was good versus bad, right versus wrong, John Wayne versus Lee Van Cleef. Skating had never attracted such vast TV audiences across the United States and there was no question as to whom the vast majority were rooting for. Kerrigan did not disappoint. Just fifty days after being clubbed on the knee, she skated to silver behind sixteen-year-old Oksana Baiul from the Ukraine. Harding could only manage eighth, having been forced to stop and restart when a lace on one of her skates broke during the warm-up. She left in floods of tears but they were just about the only ones shed on her behalf.

Three weeks later Harding entered a plea bargain to ensure that she would not be sent to prison. She pleaded guilty to conspiracy to hindering the investigation of the attack on Kerrigan and was fined $160,000 and placed on probation for three years. She also agreed to resign immediately from the US Figure Skating Association, thus barring her from competing in the forthcoming World Championships. She did not, however, admit to any prior knowledge of the conspiracy.

While Smith, Stant, Eckardt and Gillooly began jail sentences, Harding was stripped of her 1994 US figure skating title and was banned for life from the USFSA. Harding did not attend the Association's hearing which found that her conduct 'intentionally undermines the concept of sportsmanship and fair play embodied in the USFSA bylaws and rules and amateur sportsmanship in general. Ms. Harding's actions as they related to the assault on Nancy Kerrigan evidence a clear disregard for fairness, good sportsmanship and ethical behaviour.' Although Harding continued to contest Gillooly's version of events, the chairman of the USFSA panel, William Hybl, said: 'By a preponderance of the evidence, the five members of the panel concluded that she had prior knowledge and was involved in the incident. This is based on civil standards, not criminal standards.'

Things have hardly improved for Harding since the Nancy Kerrigan scandal. In August 1994 – just a month after her USFSA ban – pictures taken from the raunchy video of her and Gillooly's wedding night appeared in the 25th anniversary issue of *Penthouse* magazine and were subsequently put on the Internet. A couple of months later the Tonya Harding Fan

Club – which once boasted 2,000 members – started to disband. Booed and jeered during a two-minute performance in the build-up to a Reno Renegades ice hockey game, Harding was later convicted of assaulting her new boyfriend with a hubcap. She was placed on probation, the terms of which forbade her to touch alcohol over a two-year period, but in 2001 she failed a Breathalyser test after crashing her truck into a ditch and was jailed for ten days. Her notoriety earned her a celebrity boxing match against Paula Jones, the woman who accused President Clinton of sexual misconduct, and in February 2003 she made her official debut as a bantamweight against Samantha Browning on the undercard of a Mike Tyson fight. Harding lost . . . but then again she hasn't stopped losing since January 1994, the day of the whack on the knee that was heard around the world.

Dirt in Pocket

1994

Ball tampering had been an awkward subject in cricket for some years with the whispering campaign against Pakistan fast bowlers frequently reaching deafening proportions. Yet in the summer of 1994 it was none other than England captain Mike Atherton who found himself in the dock following the 'dirt in the pocket' affair.

Atherton had only been captain for a year when England entertained South Africa in a short series that marked the latter's readmission to international cricket. On a hot and sultry afternoon during the first Test at Lord's, television cameras spotted Atherton repeatedly dipping his hand into his right trouser pocket and appearing to apply something to the ball. When at the close of play match referee Peter Burge asked him whether he had anything in his pocket that could be used to alter the state of the ball, Atherton replied in the negative.

Although neither umpire – Englishman Dickie Bird and Australia's Steve Randell – had noticed anything amiss, television replays were damning and showed Atherton vigorously rubbing a substance on to the ball. There were clearly questions that needed answering and after England had been well beaten inside four days, the England captain faced the music.

He said that he had panicked when interviewed by Burge and had not been as open with the referee as he should have been. He went on to admit that he had some dirt in his pocket which he picked up to keep his hands dry and prevent moisture getting on the ball as he relayed it to the bowler from his position at mid-off while Darren Gough was trying to extract some reverse swing. Gough finished with eight wickets in the match and was the only English bowler to swing the ball.

Atherton explained: 'The dirt in my pocket was used to dry my fingers because it was a hot and humid day. We were trying to get the ball to reverse swing. You need one side of the ball to remain completely dry.' Pressed on suggestions that it looked as though he had been tampering with the ball, a clearly irritated Atherton replied: 'The umpires check the ball at the end of each over and they had no complaint with the condition of the ball. There was no complaint by anybody that the condition of the ball had been altered. During my career I have never used any substance to either polish the ball falsely or deteriorate the condition of the other side of the ball.'

By being 'economical with the truth' in the first instance, Atherton had left himself wide open to criticism for behaving in a manner unbecoming of an England captain. Certainly chairman of selectors Ray Illingworth took a dim view of Atherton's performance and fined him £2,000, partly for having the dirt in his pocket and partly for not being totally open with Burge. The tabloid press called for Atherton's head. The *Mirror* described him as 'the soiled skipper' while the *Daily Mail* reckoned that £2,000 was a small price for Atherton to pay for 'the deceit that has sullied the honour of the English captaincy'.

Alan Lee encapsulated the situation perfectly in *The Times*. He wrote: 'By declining to explain himself properly in private or public, until the damage was done, Atherton was not so much protecting his innocence as promoting his guilt. No matter what he was finally and reluctantly to reveal, the net result was an indisputable weakening of his authority as captain.'

The Pakistan team manager Intikhab Alam was quick to appreciate the irony of the situation. 'We have been branded cheats on numerous occasions for a crime our bowlers never committed. But that's not the point. The point is we never got caught. Atherton did.'

Atherton subsequently confessed that he was close to resignation principally because the plain-speaking Illingworth appeared reluctant to defend him in public. Although the affair soured his relations with the press and led to him being labelled 'Captain Grumpy', Atherton held on to the captaincy until 1999 and, following injury to Nasser Hussain, was even briefly reappointed two years later. The England hierarchy had obviously long forgiven him. Mud sticks, but dirt doesn't.

Crunch Time in Adelaide

1994

Recent history had shown that when the Formula One World Championship went right down to the wire, more than a hint of chicanery was guaranteed. In 1989 Frenchman Alain Prost, needing only to finish in front of Brazil's Ayrton Senna in the Japanese Grand Prix to become champion for a third time, resisted an overtaking move by his rival by turning in on him and taking both cars out of the race. Prost was champion. Each blamed the other for the collision. The following year at the same circuit the positions were reversed. This time Senna was in the driving seat and when Prost looked like beating him into the very first corner, the Brazilian put his foot down and smashed into Prost's Ferrari, taking both cars out of the race. Senna was champion. The 1994 season would see more of the same, the protagonists being Michael Schumacher and Damon Hill, as the destiny of the title rested on the final race, the Australian Grand Prix at Adelaide. It was not a place for the faint-hearted.

The season had been riddled with controversy from the moment that Senna was killed in the San Marino Grand Prix at Imola, his death casting a long shadow over the sport. Schumacher, in search of his first title, won the first four races of the year in a Benetton but by ignoring a black flag at Silverstone he not only lost his six points for finishing second but also incurred a two-race ban. Then his victory in the Belgian Grand Prix at Spa was thrown out because of technical irregularities. Schumacher's absence and misfortune allowed Hill, who had succeeded Senna as number one driver for the Williams team, to close the gap dramatically. The German became rattled and tried to put the psychological brakes on Hill with a succession of put-downs. Before the European Grand Prix at Jerez, Spain, he said:

> I don't think we would have been in this position if Ayrton Senna had been in the car. Ayrton would have been driving circles around me. That shows what I think about Damon as a driver. He has been thrown into the number one driver position but he never really was a number one driver. With David Coulthard driving quicker than him after three races, it proves he is not a number one driver… The respect is certainly not as much as I have for other drivers.

Hill remained unfazed and by the time they arrived in Australia in November, Schumacher's lead had been cut to just one point. The race around 81 laps of Adelaide's street circuit was to take place on the 13th. Who would be the unlucky driver on the day?

Schumacher made the better start but Hill, driving with tremendous determination, made steady inroads into the Benetton advantage and had closed right up by lap 36. The pressure was starting to get to Schumacher who, in those days was prone to the occasional error, and at Turn Five he momentarily lost control of the car and ran into a concrete wall, regaining the track before Hill, who had been delayed lapping Heinz-Harald Frentzen, appeared on the scene. Unaware of the extent of Schumacher's excursion or that the Benetton's suspension was badly damaged as a result, Hill tried to overtake at the next corner by diving for the inside. Suddenly Schumacher, perhaps seeing the title slip from his grasp, closed the gap by steering his ailing car sharply to the right and the pair collided. The Benetton flew into the air before ending up stuck in a tyre wall, out of the race, while the Williams limped on to the pits.

Schumacher said afterwards: 'I went to turn into the corner and suddenly I saw Damon next to me and we just hit each other. I drove over his front wheel and I went up in the air. The worst moment was not being able to continue and yet seeing my rival still driving.'

Climbing from his battered car, Schumacher stood by the track waiting for Hill to pass but then he heard that there was a problem with the Williams. Sure enough, the suspension had been damaged irreparably by the collision and when Hill did not go past for the next three laps, the German knew he was world champion by a single point.

Schumacher dismissed the coming-together as nothing more than a racing accident, caused by a damaged steering system sustained in the first crash. Possibly out of guilt, he did have the grace to apologise to Hill for having underestimated him but characteristically would not admit to any wrongdoing. 'I was still in front of Damon,' he maintained. 'It was still my corner...'

Hill was remarkably restrained in the circumstances and refused to condemn Schumacher. He said ruefully:

> At the time Michael went off the road, I had no idea what condition his car was in. I saw an opportunity and I went for it. It is very painful to look back at the replay and realise that it must have been damaged to the point where he would have been out of the race. But I did what I felt was necessary at the time. I've a bit of an empty feeling but I gave him a good run for his money. He was certainly feeling the pressure because he ended up falling off the road. I think spectators and race fans around the world will be debating what really happened at that point for a long time to come.

One team owner was in no doubt as to what had happened and accused Schumacher of acting 'like a highwayman'. In the *Sunday Times* Simon Barnes called it 'an act of pure ruthlessness'. Hill received 250 hard-luck faxes and plenty more messages from fans who thought he had been robbed of the world championship by a deliberate act of sabotage. The German media were equally unimpressed by the manner in which Schumacher had claimed victory. When he arrived at Frankfurt airport, he was greeted by a stony silence even though he was the first German to win the world championship. 'Surely he is worth a bit of applause?' one of his aides pleaded to the press corps.

Despite the overwhelming public opinion that Schumacher, his car broken, had deliberately taken his only rival out of the championship equation, team manager Frank Williams announced that he would not be lodging a protest because he didn't want to win the title by having Schumacher penalised for a third time in the season. The sport's governing body, the FIA, also decided against taking action, ruling that there was 'insufficient evidence', but, in order to avoid future world championships being decided by a collision, said it would study the possibility of empowering the stewards to allow the drivers concerned to continue the race in spare cars or hold a runoff immediately after the race. FIA president Max Mosley explained:

> We've had three now, twice with Senna and Prost, and now with Hill and Schumacher, so you start to say, 'well, maybe we can do something'. It is annoying, and there is also the question of whether he (Schumacher) did it on purpose. Even if he didn't, there is a feeling he might have, which is bad for the driver. I'm sure Schumacher wouldn't like that. I'm sure he'd have much rather beaten Hill fair and square in the race.
>
> In the end, the right man won the championship. Schumacher is the quicker driver. Maybe the route is a bit devious, but we got the right result.

Mosley's comments were hardly a ringing endorsement of Schumacher's claim of fair play and as the winter wore on Hill's generous spirit began to wane. He later reflected: 'At the time, I couldn't believe that he would do such a thing but, with hindsight, I think I was being a little naïve.'

Hill's suspicions – and those of the rest of the world – were confirmed three years later at the showdown for the 1997 World Championship as Schumacher led Canadian Jacques Villeneuve by one point going into the final round, the European Grand Prix at Jerez. When Villeneuve tried to overtake on lap 48 out of 69, Schumacher, taken by surprise, turned in on him, just as he had done with Hill in Adelaide. But this time it didn't work. For while Schumacher's car finished in the gravel and out of the race, Villeneuve was able to continue and take the title.

While Schumacher once again protested his innocence, Hill, who in the meantime had won the title in 1996, experienced a definite sense of *déjà vu*. 'Michael showed his true colours and got what he deserved,' he said. 'At least he is consistent.' And there was no sitting on the fence by the authorities who stripped Schumacher of his second place in the World Championship. Justice was done . . . albeit three years too late.

Seagulls and Sardines

1995

A Lags XI team of footballers who have served time in jail is a popular exercise for trivia fanatics. From former Arsenal and England defender Peter Storey (attempting to import porn videos and keeping a brothel) to ex-Welsh international Mickey Thomas (passing forged bank notes), there are plenty to choose from. Yet the highest-profile soccer conviction of the past decade did not actually lead to prison after the sentence was commuted to one of community service. It was an extraordinary case but then Eric Cantona was an extraordinary footballer.

Le Brat, as he was nicknamed, had a reputation for frequent temperamental outbursts in his native France where incidents included a fracas with seven opponents after an Auxerre reserve match and various violent rows with team-mates. He also had regular brushes with authority and in 1988 referred to the French national manager, Henri Michel, as a 'shitbag'. Even allowing for the translation it was scarcely complimentary. Trouble followed him to England and in 1994, playing for Manchester United, he was heavily criticised for stamping on Swindon Town's John Moncur. However, all his past misdemeanours paled into insignificance alongside the events in south London on the evening of 25 January 1995.

United were drawing 1–1 with Crystal Palace at Selhurst Park when Cantona was sent off in the 52nd minute by referee Alan Wilkie following a clash with Palace defender Richard Shaw. Cantona was no stranger to the early bath or to derision from opposing supporters who took exception to his perceived aloofness and arrogance. But as Cantona walked along the touchline, accompanied by United kitman Norman Davies who had been sent with him to unlock the door of the dressing-room, a twenty-year-old Palace season ticket holder, Matthew Simmons, ran down eleven rows to the front of the stand and began yelling abuse at the Frenchman. The precise details of the verbal assault have never been firmly established (Simmons was rumoured to have made derogatory comments about Cantona's nationality and parentage) but they were sufficient to provoke the player into a fearsome rage. Leaping over the barrier rail, he launched a two-footed kung fu attack on Simmons' chest, the force of which knocked the surprised supporter to the ground. Simmons quickly got to his feet and retaliated with a flurry of punches until a right hander from Cantona floored him again. Before any further damage could be done, United goalkeeper Peter Schmeichel managed to drag the still seething Cantona off his prey. As he was led away, Cantona had hot tea thrown at him by another supporter in the stand.

The pictures of Cantona's vicious attack shocked virtually everyone in the game. Nobody had ever seen anything quite like it. Whatever the provocation, Cantona's reaction beggared belief. In the *Sunday Times*, Hugh McIlvanney wrote: 'Few sportsmen have fallen so low by jumping so high.'

Condemnation was instant: he should be thrown out of United, he should be thrown out of football. Leading the calls for Cantona's head was Brian Clough – the same Clough that had thumped those errant supporters a few years earlier. Calling for Cantona to be kicked out of the English game, Clough ranted: 'He should have walked around the track, had a shower, put on his smart French designer clothes and waited to get on the coach. There's something wrong with the man.' The words pot, kettle and black spring to mind.

The day after the match, in what was probably a first, FA chief executive Graham Kelly spoke for many when he said: 'The Football Association believes last night's incident was unprecedented. It brought shame on those involved, and worst of all, on the game itself. We especially deplore the appalling example set to young supporters who are the game's future.' Just about the only thing that could be said in Cantona's favour was that the kick was perfectly executed.

It was not until the following morning that Martin Edwards, the United chairman, first saw the incident, on television. He recalled later: 'I realised that something had to be done and the first thing the club had to decide was "do we keep Eric or not?"' The following day United announced that they were suspending Cantona from first-team games for the rest of the season and were fining him the maximum two weeks' wages (about £20,000). Meanwhile Simmons had reported Cantona to the police and the player was given fourteen days by the FA to answer charges.

It was then that public opinion started to shift as details of Simmons' past emerged. He was branded a racist who had previously been convicted of attacking a petrol station attendant with a spanner in the course of an attempted robbery. Palace announced that they were banning him for the rest of the season and suddenly the innocent victim began to appear as a nasty aggressor who had gone running to the police when his intimidation had backfired.

To escape the brouhaha, Cantona took his pregnant wife Isabelle on a private holiday to Guadeloupe. When an ITN film crew, headed by the late Terry Lloyd, interrupted the holiday by confronting the family on the beach, Cantona again reacted angrily and lashed out. Guadeloupe police confiscated Lloyd's film and Cantona picked up the sympathy vote. Indeed, 82 per cent of *Manchester Evening News* readers now backed him over the Simmons case. His popularity continued to soar as general perception of him changed to that of a man who was simply protecting his family in the face of unwanted intrusion. Nevertheless it was somewhat alarming to read that a poll by a tour company found that 40 per cent of men would rather go on holiday with Cantona than Claudia Schiffer.

Returning to England, on 21 February Cantona was formally charged with the assault on Simmons. Three days later the FA banned him for seven months, meaning that he would miss the remainder of the season plus the first two months of the following campaign. His club manager Alex Ferguson complained: 'I don't think there will be any player ever in the history of football who will get the sentence that he got. I think it is so severe.'

Cantona appeared before Croydon magistrates on 23 March. As he arrived for the court case, a small group chanted: 'Going down! Going down!' In court Simmons denied swearing at Cantona, insisting he had merely said: 'Off you go for an early shower.' However, other witnesses testified that they had heard Simmons yell abuse at the player. After fifty minutes of deliberation, chairman of the magistrates, Mrs Jean Peach, delivered the verdict:

> You have pleaded guilty to common assault. We have heard from your counsel that you deeply regret your actions. We have taken this into account, together with your previous good character and your guilty plea. We do feel, however, that you are a high-profile public figure with undoubted gifts and as such you are looked up to by many young people. For this reason the only sentence that is appropriate for this offence is two weeks' imprisonment forthwith.

An immediate appeal allowed Cantona his freedom and, after the appeal judge commented that Simmons had indulged in conduct that would 'provoke the most stoic', the sentence was reduced to one of 120 hours' community service.

At a press conference following the court case Cantona spoke briefly and enigmatically. 'When the seagulls follow the trawlers,' he intoned, 'they do it because they think sardines will be thrown into the sea. Thank you.' As Cantona made his abrupt exit, leaving the assembled throng scratching their heads in puzzlement, the more enlightened scribes deciphered his homespun philosophy, concluding that the trawler was Eric himself, the seagulls were the press and the sardines were Cantona's words of wisdom. In this instance the seagulls were left hungry.

When Simmons appeared in court, having been charged with using threatening behaviour towards Cantona, he showed his true colours. After being found guilty, he leaped over a table towards lawyer Jeffery McCann, shouting: 'I am innocent. I swear on the Holy Bible!' It needed six officers to drag him off the shaken lawyer. Simmons was fined, banned from all football grounds for a year and jailed for seven days for contempt of court although he was released after one night. The outburst made Cantona's reaction understandable if still not justifiable.

Cantona performed his community service in exemplary fashion, teaching football to youngsters in the Greater Manchester area. Alex Ferguson was full of praise. 'He has never had one complaint about the punishment. He never says a word about it, he has just got on with life and it has taken tremendous courage from him to do that. There's not many people could handle that.'

In a rare public utterance Cantona recalled: 'The hardest thing was having to put up with the endless comments, the swift judgements, the resounding criticism.'

He returned to first-team football in October 1995 for United's 2–2 draw at Liverpool, converting a penalty and creating the other goal. He was voted the Football Writers' Player of the Year for 1995–6 and crowned a remarkable season by scoring the only goal of the FA Cup Final victory over Liverpool. As he walked up Wembley's famous 39 steps to collect the trophy, he was spat on and verbally abused by Liverpool fans. This time he simply wiped away the spit and continued serenely on his way. A lesson had been learned.

The Sacking of
George Graham

1995

The first few months of 1995 represented troubled times for British football. Quite apart from the Cantona case, Bruce Grobbelaar, John Fashanu and Hans Segers were arrested on suspicion of match-fixing, an international in Dublin was abandoned after a riot by England fans, Crystal Palace striker Chris Armstrong failed a drugs test, and George Graham was sensationally sacked as Arsenal manager amid allegations of irregular payments.

The canny Scot had brought a level of success not enjoyed at Highbury since the days of Herbert Chapman in the 1930s – two League titles, the FA Cup, two League Cups and the European Cup Winners' Cup. But that counted for nothing when the club were alerted to certain aspects of Graham's transfer dealings. As he himself later remarked: 'It took eight and a half years for me to win six trophies for Arsenal, and two and a half minutes for the club to kick me out.'

Graham's downfall stemmed from his association with Norwegian agent Rune Hauge who acted as middleman in two controversial transfers to Arsenal. In the autumn of 1991 the club signed fullback Pal Lydersen from Norwegian side IK Start and the following year they snapped up Danish international midfielder John Jensen from Brondby.

Graham's first involvement with Hauge had been over the signing of Swedish winger Anders Limpar. Then following the Lydersen transfer, the two men met again in December 1991 at London's Park Lane Hotel where Hauge handed Graham several plastic envelopes to put in his briefcase. According to Graham, the Norwegian said they were 'an appreciation of all you have done to help me open doors here in England'. When he got home, Graham found the envelopes contained wads of £50 notes, totalling £140,500. The following August – shortly after the Jensen transfer – Graham received a banker's draft for £285,000 from Interclub Ltd, a Guernsey-based company in which Hauge had interests. The first sum was paid into a bank account in Dublin; the second was paid by bank transfer to an account in Guernsey, out of reach of the taxman. Both accounts were in Graham's name. He maintained that both were unsolicited gifts, not 'bungs' connected with the transfers. Crucially, he declined to tell Arsenal about these 'gifts'.

In November 1992 Danish journalist Henrik Madsen published a book, *The Men From Brondby*, in which he investigated the affairs of the club he had supported as a boy. Discussing the role of agent Hauge in Brondby's finances, Madsen was the first to accuse Graham of profiting from the Jensen deal. Brondby said the Jensen fee was £900,000 but Arsenal actually paid £1.57 million, the difference apparently going to Interclub. This discrepancy was of particular interest to German club Hamburg who were due a 25 per cent selling-on fee for Jensen. Complaining that they should have got 25 per cent of £1.57 million instead of 25 per cent of £900,000, Hamburg took the case to FIFA and in the spring of 1993 Arsenal confirmed that they had paid £1.57 million for the Dane.

Graham's luck ran out when Arsenal were drawn against Brondby in the European Cup Winners' Cup in October 1994. At the prematch dinner the two sets of directors discussed the discrepancy between what Brondby received and what Arsenal paid. Benny Winther, the Brondby chairman, recalled: 'Some of the Arsenal directors were curious about precisely how much we paid to Hauge in the Jensen deal. When I told them we had sent all but the £900,000 Hauge had promised us to Interclub, Arsenal were very surprised. As far as they knew, they had simply paid £1.57 million for the player.'

Alerted to the situation, the Norwegian tax authorities began investigating Hauge and when they found a slip of paper with Graham's name on it along with a reference to a large sum of money, Graham was advised to notify Arsenal of these gifts in order to avoid problems with the Inland Revenue. Accordingly on 1 December 1994 consultants acting on Graham's instruction paid the £425,000 he had received from Hauge plus £40,000 interest into Arsenal's bank account.

Graham undoubtedly hoped that now he had paid the money over to Arsenal that would be the end of the matter, but the Premier League had set up a commission to investigate allegations of irregular payments and the newspapers were full of stories that the Gunners' manager was deep in the mire. Two days before the League was due to publish its findings, Arsenal chairman Peter Hill-Wood summoned Graham to his office and told him: 'We've had advance information on the Premier League report. I'm afraid their findings leave us with no alternative but to terminate your contract with immediate effect.' Graham was sacked, the club statement saying that 'the board have concluded that Mr Graham did not act in the best interests of the club'. Graham called his dismissal 'a stabbing in the back'.

Although Graham's barrister told the Premier League inquiry that the sums in question 'were paid by the agent as a mark of his gratitude' and that they 'were not paid pursuant to any arrangements connected with the transfers', Rick Parry, the chief executive of the Premier League, said that the commission 'has great difficulty in accepting that Mr Graham did not know that the payments derived directly from the transfer fees paid by Arsenal'. Three officials of IK Start had made a signed statement to Parry, which pointed the finger at Graham, insinuating that he had negotiated a deal for Lydersen that was of benefit to himself rather than Arsenal. Lydersen certainly struggled to justify the reported £500,000 fee.

Continuing to maintain his innocence, Graham called the allegations 'nonsense' and said he had been tried by a 'kangaroo court'. He demanded a full inquiry by the FA who responded by charging him with misconduct.

In July 1995 the FA inquiry into the affair found Graham guilty of misconduct over his transfer dealings and he was banned from football for a year. The three-man panel said they, too, believed that when Graham received the money he must have known it was connected with the two transfers but they were not satisfied that he had asked for the money or that he had negotiated the transfers to obtain personal gain. Although 'bitterly disappointed' with the verdict, Graham felt partly vindicated. 'I always said the payments were unsolicited; this has been proved.'

George Graham spent part of his time in exile writing his autobiography. In it he reiterated his stance. 'I did not feel I was cheating anybody,' he wrote. 'Hauge was picking my brains, and so I convinced myself that it was reasonable to accept a gift in return for my time and knowledge.'

Very knowledgeable is George.

Fifty-Seven Old Farts

1995

When Will Carling memorably described the executive of the Rugby Football Union as '57 old farts', they more than lived up to the description by instantly sacking the most successful England captain ever and then being forced to reinstate him when nobody wanted the job. The standard of bungling would have been a credit only to the Chuckle Brothers.

Despite his success on the pitch, Carling had endured a turbulent relationship with many committee members, especially since 1991 when the entire England team boycotted the post-match press conference following the Five Nations match with Wales. Rumours abounded that the boycott was the result of a pay dispute with the BBC over post-match interviews but the RFU considered that Carling, as captain, was expected to do his duty with regard to public relations.

In fact for somebody who ran a promotions company, Carling did not exactly excel at PR, his life having been one long catalogue of unwelcome headlines, whether they were for his alleged liaison with the Princess of Wales, his divorce from Julia, or being dubbed a 'love rat' by the tabloid press for deserting his fiancée and eleven-month-old child. But in sporting terms it was his relationship with the RFU that repeatedly landed him in hot water. He has since confessed that 'on one occasion, a little the worse for wear after an international against Ireland in Dublin, I grabbed a senior administrator by the throat, threatening to punch his lights out' before being pulled off by team-mate Rob Andrew. 'The run-ins were bitter and many,' added Carling. 'I had blazing rows with many RFU committee members, especially Dudley Wood, the then RFU secretary. There was never a sense of give-and-take with certain RFU officials. They were dismissive of the players as a body, scared witless of player power.'

Nevertheless his most contentious remark about the RFU executive was never intended for public consumption, the comment having been made off-air at the end of an interview with Greg Dyke for Channel 4's series *Fair Game*. In his autobiography Carling wrote: 'I had finished my interview with Greg and the production people had turned the camera off. We had both unpinned our microphones and laid them on the table. I had no idea that the mikes were still live, still recording.' It was then that Dyke asked him a general question about the merits of running sport through committees, to which Carling replied: 'If the game is run properly, as a professional game, you do not need 57 old farts running rugby.'

The interview over, Carling was simply relieved that he had not said anything controversial on tape. 'Little did I know that my remarks were going to be used over the final credits as the programme ended.'

Carling was annoyed that the comment was broadcast, but not half as indignant as the RFU. When the story broke, Carling rang RFU president Denis Easby to apologise, only for Easby to tell him that he had been relieved of the England captaincy. In high dudgeon, the RFU issued a statement:

> It has been decided with regret that Will Carling's captaincy of the England team will be terminated forthwith and an announcement concerning his replacement will be made shortly. In the light of the view recently expressed regarding administrators, it is considered inappropriate for him to continue to represent, as England captain, the RFU, England and, indeed, English sport. Will has lost the confidence of the RFU committee who appointed him in the first place. In view of his attitude to the committee, his position as England captain is untenable.

The sacking was announced just a couple of hours before that year's Pilkington Cup Final with the result that the RFU had managed to overshadow their own showpiece occasion.

Carling was stunned by the decision but was soon heartened by the support of team-mates such as Rob Andrew and Dean Richards who immediately announced that they would refuse any offer of captaincy. With the team soon to leave for the World Cup in South Africa, the RFU were faced with the prospect of going to the most important tournament in the rugby calendar without a captain. The press were merciless in their mocking of the hapless administrators, who appeared incapable of running a tombola stall at a village fête let alone a national sports team. Easby was singled out for his overreaction by *The Times*, which wrote: 'He could not leave it at a reprimand and, by taking in hand the sledgehammer of dismissal, he has created a wave of antipathy for the entire RFU.'

The RFU realised they had dug themselves into an almighty hole and with no prospect of finding an alternative captain, they were forced into a humiliating climb-down. Easby was suddenly in a more conciliatory frame of mind and told Carling that if he made a public apology he could have his job back. Carling was happy to oblige and so just two days after being sacked, he was reappointed England captain.

Thus the RFU issued a fresh statement:

> Will Carling wishes to apologise to every member of the committee for his inappropriate and gratuitously offensive comments at the end of a recent television programme. All 25 members of the England squad have indicated their support for Will Carling as captain and have respectfully requested the RFU officers to reconsider their decision to terminate his appointment. Will Carling would like to thank the squad for their support and also Denis Easby for his courage in reconsidering his original decision, thus enabling the England squad to have a settle and successful build-up to the World Cup.

As bridges were mended at breakneck speed, the RFU tried to claim that Carling had been quoted out of context initially and Easby went on to praise his captaincy record as second to none.

Carling himself remained baffled by the whole affair. 'How anyone could be so upset, react so strongly at being called old farts is beyond me.'

Still, at least he has left the world a quote to remember him by.

You've Been Tarango'd

1995

After over a hundred Wimbledon championships without a single player being disqualified, the 1995 tournament amazingly yielded three. Britain's Tim Henman was fined £1,500 and automatically disqualified after hitting the ball in anger during a men's doubles match and accidentally striking ball girl Caroline Hall. Henman duly apologised to Ms Hall with a bouquet of flowers. Then American Murphy Jensen went AWOL when he should have been playing a mixed doubles match and was disqualified and fined £750. But the most remarkable enforced exit was surely that of Jeff Tarango, the one-man temper tantrum.

Of course bad behaviour on the tennis court had been around for twenty years or so. Jimmy Connors, Ilie Nastase and John McEnroe, to name but a few, had raised the art of abusing officials to new heights. Tarango, a Californian left-hander, seemed intent on aping McEnroe's boorish behaviour but sadly not his brilliant play. Indeed, in six previous visits to Wimbledon prior to 1995, Tarango had been knocked out in the first round of the men's singles every time. Then suddenly when it looked as if he was finally going to make some progress, it all turned ugly.

Tarango was no stranger to controversy. In October 1994 he was in trouble after dropping his shorts to a Tokyo crowd after losing his serve against Michael Chang. 'I thought people were concerned because tennis isn't entertaining enough,' protested Tarango at the time. 'I played my heart out against Chang and after losing my serve against a guy I'd been a set and a break up against maybe four times, I just lost my head. My shorts came down and that was that. The gig was up.'

By the summer of 1995 Tarango was collecting fines the way Pete Sampras was collecting titles. Ranked number 80 at Wimbledon, the 26-year-old enjoyed the bonus of reaching the third round where, on 1 July, he was drawn against Germany's Alexander Mronz out on Court thirteen. Trailing 6–7, 1–3, Tarango sent down a serve that he thought was an ace, only for it to be called out. As Tarango disputed the line call at length, the crowd became impatient and started barracking him. When he yelled back at them, French umpire Bruno Rebeuh issued him with a warning for audible obscenity. Incensed, Tarango insisted that he had simply told the spectators to shut up. 'I'm not having that,' he informed Rebeuh and demanded to see the supervisor, Swede Stefan Fransson. On arrival, Fransson listened to both sides and, dismissing Tarango's demand that Rebeuh be removed from the chair, ruled that the warning should stand. Hearing this, Tarango went ballistic, screaming at Rebeuh: 'You're the most corrupt official in the game.'

Pushed too far, Rebeuh called a one-point penalty against Tarango who promptly refused to play on and stormed off the court to a chorus of jeers. Disqualification was inevitable.

While Tarango seethed, the Californian's feisty French wife Benedicte waited for the umpire and slapped him twice in the face because, as she later told the press, 'the guy deserves a lesson'. She defended her physical assault by saying: 'Players have nobody to defend them. If Jeff had done it, he would have been put out of tennis.'

Whereas most Wimbledon press conferences are mundane affairs littered with platitudes, Tarango's was an altogether more entertaining experience. He accused Rebeuh of favouring certain players, particularly French-speaking ones, in exchange for their friendship. Indeed, the animosity between the two men dated back to 1993 when Tarango first voiced his suspicions to higher-ranking officials. Speaking in measured tones, Tarango went on: 'I don't feel I should be pushed around in my whole life and let people take advantage of me. I felt I was backed into a corner and that I really had no recourse for defending myself. People always say that Jeff is a psycho, that Jeff is a hothead, that Jeff is mean. But I'm not, I'm a very rational person. I'm an intellectual person that does not fly off the handle easily.'

While an editorial in *The Times* reckoned that Tarango had livened up an otherwise dull Wimbledon, criticism of the American's outburst came from an unlikely quarter – John McEnroe. 'He has hurt himself,' said McEnroe, 'shot himself in the foot inexplicably. I just can't believe that he did that – and at Wimbledon of all places.'

Tarango's eruption cost him a £10,000 fine, suspension from the next Grand Slam tournament and also from the following year's Wimbledon. There was more to come. In August the International Tennis Federation's Grand Slam Committee, investigating the Wimbledon incident, found Tarango guilty of 'aggravated behaviour and conduct contrary to the integrity of the game' and fined him an additional £20,000. The fine plus the two-tournament suspension represented the toughest penalty ever imposed on a player.

Tarango was convinced that he was a victim of injustice. 'Goran Ivanisevic was suspended for not going to a press conference and I was suspended for going to a press conference and telling the truth. I am confused.'

The rows continued. At the 1997 French Open, Austrian Thomas Muster refused to shake hands after the American had taunted him repeatedly. Muster said: 'We know the history of Jeff. He's not an easy guy. Everybody knows that. There's no excuse for certain behaviour on the court.' Three years later he was at the centre of another Wimbledon storm after accusing opponent Paul Goldstein of faking injury. This time it was Tarango who refused to shake hands following a defeat in five sets.

With Tarango reluctant to give interviews, it has been left to his father to reflect on the effect that the 1995 fracas has had on his son's career. 'It was ugly what happened at Wimbledon,' he said. 'It was unfortunate, one of those things that happens in the heat of battle in sports. Jeff is a person who wears his heart on his sleeve but the world has not seen the real Jeff – they've just seen his dark side. Society will accept you if you're a jerk and win. But when you don't win you're not allowed to do the things Jeff has done.'

The Bite

1997

When the fighting had stopped and the boxers had been ushered out of the ring, Las Vegas hotel worker Mitchell Libonati spotted something lying on the canvas that he thought Evander Holyfield might be interested in. So Libonati, who had been working the fight as a glove cutter and ring cleaner, wrapped the object in latex gloves and took it to Holyfield's dressing room where he told his camp: 'I have something he probably wants.' Libonati was right. Holyfield did want it back. It was part of his ear – the piece that Mike Tyson had bitten off and spat out during the third and final round of arguably the most savage, disgraceful encounter since the days of bare-knuckle fights.

'I shouldn't have done that,' conceded Tyson with some understatement. 'I was just striking out and it was total hatred right there and I just forgot he was a human being. It was extremeness. There was some serious stuff going on in my head. I just snapped. I was no longer playing under the rules. Any kind of functional thinking, any kind of rational thinking, that was totally out the window.' He added that he felt 'disgust, disdain and humiliation' over his actions.

That shameful World Boxing Association heavyweight title fight with reigning champion Holyfield at the MGM Grand Garden in Las Vegas on 28 June 1997 – two days before Tyson's 31st birthday – was just the latest in a long line of scandals in the career of 'Iron' Mike. A juvenile delinquent from Brooklyn, he was befriended by trainer/manager Cus D'Amato, who channelled his aggression into the boxing ring. A world champion by the age of twenty, Tyson fell under the spell of controversial promoter Don King after D'Amato's death and for a few years appeared invincible, his snarling presence making him a truly fearsome opponent. He was a heavyweight champion with a heavyweight attitude. But following a sensational knockout defeat to James 'Buster' Douglas in 1990, Tyson lost much of his old menace and constant allegations of sexual misconduct did little for his mental state. Two years later his already flawed image took a further body blow when he was found guilty of raping Desiree Washington and sentenced to ten years in jail. He served three years before returning to the ring for a tune-up with club fighter Peter McNeeley, Tyson needing less than a round to win. He then clawed back a share of the world title with a crushing rematch win over Frank Bruno before the Tyson machine was halted in its tracks by Evander Holyfield. Their first meeting, in November 1996, was stopped in the eleventh round, Tyson for once emerging with a degree of dignity after admitting he had been beaten by the better man. The rematch was an altogether less savoury affair. If in the first fight Holyfield stripped away Tyson's veneer of toughness, in the second he exposed the monster that had always lurked within.

Like all bullies, Tyson couldn't take it in return. He enjoyed nothing more than pummelling good boxers into submission, but put him in the ring with someone who was prepared to play dirty, turn the fight into a roughhouse, and he couldn't always handle it. Even Frank Bruno, whose limitations meant that he was often best suited to being Harry Carpenter's sparring partner, met with a modicum of success against Tyson back in 1989 when advised to adopt a tough, no-nonsense approach by trainer George Francis. Holyfield's extra class made him better equipped to expose Tyson's vulnerability. In their 1996 meeting Holyfield was guilty of persistent fouling and, having got away with it once, he decided on more of the same for the rematch.

There was drama even before the fight when referee Mitch Halpern stepped down following objections by the Tyson camp and was replaced by Mills Lane from Reno. As it turned out, Tyson would not be too enamoured with Lane either.

Holyfield set out his stall from the start, using his head as a third fist. Both men received stern warnings in the opening exchanges but when Tyson was stunned by another head butt early in the second round and could feel blood seeping from his right eyelid, he saw red. The referee ruled that the collision was accidental – Tyson thought differently. He gestured angrily at Holyfield and was given time to recover, but the damage to his fragile mental state was irreparable.

Having lost the first two rounds on all three judges' scorecards, Tyson was beginning to make some headway in the third when he suddenly lost the plot. Ironically he had come out for round three without his mouthpiece and had to return to his corner for it after the omission had been pointed out by Holyfield. With the fighters clinching, Tyson suddenly sank his teeth into Holyfield's right ear and spat an inch-long lump of it out on to the canvas. Holyfield immediately pulled away and leaped into the air, twisting and writhing in obvious pain and anger. While facing his corner, he was then violently shoved in the back by an enraged Tyson. The referee halted the fight and escorted Holyfield to his corner where he was treated for his bleeding ear. Lane told Tyson: 'One more like that and you're gone.' He also deducted two points from Tyson's score, which made it impossible for him even to share the round unless Holyfield took a count.

After examining Holyfield's wound, the ringside doctor Flip Homansky pronounced him fit to continue but before the two men were called back to the centre of the ring, Holyfield told his trainer Don Turner: 'I'm going to knock Tyson out.' Although his fury was understandable, Holyfield was strongly advised by his corner to 'cool it'.

Following a four-minute delay, the fight resumed but before Holyfield had the opportunity to carry out his threat, Tyson spat out his mouthpiece and bit him in the other ear. As the bell sounded, referee Lane examined Holyfield's left ear and instantly disqualified Tyson. All hell broke loose. After being restrained from reaching Lane, Tyson, his face contorted with fury, tried to get at Holyfield and struggled with several officials who kept him away from the champion. Dozens of Las Vegas police officers poured into the ring and wrestled with Tyson and his entourage before diving into the audience to make arrests. While Holyfield left the ring to cheers, Tyson was bombarded with abuse and debris, leading to further arrests and scuffles on the way to his dressing room.

The violence spread to the MGM Grand. Near-riots broke out as people ducked for cover under blackjack tables and behind slot machines when men were seen brandishing guns. Witnesses reported that shots were fired after a fight between several men. Police eventually shut down the casino, ordered thousands of customers to leave, and barricaded adjoining streets.

Holyfield was taken to hospital for treatment to his bitten ears. Before leaving he told reporters:

> When he bit me for the first time, I couldn't believe it. They have rules and regulations for this. After he bit me, I went back to my corner and they told me to take a deep breath and concentrate. He caught me with a good shot, bit my ear and spat it out. Look at the bite. I'm missing part of my ear. I heard Mills Lane tell him one more time and he's gone. He continued to foul and that was it. I can't understand the biting and he was trying to break my arm. He fouled in every way. He had no real courage. I think what he did was caused by fear. I'm just thankful we had a referee like Mills Lane.

The referee proceeded to explain his decision:

> I deducted two points from Tyson in the third round, first for biting Holyfield's right ear, then for pushing him in the back. At the end of the round I could see that Tyson had bitten Holyfield's other ear and I had no option but to disqualify him. The second bite was the end of the stretch. How many times do you want a guy to get bit? There's a limit to everything, including bites.

Tyson was still wild-eyed and ranting when fulfilling an interview obligation to Showtime, the cable TV network in which Don King had interests. Pointing to the two-inch gash in the lid of his right eye caused by the second-round butt, Tyson growled:

> Look at this. How much was I expected to put up with? He (Holyfield) was butting me all the time. He butted me in the first round and in the second round again. He kept going down and coming up on me. I was left with only one eye. My career was on the line. I've got kids to bring up. Who cares about me and my children?
>
> The referee didn't listen to my protests. When Richie (Tyson's trainer, Richie Giachetti) complained about the butt he was told it

was accidental. That was ridiculous, an insult. I had one eye, Holyfield had two ears. What else was I supposed to do? I had to retaliate.

The most objective comment came from Holyfield's trainer, Don Turner. 'This is a sad day for boxing, there's no doubt about that,' he said. 'But don't blame the sport. Blame the people in the sport.' It didn't take a genius to work out who he was referring to.

It was only when he had calmed down and realised the enormity of his crime that Tyson started to express a degree of contrition. By then his $30 million purse for the fight had been frozen by the Nevada State Athletic Commission and the press on both sides of the Atlantic were baying for blood.

'There can be no escape for Mike Tyson now,' wrote Ken Jones in the *Independent*. 'His ill-starred career in jeopardy, his behaviour so savagely bizarre that all sympathy for him has gone. Who but that squalid crew of associates and hangers-on can defend him now?'

A *Times* editorial said: 'Tyson's behaviour has again put the sport on the ropes... There is only one response that will save boxing from this stain and the world from further obscenity. Tyson should be banned from the ring for life.'

The following month Tyson was fined $3 million and suspended from boxing not for life, but for fifteen months. After serving another spell in prison on assault charges, he returned to the ring in 1999 and promptly announced to an astounded boxing world that he would resort to biting again if necessary:

I would do it again if provoked. Mills Lane was not protecting me from Holyfield's head butts. He wasn't controlling the situation appropriately. I would do it again if I see myself bloody and cut up. If my opponent is rough and there's some fouling going on, the referee is going to be paralysed and not act. Nobody ever has any sympathy or pity for me. In retaliation, I'll fight back because nobody is fighting for me.

Tyson proved that while his fists may not have been as lethal at the age of 36, his teeth were still in good working order when, during the infamous brawl before his 2002 defeat to Lennox Lewis, he managed to bite his opponent on the thigh. Inevitably the incident sparked reminders of the Holyfield fight.

Evander Holyfield has long since forgiven Tyson. Some might argue that it is more perhaps than he deserves.

Hoddle in a Muddle

1999

Glenn Hoddle's standing as England soccer manager took a sharp downward turn in the months following the 1998 World Cup. Apart from disappointing results, there was unrest at the publication of his World Cup diary for which he was paid a reported £200,000 in return for, as his detractors put it, 'selling players' secrets', including how the fragile Paul Gascoigne had flown into a rage at being excluded from the final squad. However, the gravest area of concern surrounded Hoddle's relationship with Eileen Drewery, a former Harlow pub landlady turned faith healer.

Hoddle first hobbled into Drewery's life back in 1976 when, as a seventeen-year-old prodigy with Tottenham Hotspur, he was dating her daughter Michelle. Initially spooked by her offer of psychic help to repair his torn leg muscle, he was nonetheless impressed when her use of what she called remote access or 'distance' healing appeared to clear up the young player's injuries. In 1986 Hoddle found God. As comedian Jasper Carrott remarked: 'That must have been one hell of a pass.' Hoddle explained the 'wonderful feeling of peace' he had found to Mrs Drewery, who in turn claimed to have used 'the channelled energy of God' to bring her husband Phil back from the brink of death on three separate occasions. Hoddle became a firm disciple of Mrs D and in 1998 brought her into the England setup as an advisor, telling sceptical journalists who failed to see where a faith healer would fit into a 4-4-2 formation that she was 'more of an agony aunt'. Several players were sent to her amid a growing fear that refusal might result in omission from future England squads. Darren 'Sicknote'

Anderton, who would have been put down years ago had he been a racehorse, found the consultation beneficial; Robbie Fowler was less impressed, saying he spent his visit watching television with Mr Drewery.

Following an indifferent performance at the World Cup, Hoddle was roundly criticised when his diary contained frequent references to Mrs Drewery and the startling admission that his one big mistake of the tournament had been in not taking her to France. He was now being held up to ridicule by the media as concerns grew that the faith healer's opinion was a key factor in selecting members of the England squad. The end of August brought 'Hodgate' after Hoddle and Drewery's plans to open a fee-paying spiritual sanctuary came to light. Commercial as well as psychic forces appeared to be at work.

With Hoddle attracting almost exclusively negative publicity, in January 1999 the FA decided to launch a charm offensive in the build-up to the friendly international with France. Acting chief executive David Davies had detected a distinct note of hostility in *The Times'* assessment of the England manager and made a phone call to the newspaper's sports editor David Chappell to arrange for Hoddle to do an interview before the France game. Ironically the FA's well-intentioned initiative plunged it into a crisis that would cost Hoddle his job.

The interview with *Times* reporter Matt Dickinson was conducted over the phone. After discussing the France game, Dickinson asked Hoddle about his views on reincarnation. 'He said he was interested,' claimed Hoddle afterwards. 'I tried to help him. I tried to give him a bit of an understanding.'

Hoddle's thoughts appeared in print on Saturday 30 January. He was quoted as saying: 'You and I have been physically given two hands and two legs and half-decent brains. Some people have not been born like that for a reason. The karma is working from another lifetime. I have nothing to hide about that. It is not only people with disabilities. What you sow, you have to reap. You have to look at things that happened in your life and ask why. It comes around.'

Hoddle's comments, interpreted as suggesting that disabled people are being punished for sins in a former life, were greeted with a mixture of horror and disbelief by action groups and ministers alike. Freda Murray, chairwoman of the Disabled Supporters' Association, immediately called on Hoddle to resign, saying: 'It is disgusting for a man in his position to be talking like this. I take a boy in a wheelchair and a boy with Down's syndrome to matches. What are they going to think?' A spokeswoman for Disability Action added: 'How can he look in the face of all those disabled people who line the pitch at Wembley after what he has said?' And Eddy Burns, chairman of Incapacity Action, came quickly to the point. 'Glenn Hoddle,' he said, 'is clearly off his rocker.'

Burns was not alone in his opinions although others fought shy of expressing them quite so bluntly. Margaret Hodge, Minister for the Disabled, joined the chorus for Hoddle to stand down as England manager. 'There are probably over six million disabled people in Britain today,' she said, 'and to suggest to them that somehow it is their fault, or somehow they have a lesser contribution to make to society, is deeply insulting.' Sports Minister Tony Banks weighed in with a typically flippant appraisal: 'If his theory is correct, he is in for real problems in the next life. He will probably be doomed to come back as Glenn Hoddle!' More worryingly for the FA, the Nationwide Building Society, new sponsor of the England team, indicated that unless Hoddle were reprimanded, the society's £15-million-a-year deal with the Football Association could be in jeopardy. The Nationwide's Mike Lazenby said: 'On the day we announced our sponsorship, we said we wanted football to clean up its act, and Mr Hoddle's comments are not helpful.' He called for the manager 'to ensure that his personal views are not confused with those of the England team or its sponsor', adding ominously: 'If he did repeat these comments I think we would need to talk very seriously with the FA about the implications.'

On the ropes, Hoddle fought back, labelling *The Times* article 'scandalous and disgraceful' and added: 'My support and care for disabled people is well known. What disabled people must know is that they will always have my overwhelming support, care, consideration and dedication.' Without doubt he was stunned by the ferocity of the reaction to *The Times* piece, not least because he had said much the same about disability in an interview with Radio 5 the previous May. However, on that occasion his comments had not been picked up by the national press.

As the storm intensified, David Davies made calls to senior members of the FA's international Committee on the Sunday afternoon and arranged a meeting at Whites Hotel, near the FA offices in London's Lancaster Gate, for the following day. On the Monday Hoddle, battling to keep his £350,000-a-year job, gave an interview to ITN that, drawing freely from the Football Manager's Book of Clichés and dotted with his own bad grammar, proved conclusively that his was a mind not burdened by excessive intellect. In it he said:

> The only reason people are saying I should resign is that they are saying I have come out and said that people disabled and handicapped have been paying for their sins and I have never ever said that. I don't believe that. At this moment in time, if that changes in years to come I don't know, but what happens here today and changes as we go along that is part of life's learning and part of your inner beliefs. But at this moment in time I did not say them things and at the end of the day I want to put that on record because it has hurt people.

As an explanation, it left people more baffled than ever.

While Hoddle now accused reporter Dickinson of misinterpreting – rather than misquoting – him and tried to claim that their conversation was off the record, *The Times* stood by its story. Dickinson himself wrote: 'Glenn Hoddle has changed his story so many times that I have lost track. Instead of issuing a proper denial, he is in denial.' Predictably Eileen Drewery defended Hoddle, complaining that he was being treated 'worse than Saddam Hussein', and the manager's thirteen-year-old daughter Zara wrote a letter to the BBC's Ceefax service pleading for him to be kept on. But Prime Minister Tony Blair, speaking on ITV's *This Morning with Richard and Judy*, entered the debate with the view that Hoddle should resign if he had made the controversial comments. Even former Tottenham manager Terry Neill, who had given Hoddle his debut as a player, was forced to admit: 'He screwed up. As a person, he comes across as a crank.' On the Monday night

Hoddle joined the fifteen-man FA panel for half an hour to be told his position was in peril.

The Tuesday morning newspapers offered no respite for the beleaguered England manager. Those that did not demand he resign called for his sacking. The *Sun*, who had earlier mocked him as 'Mad Hod', filled its front page with the emphatic headline, GO, and wrote in a leader: 'Hoddle was already a joke with the players, who laughed at his ridiculous antics with a barmaid turned faith healer. Now he is a figure of hate for the fans.' The *Express* produced a reader poll that put dissatisfaction with Hoddle at eighty per cent and stated that he was 'unfit to bear the responsibility of being England coach'. The *Guardian* called for his head on the grounds that he had become 'a bit of a laughing stock'. Only the *Mirror*, which had secured an exclusive three-page interview with Hoddle, offered any editorial support suggesting in its leader headline: 'HONEST HOD IS WORTH ONE LAST CHANCE'.

Had Hoddle's England team been carrying all before them, he might just have managed to ride the storm. But a poor start to their qualifying campaign for Euro 2000 – defeat in Sweden followed by a goalless draw with Bulgaria at Wembley – made it easy for the FA to go with the flow. After reconvening their meeting on Tuesday morning, the FA delivered the news that most had been expecting – and Hoddle had been dreading – early that evening. In a statement announcing that Hoddle's contract was being terminated by mutual consent, the FA said his position had become untenable. The statement, read by Davies, went on: 'After more than 24 hours of meetings and discussions it became apparent to all those concerned that this was the right decision for English football... The past few days have been painful for everyone involved, but that is as nothing compared to any offence that may have been caused to disabled people in our community and in our country. We accept this wasn't Glenn's intention.'

Hoddle finally apologised for making a serious error of judgement but still felt that he had been hard done by. 'If you lose your job over a football-related thing, fine,' he said. 'But with this it's an injustice.' Asked whether sacrificing Drewery might have saved his skin, he replied: 'I said to the FA six months ago that Eileen Drewery was helpful. I said she was helpful to the players and staff. I'd done it at club level and seen the fruits of it. The press ridiculed it, used it as a vehicle to have a pop at me. That's where you stand up for your principles.'

The Brookline Bear Pit

1999

It is hard to believe that a competition devised by a Hertfordshire seed merchant could arouse such feelings of fierce commitment and intense nationalistic rivalry as does the Ryder Cup. Over the past twenty years golf's premier team event has become a breeding ground for the worst aspects of patriotism. Normally mild-mannered players are turned into whooping and hollering dervishes, punching the air in triumph where once they would have quietly shaken hands, while the galleries behave as if they are on one long stag night.

It wasn't always thus. When the Ryder Cup was fought out between the USA and Great Britain & Ireland, it was an altogether more dignified affair. Every two years – give or take the odd surprise – the British would turn up and be routinely slaughtered. The Americans were happy to win and the British were just happy to be taking part. We knew our place – and in the Ryder Cup it was that of runners-up. But then the contest became so one-sided that even the Americans began to lose interest in winning. To breathe new life into the contest, the British & Irish team was expanded to include Europe and the addition of the cream of Spain and Sweden at last threatened American supremacy. The Americans suddenly realised that hollow victories were vastly underrated while the Europeans relished the chance to topple some of the Yankee big guns. The friendly contest was now a very serious business indeed.

At The Belfry in 1989 some European spectators cheered when American players drove into the water. Unaccustomed to defeat and nursing wounded pride, the Americans responded with the 'War on the Shore' at Kiawah Island where their players wound up the crowds by wearing Desert Storm hats from the Gulf War. With the likes of Corey Pavin strutting belligerently around the course as if taking part in a real war, that year's Ryder Cup made for unpalatable viewing and led to calls for better crowd control in future.

The 1999 Ryder Cup – the 33rd in total – was to be staged at the Brookline Country Club, near Boston, Massachusetts, and having lost the previous two contests, the US team were determined to regain the trophy. The European captain Mark James, himself a spiky competitor, had chosen an inexperienced line-up, leaving out such old hands as Nick Faldo, Ian Woosnam and Bernhard Langer and instead choosing the eccentric Swede, Jesper Parnevik, and Scotland's Andrew Coltart as his two wild card selections. The foursomes and fourballs – traditionally the European strength – began well for the visitors with Europe leading 6–2 at the end of the first day. The Saturday foursomes and fourballs were squared so that Europe were ahead 10–6 going into the final day's twelve singles matches, needing just four more points to retain the Ryder Cup.

Despite the gloomy predicament, US captain Ben Crenshaw remained confident. 'I have a good feeling about this,' he told journalists even though only five teams in the history of the Ryder Cup had won the trophy after trailing going into the singles. On the Saturday evening Crenshaw enlisted the services of vote-hungry Texas governor George W Bush to read to the US players from the memoirs of a soldier who was at the siege of the Alamo. Even though some of them probably had to help him with the long words, the reading apparently got them fired up and ready for battle on the golf course the next day. As an added inspiration, Crenshaw dressed his team on the final day in shirts bearing a montage of photographs of past American Ryder Cup wins.

Come the Sunday and the US players were ready to die for their country. David Duval was so pumped up he looked ready to burst and Hal Sutton shamelessly whipped up the galleries. He admitted later: 'We knew we had to set the pace and get the crowd involved.' Crenshaw's masterstroke was to send his best six players out first and as the European rookies began to crumble under the onslaught, mindless chants of 'U-S-A!

U-S-A!' from cheerleaders who had seen better days echoed around the course. The first point was posted by Tom Lehman, who beat Europe's Lee Westwood 3&2. A man who usually bore the air of a shy turtle, Lehman was transformed into a raging bull for the occasion and became the brunt of much of the European criticism following the disgraceful scenes towards the end of the contest. Other US players took their cue from Lehman and soon Sutton, Phil Mickelson, Davis Love III, Tiger Woods, Duval, Steve Pate and Jim Furyk had all recorded wins. Crenshaw said afterwards that the performances of his top players had 'ignited everybody'.

The American spectators were highly combustible, nowhere more so than in the presence of the man they love to hate – Scotland's Colin Montgomerie. Red-faced and irascible, Montgomerie represents an easy target for brainless morons and found to his disgust that Brookline seemed to be holding a convention for the species that afternoon. Such was the venom hurled at 'Monty' that his father had to leave the course after seven holes, unable to listen to any more abuse being directed at his son. Montgomerie conceded that the heckling was 'very hurtful' – a view shared even by his opponent, the late Payne Stewart. Incensed by the crowd's behaviour, Stewart later apologised to the Scot. A saddened Mark James noted: 'The rowdiness and disorder was by no means restricted to the crowd. I saw marshals repeatedly turn to the crowd and pump their fists in the air. Those who were supposed to be controlling were actually inciting.'

With spectators making a habit of shouting out just as the Europeans were about to play, the overall balance of the Ryder Cup was swinging in the Americans' favour. A key match was the one immediately ahead of Montgomerie–Stewart, the battle between José Maria Olazábal and Justin Leonard. The Spaniard had been four up after eleven holes but then made bogeys on 12 and 13, and when Leonard sank a birdie on the 14th, the deficit was reduced to one. Leonard squared the match with a long birdie putt on the 15th and, with other results going the Americans' way, the position was that if Leonard could avoid defeat the Ryder Cup would be changing hands.

So there was everything to play for as Olazábal and Leonard reached the seventeenth green. Leonard was the further from the hole and faced a 45ft putt for a birdie. Allowed the common courtesy of silence as he lined up his putt, Leonard proceeded to sink it – a magnificent shot under enormous pressure. As ignorant of the basic rules of the game as they were in their behaviour, the Americans poured on to the green in victory celebrations – players, caddies, wives and officials. They thought the Ryder Cup was theirs, forgetting that Leonard could still be beaten if Olazábal sank his putt to halve the hole and then went on to win the eighteenth. Not that there was much chance of Olazábal being able to hole his putt as the American invaders had already run across his line and wrecked his concentration in their rush to embrace Leonard. The worst transgressor was born-again Christian Tom Lehman. Europe's vice-captain Sam Torrance snapped: 'Calls himself a man of God? That was the most disgraceful thing I have ever seen.'

Back down the fairway, Montgomerie, having witnessed the scenes from a distance, fully expected the players to walk on to the next tee. 'Then I saw Olly standing there on his own trying to make a putt and I thought it was unbelievable.'

Inevitably Olazábal missed his putt, his first attempt to line up being interrupted by yet more shouts of 'U-S-A! U-S-A!' When the ball stayed out, Crenshaw bent down and kissed the green. In the event Olazábal birdied the eighteenth to halve his match but it could not prevent the USA from winning $14^{1}/_{2}$ – $13^{1}/_{2}$. The shaken Spaniard told reporters: 'It was very sad to see an ugly picture. That was no way to behave. Showing emotions is fine but we are playing a match and we should show respect to each other.'

Sir Michael Bonallack, secretary of the Royal and Ancient Club of St Andrews, likened the scene to a 'bear pit'. He went on: 'I felt embarrassed for golf. It went way beyond the decency you associate with proper golf. I love the Ryder Cup, but I do not want to see it degenerate into a mob demonstration every time we play it.' James warned that some of Europe's leading golfers might avoid playing tournaments in the United States because of the abuse and said of the Americans' behaviour: 'We are going to get into a situation where fights will break out if we don't stop this type of thing now.'

Crenshaw subsequently apologised to the Europeans. 'There was no call for it,' he admitted. 'Celebrating started spilling over and for this we are truly sorry.' Lehman was similarly contrite. 'That was overexuberance,' he explained, 'there is no question about it. It wasn't a good thing, but what is done is done. You wish you could have contained yourself but sometimes you get carried away.'

James cut a sad and lonely figure in defeat. He later wrote: 'I was not really sure where to go or what to do. I had never previously experienced anything like it. I could cope with the disappointment of defeat... but to be so closely involved in something which was so alien to my sport, so degrading and intolerable, left me drained and empty inside.'

While the jingoistic American press accused the Europeans of being sore losers and 'crybabies', the British media savaged the buffoonery at Brookline. The *Daily Telegraph* wrote: 'The Americans not only indulged in the worst excesses of triumphalism during and after the match, but also turned in a repulsive display of bad manners.' In *The Times* John Hopkins warned: 'I fear that the last Ryder Cup of the millennium may also mark the last Ryder Cup that contains the essential charm, skill and grace under pressure that have marked so many contests in the past.' These views were shared by the *Mirror*, who reported: 'Football hooligans act better than the way Americans have treated the Ryder Cup over the last three days. Their antics whipped the crowd into uncontrolled boorish behaviour. Sporting relations between the two nations have slipped to an all-time low.'

Eleven days later Tom Lehman came to St Andrews for the Dunhill Cup competition and was taken aback by the frosty reception awaiting him. 'It concerns me that my reputation seems to have been somewhat damaged,' he wailed. 'I'm not a monster, I'm not a rogue, I'm not a hooligan.' He pleaded that he wanted to be allowed to put the Ryder Cup behind him, but Mark James was in unforgiving mood. 'You can't pretend that nothing has happened,' he retorted. 'What we saw and experienced at Brookline was very sad. I don't think we should forget about it. Golf definitely has a problem and we need to address it.'

Lehman subsequently wrote a letter of apology to Olazábal and ironically it was James who soon found himself in hot water following the publication of *Into the Bear Pit*, his account of that year's Ryder Cup. In the book James accused Nick Faldo of undermining team morale in the run-up to the match and described how he had thrown away a good luck note from Faldo on the eve of the battle of Brookline. A furious Faldo responded by accusing James of bringing both the Ryder Cup and the European Tour into disrepute and demanded that disciplinary action be taken. Following much petty squabbling, Faldo got his way and James was removed from his position on the Tournament Players' Committee. As another instance of the game of golf being elbowed from centre stage by the folly of human behaviour, it pretty much summed up everything connected with the 1999 Ryder Cup.

Siding with Satan

2000

On the morning of 1 June 2002 the body of former South Africa cricket captain Hansie Cronje was recovered from a plane crash in the country's Western Cape province. Under ordinary circumstances the sudden death at the age of just 32 of a prominent sportsman would provoke fulsome tributes and national mourning, but Cronje was never likely to be remembered for any of his positive contributions to South African cricket – only for the match-fixing scandal of two years earlier that cast a shadow over the entire sport. As the BBC's Jonathan Agnew said on hearing of Cronje's death: 'It's a tragic end to a tragic story.'

That story began on 25 September 1969 when Wessel Johannes Cronje was born in Bloemfontein of solid Afrikaner stock. An unsmiling and, outwardly at least, uncomplicated leader of men, Cronje captained his province, Orange Free State, at the age of 21 and was earmarked as a future South Africa captain from the moment he made his Test debut in 1991. He first deputised as national captain at 24 before succeeding Kepler Wessels a year later. With South Africa returning to the sporting fold in 1992 following years of isolation, Cronje became the country's most admired cricketer – a man driven by the desire for success. Under his inspirational leadership, South Africa rose to number two in the world rankings and threatened to knock Australia from their pedestal. As a born-again Christian, Cronje was equally uncompromising off the field and declared himself committed to the highest personal moral code. He reacted angrily in New Zealand when the United Cricket Board of South Africa attempted to incorporate as a hollow gesture non-White cricketers clearly not up to international standard, and also offered to step down from the captaincy during an England tour of South Africa when his form temporarily deserted him. On the face of it, therefore, Hansie Cronje represented all that was good about South African cricket, which explained why the sensational revelations of April 2000 were treated initially with such incredulity.

The news first broke on 7 April when Delhi police released details of a recording of a conversation on a mobile phone during the one-day series between India and South Africa the previous month, which they said pointed to match-fixing. The Delhi authorities claimed that the two voices on the tape were those of Cronje and a representative of an Indian betting syndicate. The two individuals were heard to agree that South Africa's Herschelle Gibbs should not score more than twenty runs in one match. The man said to be Cronje also divulged useful information regarding the team, including a suggestion that off-spinner Derek Crookes might open the bowling later in the series. An astounded Crookes did indeed open the bowling in the final match, conceding 53 runs in just six overs.

Reacting to the allegations, Cronje said: 'I am stunned. They are completely without substance. I have been privileged to play for South Africa and I want to assure every South African that I have made a hundred per cent effort to win every match that I have played.' Assured by his captain that the accusations were totally unfounded, Dr Ali Bacher, managing director of the UCBSA, issued a strong denial, concluding: 'Hansie Cronje is known for his unquestionable integrity and honesty.'

The South African press also stood up for Cronje. Veteran cricket journalist Trevor Chesterfield angrily denounced the tapes as poor fakes, pointing out that the supposed Cronje spoke with an Indian accent. It later transpired that Chesterfield had not heard the original tape at all, but a reading of the transcript. On 9 April in the presence of Bacher and UCBSA president Percy Sonn, Cronje reiterated his innocence at a press conference in Durban. 'I want to make it a hundred per cent clear,' he stated, 'that I deny ever receiving any sum of money during the one-day international series in

India. I want to also make it absolutely clear that I have never spoken to any member of the team about throwing a game.'

So that was that. The Indian police had done their worst and Cronje had denied everything with such conviction that even those who adhered to the old principle that there was no smoke without fire must have believed that the fuss might soon blow over. Then at 3 a.m. on 11 April Dr Bacher was woken by a phone call. It was Cronje, confessing that he had not been 'entirely honest' when issuing his denials. He now admitted to having accepted between US$10,000 and $15,000 from an Indian bookmaker called Sanjay – but for 'forecasting' results, not match-fixing. Acknowledging an 'error of judgement', Cronje wrote a bizarre confession in which he blamed the devil:

> It has been a tough weekend but also a great weekend for me in that I now have the opportunity to face myself in the mirror again for the first time since the Indian tour. I have been a role model for many people in South Africa and this was a lesson for all of you out there: when Satan comes knocking on the door, always keep your eyes on the Lord Jesus Christ and ask him to protect you from any wrong. The moment I took my eyes off Jesus, my whole world turned dark and it felt like someone had stuck a knife through my chest.

Ali Bacher knew precisely how Cronje felt. Declaring that the UCBSA had been 'deceived', Bacher, previously Cronje's staunchest ally, now announced his sacking as captain of South Africa.

Although Cronje still denied fixing or manipulating matches, his partial confession and summary dismissal shook the nation. While Cronje frantically tried to cover his tracks by throwing away incriminating mobile phones and hiding money that had been given to him by bookmakers, doubts began to surround England's morale-boosting victory in the fifth Test at Centurion Park in January 2000. After South Africa had posted a respectable score, the match was ruined by rain, no play being possible on days two, three or four. With South Africa having already clinched the series, the game seemed certain to end in a draw, but then Cronje, who habitually gave no quarter on the cricket field, suddenly tried to set up a result by suggesting that England forfeit their first innings and South

Africa their second – a move unprecedented in the history of Test cricket. He went on to offer England captain Nasser Hussain a target of 270 runs in 73 overs and when this was rejected he came back with a revised 255 in 73 overs. When that, too, was turned down, a seemingly desperate Cronje made Hussain a third offer – 249 runs in 76 overs. The deal was done and England got home with five balls to spare. A number of the South African players were less than happy at the outcome. Daryll Cullinan later said: 'I would like to think that Hansie was acting in the best interests of the game and doing something for the public, but it totally went against the guy I knew. He wasn't in the habit of giving something to the other side or making a game of it.'

When the official inquiry into the match-fixing allegations began in Cape Town on 7 June, presided over by retired judge Edwin King, former South African Test spinner Pat Symcox confirmed an old story that the team were offered $250,000 by Indian bookmakers to throw a one-off international against India in Bombay in 1996. Cronje had always maintained that the players simply 'laughed it off', but now it emerged that the offer had been discussed at three team meetings with Cronje eventually getting the price raised to $350,000. However, it fell through because several senior players were vehemently opposed to the idea. Nevertheless it was obvious that, far from the Indian series of 2000 being a momentary aberration, Cronje had long been susceptible to corruption. He had evidently taken his eyes off Jesus for some time.

Next Herschelle Gibbs confessed to agreeing to his former captain's bribe of $15,000 to score fewer than twenty runs in the final one-day international against India at Nagpur on 19 March 2000. With South Africa already beaten in the series, Cronje also persuaded Henry Williams to agree to concede in excess of fifty runs from his allotted ten overs. In the event Gibbs found that the thrill of scoring runs outweighed any financial consideration and he went on to compile a majestic 74 off 53 balls and when South Africa came to bowl, Williams, too, failed to deliver his side of the bargain, retiring injured at the end of his second over. South Africa ended up winning by ten runs. Although the betting coup was foiled, Gibbs and

Williams were subsequently banned from international cricket for six months for their involvement in the affair.

Taking the stand, Cronje admitted receiving a phone call from a gambler named Marlon Aronstam urging him to 'make a game' of that fifth Test against England. Cronje's reward for contriving a result was a small financial bonus plus a leather jacket for his wife. In the face of further damning evidence, Cronje was offered immunity from prosecution if he made a full disclosure of his role in match-fixing. He said he had first been approached in 1995 by 'an Indian or Pakistani' called 'John' (Indian police allege that 'John' was really a mysterious individual named Mukesh Gupta) and had since received some $140,000 from bookmakers for supplying information and asking team-mates to play badly. He told the King Commission how he had hidden money from his wife at their home and had tried to convince her that their new-found wealth had been earned legitimately from benefits and bonuses. Of the moment when the scandal first broke he recalled: 'I had this horrible sinking feeling in my stomach that my cricket career would be over. Everyone would get dragged into it...but my first thought was of self-preservation.' Led away in tears after completing his evidence, Cronje announced his intention to put his ill-gotten gains to good use 'to try to redress the wrongs I have done to my game and my country'.

In October 2000 Cronje was banned from cricket for life by the UCBSA, a decision later endorsed by the game's governing body, the International Cricket Council. He thus remained an outcast until his premature death. The *Natal Witness* described his demise as bringing 'the finality of a Greek tragedy to the saga of a flawed hero...who fell from grace because of a fatal love of the money offered to him by dubious bookmakers' while an editorial in *Die Burger* said that 'in Hansie, South Africa has lost a sinner-hero'. The Indian press echoed the sentiments. The *Times of India* wrote: 'Tragic as Cronje's untimely death is, what is even more tragic is the way he will be remembered – an example of what happens when talent succumbs to temptation. The legend of Hansie Cronje died long before he did. But his career will, hopefully, serve as a cautionary tale for those tempted to ignore the virtues of playing with a straight bat.'

The Spanish Inquisition

2000

The Olympics may have been tainted for a number of years but it was always hoped that at least the Paralympic Games – that platform for nobility and courage – might remain unimpeached by accusations of cheating and malpractice. Surely this, more than any other sporting competition, represented the original Olympic ideal that it was the taking part that mattered. Unfortunately nobody had told the Spanish Paralympic basketball team.

In the wake of the hugely successful Sydney Olympics of 2000, the following month's Paralympic Games in the same city attracted greater media attention than usual. The surprise packages were Spain whose haul of 107 medals – 37 gold – put them third in the final medals table behind Australia and Great Britain. It was Spain's most successful Paralympics by some distance.

Among Spain's golds was an 87–63 victory over Russia in the final of the intellectual disability basketball tournament. But then it emerged that ten of the twelve-strong Spanish squad had no disability whatsoever. The medals were handed back and a leading Spanish official was forced to resign.

The man who blew the whistle on the Spanish basketball team was one of its players, Carlos Ribagorda, who also worked as a journalist on the business magazine *Capital*. Despite having no mental handicap, Ribagorda had been playing for Spain's intellectually disabled national team for two years when Paralympic officials approached him about playing in Sydney. He decided to accept the offer with a view to exposing the scandal afterwards.

Ribagorda's story appeared in *Capital* a month after the Games. Under Paralympics rules, a player had to have an IQ of 70 or less to be eligible for intellectually disabled competition, but Ribagorda said that nobody ever tested him or asked him to provide any documentation to prove his disability. He claimed that at least fifteen athletes with no incapacity at all, including ten basketball players, were signed up by the Spanish Federation for Mentally Handicapped Sports (FEDDI) and told to pretend they were handicapped. The goal, he said, was to win more medals so that the federation would qualify for additional funding. Ribagorda wrote:

> The FEDDI did not hesitate in signing up athletes without any type of handicap. They just sent them an official letter. The aim of this policy was to win medals and gain more sponsorship. The FEDDI discovered that it could benefit from signing up athletes who had no physical or mental handicap. The only test they did was to make me do half a dozen sit-ups and take my blood pressure. We never had any medical or psychological tests but we were told to slow the rhythm of our play so as not to awaken suspicions.

Igor Kopylov, who was in charge of the beaten Russian team, admitted: 'After the competition there were no protests from anyone, so the whole thing is a bit surprising although we suspected some discrepancy with members of the Spanish team. As far as individual skills and physical attributes like players' height, both teams were pretty much evenly matched. But tactically they were much better than us, which can only suggest one thing – they had good mental capacity.'

Apart from Ribagorda himself, the Spanish Paralympic basketball squad also included a lawyer, an engineer and a number of students. Ribagorda claimed that members of the Spanish table tennis, track-and-field and swimming teams at Sydney were not disabled intellectually or physically either.

In the ensuing hullabaloo an American Paralympic coach said that some nations allowed athletes who suffered only from dyslexia to play in basketball teams.

The Spanish Paralympic Committee reacted to the scandal by ordering the victorious basketball team to return their gold medals. Fernando Martin Vicente, president of FEDDI, was forced to resign 'for actions that were clearly contrary to the interests of the Spanish and international Paralympic movement'. And in January 2001 the International Paralympic Committee announced that it would no longer include athletes with intellectual or mental disabilities in its activities. A sporting outlet had been closed to many because of the actions of an unsporting few.

Freddie the Fix

2001

Until 1999 a sad omission from the sporting calendar was an event that allowed owls, lions, bears, swans, extinct dinosaurs and merry mariners to compete on an equal footing. Then Huntingdon racecourse manager Jim Allen came up with the idea of the Mascot Grand National, involving the cream of British sports' team mascots but predominantly from the world of football. Running over a course featuring six fences (somewhat smaller in size than those negotiated by real horses), seventeen mascots took part in the inaugural competition, which was won by Beau Brummie Bulldog of Birmingham City.

The success of the event prompted a bumper turnout for the following year and, although there was a hint of sabotage in the build-up to the big race with a couple of mascots reporting that their heads had been stolen, 49 lined up at the start. Victory went to Watford FC's heavily backed Harry the Hornet, who stung bookmakers to the tune of £5,000 with a late swoop to pip Swansea City's belligerent Cyril the Swan. But the surest indication that the Mascot Grand National was being taken seriously occurred in 2001 when the race was the subject of an attempted betting coup, which resulted in the winner being sensationally disqualified.

Before the race, which took place at Huntingdon on 30 September, much interest surrounded Freddie the Fox, the entry of the Countryside Appreciation Group. Not only was Freddie backed down from 33–1 to 10–1 but also it was observed that he was wearing spikes rather than traditional mascot boots. Yet the cunning fox managed to grab a place on the front line reserved for those mascots in heavy footwear and sprinted away to an effortless victory.

Immediately after the race, rumours circulated that the fox was part of a betting coup by a professional gambler, prompting an official inquiry. The fur flew when Freddie's costume was found to contain Olympic 400 metres hurdler Matthew Douglas – a semifinalist at the Sydney Olympics. Furthermore the Countryside Appreciation Group proved to be a fictitious organisation. While Douglas confessed that he had been asked to run to raise money for a cancer charity, Freddie was disqualified and first place awarded to Rushden & Diamonds mascot Dazzler the Lion, a 33–1 shot. Oldham Athletic's Chaddie the Owl was promoted to runners-up spot.

Jim Allen told reporters: 'It was a shame that Freddie spoiled the day for many mascots and spectators, but we must look on the bright side and feel proud that we have attracted an Olympic semifinalist to the event. I have already received an entry form for next year's race from the USA Athletics Association mascot Michael the Johnson. We will of course be checking his credentials.'

Skategate

2002

Commentators threw up their hands in horror; the Salt Lake City crowd registered disapproval with a chorus of boos. The decision to award the pairs gold medal in the figure skating competition at the 2002 Winter Olympics to Russians Elena Berezhnaya and Anton Sikharulidze was definitely not a popular one. Most observers thought gold should have gone to the Canadians Jamie Sale and David Pelletier who skated faultlessly whereas the Russian duo slipped up badly at one point in their routine. But sport is sometimes all about differing opinions and controversial judgements, as a result of which it seemed that the Canadians would have to accept defeat with good grace. Then a strange thing happened. The next day the French judge, Marie-Reine Le Gougne, suddenly broke down in front of her fellow officials and revealed that she had been pressured into voting for the Russians. This disclosure was dramatic enough in itself but would be just the first in a scandal that has brought accusation and counteraccusation plus allegations of a link to a Russian crime boss. Not since the days of Tonya Harding has ice skating attracted so much unwelcome publicity.

Le Gougne spoke out after the Russians had taken the gold in a 5–4 judging split. She claimed that the French federation president, Didier Gailhaguet, had ordered her to vote for Berezhnaya and Sikharulidze as part of a deal that had been struck between the two countries. The favour was apparently due to be returned when France's Marina Anissina (who happened to be Russian-born) and Gwendal Peizerat took part in the ice dancing competition a week later. Sure enough,

Anissina and Peizerat won France's first gold in figure skating since 1932 – also on a 5–4 split – although the Russian judge did not vote them first.

By then, in a virtually unprecedented step, the IOC had awarded duplicate gold medals to the Canadian pair – an indication that great significance was being attached to Le Gougne's allegations. This infuriated Russian officials who demanded that their skater, Irina Slutskaya, placed second in the women's figure skating to the sixteen-year-old American Sarah Hughes, be awarded a joint gold on account of 'biased judging'. 'Canadian pair skaters were awarded their gold medals,' said the head of the Russian delegation. 'Now that subjective judging harmed us, we want the same for Slutskaya.' When the protest was rejected, the Russians threatened to walk out of the Games, citing a 'witch hunt' against their competitors.

The waters became even murkier when, in an interview with the French sports newspaper *L'Equipe*, Le Gougne retracted her story, claiming that she had been under emotional duress and had been harassed by International Skating Union officials, including Britain's Sally Stapleford, into making false accusations against Gailhaguet. Le Gougne said: 'Physically, I felt threatened. She (Stapleford) criticised me for having voted for the Russians. That's why I broke down.' She also inferred that Stapleford wanted Sale and Pelletier to win because the Briton's father is Canadian. An angry Stapleford rejected the allegations as 'completely unfounded and untrue' and likened the scenario to something out of *Dallas* or *Dynasty*.

Rumours of corruption within skating rumbled on for a further ten weeks until, at the start of May, an ISU hearing in Lausanne banned Le Gougne and Gailhaguet from the sport for three years and barred them from officiating at the next winter games. They were the harshest punishments imposed in the history of skating. Le Gougne was found guilty of misconduct on two counts – voting for the Russian pair on Gailhaguet's orders and not reporting him to the ISU. Gailhaguet was suspended for instructing Le Gougne to give first place to the Russians. Afterwards Le Gougne protested: 'I've been the scapegoat from the beginning. Some people have said, "You are the Bin Laden of figure skating." My God, how is it possible to say such an insult?'

Just when it seemed that the vote-rigging scandal had been laid to rest, the story took on another bizarre twist when in July 2002 a reputed Russian crime baron was charged with engineering the whole plot. Alimzan Tokhtakhounov was arrested at the resort of Forte dei Marmi in Northern Italy after Italian wiretaps in an unrelated investigation captured a series of telephone calls, apparently between himself and unnamed conspirators during the Winter Olympics. Tokhtakhounov, described as a 'major figure in international Eurasian organised crime' and who was rumoured to have fixed Moscow beauty pageants in the early 1990s, was charged with conspiracy to commit wire fraud and conspiracy to commit bribery relating to sporting contests. It was said that his motive for fixing the pairs and the ice dancing competitions at the Winter Olympics was that he hoped to gain favour with the French authorities to have his French visa extended.

'We are going to make Marina an Olympic champion,' he allegedly told Annisina's mother in one of the taped conversations. 'The French helped us in pairs skating. They gave us the last vote and said that for that, we have to make sure that Marina gets first place, even if she falls.'

'It was a classic quid pro quo,' said Manhattan US Attorney James Comey. 'Everybody will go home with the gold and maybe there'll be a little gold for me.'

To the outsider it seems inconceivable that such dark forces could be at work behind the awarding of marks in figure skating. But as David Pelletier told Canadian television: 'Corruption has always been there. It is always going to be there, let's not kid ourselves. You just hope it isn't going to happen to you.'

F1's Day of Shame

2002

The 2002 Austrian Grand Prix had all the makings of a rare victory for one of the nice guys of Formula One – Ferrari driver Rubens Barrichello. With only one win to his name in his nine-year F1 career, the Brazilian dominated the weekend at the A1-Ring, qualifying on pole and leading from the off. He was still there on the final straight, ahead of team-mate and comfortable World Championship leader Michael Schumacher. But then yards from the chequered flag, and to the dismay of the crowd as well as the millions of television viewers around the world, Barrichello was ordered by his team to take his foot off the accelerator, pull over and allow Schumacher through to win. It was a Ferrari one-two, but not in the rightful order.

The nature of Schumacher's win – his fifth in the six races that season – prompted booing from spectators as he stepped on to the victory stand. The ceremony itself was a farce with a faintly embarrassed Schumacher hauling Barrichello up to share the top of the podium for a few moments before handing him the trophy and telling him to keep it.

Barrichello realised that, as Ferrari's number two driver, there was no point in arguing about team orders. 'I did as I was told,' he said philosophically, 'even if I would have preferred not to have been asked to move over.' Schumacher, too, professed himself surprised by the contrived result. 'It was a team decision,' he confirmed. 'I didn't believe it. Suddenly they told me Rubens would move over. I am not very pleased about it either but we have to look at what are the team's ambitions. They are out to win the championship. Imagine if we had lost the championship by this number of points at the end of the season – the team would look stupid. I have to thank Rubens. I don't take a lot of joy from the victory.'

He was in good company. While the fans at the circuit let their feelings be known, Williams' technical director Patrick Head called it the most disgusting thing he had seen in 22 years of motor racing. Sweden's state-run gambling agency, Svenska Spel, said it would pay winning bets on both Schumacher and Barrichello but Fernando Henrique Cardoso, President of Brazil, faced no such dilemma, issuing an unequivocal statement in which he simply called Barrichello the winner. Emerson Fittipaldi, Brazil's two-time world champion, raged: 'I wouldn't have let Michael Schumacher past. It's a disgrace, it's absurd.'

Media condemnation was universal, even in Ferrari's home country where some Italian journalists wrote that Ferrari red was now a blush of shame. The *Gazzetta dello Sport* said: 'It could have been a great day for Ferrari. Unfortunately it turned into a nasty day of shame.' The German paper *Bild* lashed Schumacher. 'Sport was the loser,' it wrote, 'because victory and defeat were not decided on the track but in the stands. Schumi is the loser because his so-called victory was nothing other than a betrayal of his millions of supporters.' *France Soir* called Ferrari's action 'shameful, scandalous, depressing and unworthy of all those who love sports' while *L'Equipe* described the orders as a 'monumental gaffe'. In Britain the *Daily Mail* attacked 'a crassly cynical sporting "fix" orchestrated by the Ferrari team with complete disregard for fair play and decency' and the *Sun* headlined its report of the race: DAY F1 DIED OF SHAME.

Ferrari sporting director Jean Todt, who made the controversial decision, defended his actions: 'In the past we lost the title in the last race three times in a row (from 1997 to 1999) and we have to make the most of every situation.' He was backed by Ferrari chairman Luca Di Montezemolo who insisted that, despite the fans' disappointment, the orders were correct. While they had acted within the rules as they stood, Ferrari had underestimated the level of public discontent, but they received a sharp reminder when Schumacher was loudly booed at the next Grand Prix in Montreal. Accustomed to playing the role of the hero, the German was clearly taken aback to be deemed the villain of this particular piece.

There was further outrage when the sport's governing body, the FIA, met in Paris at the end of June to discuss what penalties – if any – to impose upon Ferrari. Unable to find the team in breach of any rule on the track, although it 'deplored the manner in which team orders were given and executed at the Austrian Grand Prix', the FIA had to settle for fining Ferrari and both drivers for breaking with protocol on the victory podium. The statement read:

> The podium procedure was not followed. Having finished second, Barrichello, who is a Brazilian national, stood on the top step while the German national anthem played for Michael Schumacher. Michael Schumacher then ascended the top step and both drivers, rather than just the winner, stood there while the Italian national anthem was played. Michael Schumacher took the trophy for first place from the Austrian Chancellor, did not acknowledge him, handed the trophy to Rubens Barrichello and then took the second place trophy from the Austrian Deputy Chancellor.

The message was clear: in the world of F1 it was perfectly acceptable to insult the public, many of whom had paid a small fortune for tickets, but on no account must a dignitary be snubbed.

Predictably Schumacher cruised to a fifth world title in a season rendered achingly dull by his total domination. In fact the destiny of the drivers' championship was already decided with nearly half the season left, meaning that a hefty points deduction for the Austria fiasco might have livened things up a little. Whether out of guilt for the earlier transgression or because his hide is so thick that he really has no appreciation of public opinion, Schumacher foolishly tried to engineer another contrived finish in the penultimate Grand Prix of the season, at Indianapolis. This time he attempted to create a dead heat with Barrichello, who had been running second all race, but mistimed it, the Brazilian being declared the winner by 0.11 seconds. This latest Ferrari farce was too much for Canadian driver Jacques Villeneuve who branded the antics 'embarrassing', saying that they 'just turned the sport into a joke'.

The Indianapolis incident also represented the last straw for FIA president Max Mosley who finally realised that unless he did something to prevent a repetition of these non-finishes, a billion-dollar sport would vanish under a tidal wave of public apathy. So among a number of new measures introduced for the 2003 season was a rule banning teams from manipulating the climax to a Grand Prix. Hopefully we will never again be subjected to scenes such as those witnessed at the A1-Ring in May 2002.

Showdown in Sapporo

2002

Roy Keane and Mick McCarthy had never exactly been bosom buddies. The ill feeling between them started back in 1992 when Keane, a newcomer to the Irish squad, kept the team bus waiting en route to a friendly in Boston, Massachusetts. McCarthy, one of the senior players, gave Keane an earful for showing disrespect to manager Jack Charlton, whereupon the youngster returned it with interest. McCarthy probably gave the incident little more thought but Keane never forgot a feud – ask Alf Inge Haaland.

A complex, introverted character, Keane had no time for either McCarthy or Charlton. As a player McCarthy was not really fit to be in the same team as the classy Keane. He was a solid, uncompromising defender but one whose passes were as likely to end up in Row Z as with a team-mate. He believed in kicking the ball the way he was facing and as such was a man very much in the mould of his manager. There were no frills with McCarthy. What you saw was what you got. If Keane were a restaurant, he would be the Savoy Grill; McCarthy would be a Happy Eater. As for Charlton, Keane detested his haphazard approach, how the Irish always seemed to muddle through in that endearing way of theirs. As a driven professional, Keane was never willing to settle for second best and considered Charlton to be a clown, an impostor.

When Charlton stepped down as the most successful manager in Irish history, McCarthy, his loyal lieutenant, took over. With his broad Yorkshire accent he was hardly any more Irish than his predecessor, but if he brought the country similar glory, only Roy Keane and a few nit-picking journalists would object. Although he had met with some success as a club manager with Millwall – where he had proved himself a fine motivator if not always crowning himself with glory in the transfer market – McCarthy faced a tough job inheriting an ageing Irish side from a legend like Charlton. Yet not only did he adequately replace the old pros but he also transformed the team's playing style from long-ball to a smooth, passing game and, despite being drawn in a tough qualifying group with Portugal and Holland, the Republic of Ireland reached the finals of the 2002 World Cup in Japan and Korea. McCarthy was hailed as a national hero. But while he celebrated his finest hour in management, the brooding figure of Roy Keane was lurking in the background ready to spoil the party.

When travelling abroad with his club, Manchester United, Keane was accustomed to first-class preparations but, as far as he could see, Ireland in the McCarthy era was every bit as ramshackle as under Charlton. The other players didn't appear to mind but Keane was a perfectionist and, as the only world-class member of the squad, had higher standards to live up to. The first indication of the problems ahead began at the end of the seventeen-hour flight that took the Irish to the Western Pacific island of Saipan, where they were to spend a week preparing and acclimatising for the tournament. On the first day of training, they found a bumpy pitch, no spare goalposts and no footballs. Furthermore the special drinks that the Football Association of Ireland were supplying to help the players cope with dehydration had not yet arrived. Keane was distinctly unimpressed.

The footballs duly arrived but Keane's anger boiled over during a seven-a-side match on a sweltering hot afternoon. Learning that the exhausted goalkeepers, who had been training earlier in the day, were excused the match, Keane protested furiously to coach Packie Bonner that there was no point playing a game with outfield men in goal. When his complaints were overruled, he played on grudgingly before storming off to the team bus. That evening the players were told that Keane had decided to return home for 'personal reasons'.

The FAI spent the night trying to persuade Keane to reconsider, which he eventually did following a phone conversation with his club manager, Sir Alex Ferguson, but not before a fax had been sent to Preston's Colin Healy, calling him up as a last-minute replacement. McCarthy was thus left to tell a disappointed Healy that Keane had done a U-turn.

The simmering resentment, the bitterness and the frustration all blew up two days later on 23 May, by which time it was too late for Healy to be included in the official squad. A furious McCarthy read an interview Keane had done for the *Irish Times* in which he slated the manager's World Cup preparations and questioned the team's ability. Summoning the players to a meeting, McCarthy produced a copy of the article and asked Keane to air his grievances there and then rather than through the media. Keane exploded with rage, the vein on his temple standing out in relief from his face. How dare McCarthy criticise him in front of the rest of the team? He then embarked on a ten-minute rant in which he verbally destroyed McCarthy with a string of choice adjectives such as 'spineless', 'gutless', 'incompetent' and 'ignorant', detailing every perceived slight from that day in Boston to the shambolic training at Saipan. While the rest of the squad sat open-mouthed scarcely able to believe the intensity of the invective, McCarthy could not get a word in. When he did finally manage a reply, he asked Keane whether he had deliberately opted out of the World Cup play-off game in Iran. The mere suggestion sent Keane apoplectic. As the abuse continued, McCarthy could take no more and told him to go. 'You're a f***ing wanker,' Keane yelled. 'I didn't rate you as a player, I don't rate you as a manager and I don't rate you as a person. You're a f***ing wanker and you can stick your World Cup up your arse. I've no respect for you.' And with that, Roy Keane marched out of the World Cup.

The room was filled with an awkward silence until reserve goalkeeper Dean Kiely broke the ice. 'Mick, can I offer my services to fill that midfield dynamo role?' The players dissolved into nervous laughter.

As news of the storm broke, McCarthy defended his move to the waiting press. Branding Keane a 'disruptive influence', he went on: 'I have never witnessed such an attack from any human being. It was vicious and it was unjust. I cannot and will not tolerate that level of abuse being thrown at me so I sent him home. I have made the right decision, not only for the benefit of me but for the squad. This is a huge decision but I am happy to go to the World Cup one man down rather than with a man who shows utter disregard and disrespect for me.'

The FAI declared that it fully supported McCarthy's stance, as did the remaining players. Keane's successor as captain, Steve Staunton, said of the diatribe: 'I've never witnessed anything like it in my life and there is a line, which you can't cross, and unfortunately Roy has crossed it.'

For his part, Keane, who had been flown home on a private jet chartered by Manchester United, muttered that 'my sanity is more important' than staying with the squad. 'The final straw was when I was accused of being disloyal, faking injury and going against my team-mates, in front of everybody, and I wouldn't accept it. I still don't accept that. I have a clear conscience. I don't feel an ounce of guilt about my part in what has happened. I have nothing to be ashamed of.'

McCarthy expressed the hope that with Keane gone he could at last begin to enjoy the World Cup. 'Roy Keane is history,' he declared with commendable optimism, but he must have known deep down that the story would not fade away overnight. Indeed, no sooner had Keane arrived back in England than Irish Prime Minister Bertie Ahern, who was said to be 'very disappointed' by the decision to send the country's number one player home, was offering to mediate between the two parties with a view to securing Keane's immediate return to the squad. McCarthy did not welcome the political intrusion. 'As long as I'm in charge of Ireland's team, he will not play for us. After what he said to me, I could not tolerate his return to the squad. Earlier this week I listened to people telling me he wanted to reverse his decision and come back into the fold first time around. This time he has no chance. I'm in charge of team affairs and if it ever happens that someone else tries to force a player on me, I will quit.'

By now the Irish camp was hosting one long round of Chinese whispers. On 28 May word reached McCarthy that Keane was thinking about apologising. Magnanimously McCarthy offered a tentative olive branch by saying that if

Keane apologised and the players wanted him back, then he was willing to consider his wayward star's return to the fold. But when the players made it clear that they did not want him back, Keane issued a curt statement putting an end to the speculation: 'I do not consider that the best interests of Irish football will be served by my returning to the World Cup. The damage has been done.'

The spectre of Roy Keane continued to haunt the World Cup but not for the first time the Irish gained strength from adversity. Displaying tremendous team spirit that was a tribute to their manager, the players did McCarthy proud, reaching the second round before going out to Spain on penalties. Yet always there was the nagging doubt: how much further could they have gone with Keane in the side?

Back in Ireland opinion was sharply divided between the Keane and McCarthy camps to the extent that some Keane supporters were actually glad when Ireland were knocked out. Keane himself put the boot in by claiming that 'a more astute manager would have won the game' against Spain.

McCarthy and his players received a heartening welcome on their return to Ireland, with around 100,000 people turning out to greet them in Dublin's Phoenix Park, but, like any manager, he was aware that he would only ever be as good as his last result. Moreover, even some of those who thought Keane's banishment was wholly merited could not reconcile themselves to the prospect that he would never again wear the green shirt. But since both sides had made it abundantly clear that they could not work together again, the argument boiled down to who was more important to the cause – the manager or the star player?

The old wounds were reopened in the autumn with the publication of their respective accounts of the blarney barney. Keane complained: 'It was a setup. Humiliation in front of the whole party was the result he was seeking. I know that time is a great healer and all that but it is still very raw to me. It still hurts me and I still feel bitter.' Asked about his present feelings towards McCarthy, Keane replied: 'He can rot in hell.'

McCarthy in turn admitted: 'It sounds daft now, but I never realised I had a problem with Roy Keane. I never saw it coming. But ask me if I'd handle things the same way again, and I'd have to say, "Yes. Exactly the same." I've got no regrets on that score. None at all.'

His job should have been watertight after the success of the World Cup but the Keane affair had seriously destabilised his position. Even some of those who publicly supported the manager were said to be working behind the scenes on ways of finding a compromise so that Keane could return to the side. At least McCarthy knew who his enemies were; it was his friends he had to worry about.

Meanwhile pro-Keane sections of the Irish press were actively waiting for McCarthy to fail...and did not have to be patient for long. Without Keane (who was injured anyway), the team made a poor start to qualifying for the 2004 European Championships and in November McCarthy resigned as Ireland manager 'for the good of the team', citing outside pressures. But as he rightly said: 'I can walk away with my head held high.'

Speculation as to whether his successor, the little-known Brian Kerr, would be to Keane's liking was rendered irrelevant in February 2003 when Keane announced his retirement from international football. He said the decision had been taken on medical advice so that he could prolong his career with Manchester United. The irony would not have been lost on Mick McCarthy.

Bibliography

Barrett, John, *Wimbledon*, Collins Willow, 2001.

Barrett, Norman (ed.), *The Daily Telegraph Chronicle of Cricket*, Guinness, 1994.

Bath, Richard (ed.), *The Ultimate Encyclopedia of Rugby*, Carlton Books, 1997.

Butler, Bryon, *The Official History of the Football Association*, Queen Anne Press, 1991.

Carling, Will, *Will Carling: My Autobiography*, Hodder & Stoughton, 1998.

Cohen, Richard, *By The Sword*, Macmillan, 2002.

Coldham, James P, *Lord Hawke: A Cricketing Biography*, Crowood Press, 1990.

David, Roy, *The Shergar Mystery*, Trainers Record, 1986.

Edworthy, Niall, *Football Stories: Bad Boys and Hard Men*, Channel 4 Books, 2002.

Eliot, Elizabeth, *Portrait of a Sport: The Story of Steeplechasing*, Longmans, 1957.

Fife, Graeme, *Tour de France*, Mainstream, 1999.

Fotheringham, William, *Put Me Back On My Bike: In Search of Tom Simpson*, Yellow Jersey Press, 2002.

Gower, David, with Johnson, Martin, *Gower: The Autobiography*, CollinsWillow, 1992.

Graham, George, *The Glory and The Grief*, André Deutsch, 1995.

Hennessey, John, *Eye of the Hurricane: The Alex Higgins Story*, Mainstream, 2000.

Hoddle, Glenn, with Davies, David, *Glenn Hoddle: My 1998 World Cup Story*, André Deutsch, 1998.

Holland, Anne, *Grand National*, Queen Anne Press, 1988.

Hopcraft, Arthur, *The Football Man*, Harper Collins, 1971.

Hunn, David, *Epsom Racecourse*, Davis-Poynter, 1973.

James, Mark, *Into the Bear Pit*, Virgin, 2000.

Karter, John, *Lester: Return of a Legendary Headline*, 1992.

Kelly, Stephen F, *Back Page Football*, Aurora, 1988.

Kelly, Stephen F (ed.), *A Game of Two Halves*, Mandarin, 1993.

Kent, Graeme, *Boxing's Strangest Fights*, Robson Books, 1991.

Kurt, Richard, *Red Devils: A History of Manchester United's Rogues and Villains*, Prion, 1998.

Le Quesne, Laurence, *The Bodyline Controversy*, Secker & warburg, 1983.

Lindsay, Nigel, *America's Cup*, Heath Cranton Ltd, 1930.

Longrigg, Roger, *The History of Horse Racing*, Macmillan, 1972.

Lowe, Douglas and Brownlie, Alex, *The Open Championship*, Black and White, 2000.

Lyle, R C, *Royal Newmarket*, Putnam and Co., 1945.

Marqusee, Mike, *Redemption Song: Muhammad Ali and the Spirit of the Sixties*, Verso, 1999.

McGregor, Adrian, *Greg Chappell*, Collins, 1985.

Moorhouse, Geoffrey, *A People's Game – The Official History of Rugby League*, Hodder & Stoughton, 1995.

Mortimer, Roger, *The Jockey Club*, Cassell and Co., 1958.

Onslow, Richard, *Great Racing Gambles and Frauds*, Marlborough Books, 1991.

Orchard, Vincent, *The Derby Stakes (1900–1953)*, Hutchinson, 1953.

Osbaldeston, Squire George, *Squire Osbaldeston: His Autobiography*, John Lane, 1926.

Plumptre, George, *Back Page Racing*, Aurora, 1996

Powell, Jeff, *Bobby Moore: The Life and Times of a Sporting Hero*, Robson Books, 1993

Rae, Simon, *It's Not Cricket*, Faber and Faber, 2001.

Retter, Jack, with Taylor, Paul, *Mansfeld Town – The First 100 Years*, Glen Publications, 1997.

Riccella, Christopher, *Muhammad Ali*, Holloway House, 1991.

Riggs, Doug, *Keelhauled: Unsportsmanlike Conduct and the America's Cup*, Stanford Maritime Ltd, 1986.

Rilhn, Christov (ed.), *Le Foot: The Legends of French Football*, Abacus, 2000.

Scott, John, *Caught in Court*, André Deutsch, 1989.

Smith, Sean, *The Union Game*, BBC Books, 1999.

Startt, James, *Tour de France: Tour de Force*, Chronicle Books, 2000.

Steen, Rob, *David Gower: A Man Out of Time*, Victor Gollancz, 1995.

Swales, Andrew, *Golf Facts and Feats*, Guinness, 1996.

Swanton, E W (ed.), *Barclays World of Cricket*, CollinsWillow, 1986.

Tibballs, Geoff, *Motor-Racing's Strangest Races*, Robson Books, 2001.

Tinling, Teddy, *Sixty Years in Tennis*, Sidgwick & Jackson, 1983.

Wallechinsky, David, *The Complete Book of the Olympics*, Aurum Press, 1992.

Welcome, John, *Infamous Occasions*, Michael Joseph, 1980.

Williams, Marcus (ed.), *Double Century: 200 Years of Cricket in The Times*, CollinsWillow, 1985.